D1555201

Songs of American Experience

American University Studies

Series XXIV
American Literature

Vol. 24

PETER LANG
New York • Bern • Frankfurt am Main • Paris

Marc Maufort

Songs of American Experience

The Vision of O'Neill and Melville

PETER LANG
New York • Bern • Frankfurt am Main • Paris

Library of Congress Cataloging-in-Publication Data

Maufort, Marc.
  Songs of American experience : the vision of O'Neill
and Melville / Marc Maufort.
     p.   cm. — (American university studies. Series
XXIV. American literature : vol. 24)
Includes bibliographical references and index.
  1. American literature — History and criticism.   2. National
characteristics, American, in literature.   3. O'Neill,
Eugene, 1888-1953 — Knowledge — United States.
4. Melville, Herman, 1819-1891 — Knowledge — United
States.   I. Title.   II. Series.
PS169.N35M38   1990   810.9 — dc20   90-41225
ISBN 0-8204-1407-7   CIP
ISSN 0895-0512

© Peter Lang Publishing, Inc., New York 1990

Printed in the United States of America.

ACKNOWLEDGMENTS

Ouvrage publié avec le concours de la Direction Générale de l'Enseignement Supérieur et de la Recherche Scientifique du Ministère de l'Education Nationale, Bruxelles (book published with the support of the Research Department of the Ministry of National Education, Brussels, Belgium).

Ouvrage publié avec le concours de la Fondation Universitaire de Belgique (book published with the support of the University Foundation of Belgium).

1. UNPUBLISHED WORKS BY O'NEILL AND FACSIMILE REPRODUCTIONS

Quotations from O'Neill's Introduction to Hart Crane's *White Buildings* are printed with the kind permission of The Henry W. and Albert A. Berg Collection, The New York Public Library, Astor, Lenox, and Tilden Foundations; and with the permission of the Yale Committee on Literary Property.

The quotation from the manuscript material of O'Neill's *Mourning Becomes Electra* is printed with the permission of the Collection of American Literature, Beinecke Rare Book and Manuscript Library, Yale University and the Yale Committee on Literary Property.

O'Neill's drawings of clipper ships and the reproduction of the front page of his "Thomas Jefferson Play" are printed with the permission of the Collection of American Literature, Beinecke Rare Book and Manuscript Library, Yale University and the Yale Committee on Literary Property.

The manuscript front page of O'Neill's *The Long Voyage Home* is printed with the permission of The Theatre Collection of the Museum of the City of New York.

2. PUBLISHED WORKS BY O'NEILL

Excerpt from *Poems 1912-1944* by Eugene O'Neill, edited by Donald Gallup. Copyright 1979 by Yale University. Reprinted by permission of Ticknor and Fields, a Houghton Mifflin Co., and of Jonathan Cape, Ltd.

Quotations from *Beyond the Horizon*, *Chris Christophersen*, *The Iceman Cometh*, *The Hairy Ape*, *All God's Chillun Got Wings*, *Desire under the Elms*, *Marco Millions*, *The Great God Brown*, *Strange Interlude*, *Mourning Becomes Electra*, *The Long Voyage Home*, *Bound East for Cardiff*, *The Rope*, *Ile*, *Where the Cross Is Made*, and *Fog* are reprinted from *The Plays of Eugene O'Neill*. Copyright 1928 by Eugene O'Neill and renewed 1956 by Carlotta Monterey O'Neill. Reprinted by permission of Random House, Inc. and of Jonathan Cape, Ltd.

Quotations from *Anna Christie* (copyright 1922, renewed 1949; from *The Hairy Ape and other Plays*, London, Jonathan Cape, 1936) and from *Dynamo* (copyright 1929, renewed 1957; from *Lazarus Laughed and other Plays*, London, Jonathan Cape, 1929) are printed with the kind permission of Random House, Inc. and of Jonathan Cape Ltd. Acknowledgments are made to the Estate of Eugene O'Neill.

Excerpts from *The Calms of Capricorn* by Eugene O'Neill. Copyright 1981 by Yale University. Reprinted by permission of Ticknor and Fields, a Houghton Mifflin Co.

3. WORKS BY HERMAN MELVILLE

4. PARTS OF THIS BOOK PREVIOUSLY PUBLISHED IN PERIODICALS (IN MODIFIED VERSION)

TABLE OF CONTENTS

Foreword xi

Abbreviations xiii

Chapter I. The Vision of O'Neill and Melville 1

Chapter II. Autobiographical Journeys 19

Chapter III. Mariners and Mystics 39

Chapter IV. Tragic Tensions of Land and Sea 65

Chapter V. Tales of Yankees and Puritans 99

Chapter VI. An American Tragedy 125

Chapter VII. In Search of Poetic Realism 147

Chapter VIII. Songs of American Experience 163

Appendix: illustrations 169

Endnotes 175

Selected Bibliography 197

Index 217

TABLE OF ILLUSTRATIONS

1. Draft of "Thomas Jefferson Play"   169

2. Sketches for the "Cycle Plays"   170

3. Design for *The Calms of Capricorn*   171

4. Design for *The Calms of Capricorn*   172

5. Front page of the manuscript of *The Long Voyage Home*   173

O'Neill's manuscripts are extremely difficult to reproduce in photographic form. Written in pencil, in a tiny handwriting, they faded quickly with the passing of time. Accordingly, some of those manuscripts, and particularly the illustrations included in this book, are of a faint color and must be examined with a magnifier. However, their value as research tools can hardly be denied, even if their photographic reproduction lacks in technical quality.

FOREWORD

This study aims-at a re-evaluation of Eugene O'Neill's achievements, a necessary task after the 1988 celebration of the playwright's centenary. I have deemed it essential to consider O'Neill in a new context, one that places him among American writers and that throws light on his vision of American experience. Ironically, up to now very few American critics have examined O'Neill from that perspective. Even John Henry Raleigh devotes only one chapter to that topic in his book on the dramatist. Drawn by motives which may appear surprising for a European, I have sought to illuminate O'Neill's link with his national literary tradition, a topic little heeded hitherto. This book, based on the methods of comparative literature, does not always rely on verified elements of influence between Melville and O'Neill. Rather, traces of confluence between the two writers are investigated in detail. I contend that such a technique allows the critic to delineate more clearly the richness of O'Neill's craft.

At the outset, I would wish to extend my gratitude to three of my mentors: to Professor Gilbert Debusscher, of the Free University of Brussels, who first introduced me to American drama and encouraged me to pursue studies in the United States; without his valuable advice, this study could not have been completed; to Emeritus Professor Esther M. Jackson, of the University of Wisconsin-Madison, who led me to appreciate the plays of O'Neill and made me discover the "Americanness" of the dramatist's achievements; and to Professor William Lenehan, of the University of Wisconsin-Madison, with whom I studied the American literature of the nineteenth and twentieth centuries.

Further, I wish to acknowledge the help of the Belgian American Educational Foundation, which enabled me to pursue research in the United States during the academic year 1981–1982. I am also deeply indebted to the "Fonds National de la Recherche Scientifique" for several research appointments which subsequently allowed me to write this book. The publication of this study was made possible through grants from the "Direction Générale de l'Enseignement Supérieur et de la Recherche Scientifique" (Ministry of Education, Belgium) and the "Fondation Universitaire" (University Foundation, Belgium). I would also like to thank Dr. Donald Gallup, Dr. David Schoonover, and Mrs. Patricia Willis, past and present Curators of the Collection of American Literature, The Beinecke Rare Book and Manuscript Library, Yale University, for permission to study the O'Neill material of their Institution. Likewise, I wish to acknowledge the collaboration of Mr Robert Taylor, Acting Curator of the Theater Collection of the Museum of the City of New York, who granted me the permission to examine the manuscripts of O'Neill's early plays. In addition, I am grateful to Dr. Jeanne Newlin, Curator of the Harvard Theater Collection; to Miss Jean Preston and to Princeton University Library for kindly allowing me to have access to their O'Neill material; and finally, to the Curator of the Henry W. and Albert A. Berg Collection, The New York Public Library, Astor, Lenox and Tilden Foundations, who facilitated my study of his O'Neill Collection.

In addition, I thank all those who contributed to my work through encouragement and advice: my parents, Mrs. J. Delrue, the late Mrs. A. Deflandre, and Professor Paul Lilly. I consulted various specialists while at work on this book, namely Professors Jean Weisgerber (Free University of Brussels), Kristiaan Versluys (University of Ghent) and Michael Manheim (University of Toledo). Through their insightful comments, they in many cases helped me to strengthen the argument of this study.

My deepest debt, however, is to my wife, Joëlle, whose patience and understanding facilitated the completion of my task. This book is naturally dedicated to her.

Marc Maufort
Chargé de Recherches FNRS
Brussels, June 1990

ABBREVIATIONS

Listed here only are the titles of O'Neill's plays abbreviated for the purposes of my study. The sequence in which these titles are ranked is chronological rather than alphabetical.

The concision of Melville's titles, and their relatively less frequent occurence, have prompted me to avoid any shortening, except in the case of *Israël Potter* and *The Confidence-Man*.

Children of the Sea	*Children*
Bound East for Cardiff	*Cardiff*
The Sniper	*Sniper*
In the Zone	*Zone*
The Long Voyage Home	*Long Voyage*
The Moon of the Caribbees	*Caribbees*
The Rope	*Rope*
Beyond the Horizon	*Horizon*
Where the Cross Is Made	*Cross*
Chris Christophersen	*Chris*
Anna Christie	*Anna*
The Emperor Jones	*Emperor*
The Hairy Ape	*Ape*
All God's Chillun Got Wings	*Chillun*
The Ancient Mariner	*Mariner*
Desire Under the Elms	*Desire*
Marco Millions	*Marco*
The Great God Brown	*Brown*
Strange Interlude	*Interlude*
Mourning Becomes Electra	*Electra*
Days Without End	*Days*
A Touch of the Poet	*Touch*

More Stately Mansions	*Mansions*
The Calms of Capricorn	*Capricorn*
The Iceman Cometh	*Iceman*
Long Day's Journey into Night	*Journey*
A Moon for the Misbegotten	*Misbegotten*
Israël Potter	*Israël*
The Confidence-Man	*Confidence*
Beinecke Rare Book and Manuscript Library	Beinecke

Songs of American Experience

CHAPTER I. THE VISION OF O'NEILL AND MELVILLE

Over the years, the romantic genius of Eugene O'Neill (1888–1953), America's first dramatist, has elicited the interest of American critics. Biographers have carefully recorded the details of his early life, including his experience at sea, his travel to South America, and his aborted suicide attempt on the New York waterfront. Likewise, his daringly innovative plays have constituted the focus of numerous critical investigations. His first commentators have considered him through an essentially European looking glass. They have emphasized, and still do, the evident relationship between O'Neill and writers such as Nietzsche, Ibsen, Strindberg, Synge, Kaiser, and Toller. O'Neill shares with them not only a common philosophical vision, but also a cluster of characteristics drawn from styles as varied as naturalism, symbolism, and expressionism.

However valuable, these studies have left obscure the link between O'Neill and his own literary tradition. The playwright underwent a great number of influences, both from European and American writers, and amalgamated these sources into the complex artistry of his masterpieces. His American sensibility reveals itself in certain elements of confluence, reflected in his plays, with the writers of the "American Renaissance," i.e., Ralph Waldo Emerson, Henry David Thoreau, Nathaniel Hawthorne, Herman Melville, and Walt Whitman. But although O'Neill seems to have read and admired all these nineteenth century American artists, his most direct forebear was undoubtedly Melville (1819–1891). With him, he shared a satirical vision of American Puritanism. Like the author of *Moby Dick*, he developed an intensely personal concept of tragedy and was fascinated by the sea. In other words, both writers attempted, through a strikingly similar sense of vision, to define the reality with which their contemporaries were confronted and thus to create compelling songs of American experience.

Recent critical studies about O'Neill have offered new literary interpretations of his work, such as James A. Robinson's *O'Neill and Oriental Thought. A Divided Vision*; Laurin Porter's *The Banished Prince*, or Peter

Egri's *Chekhov and O'Neill* and *The Birth of American Tragedy*.[1] Others have concentrated on aspects of the dramatist's reception abroad, such as Ward B. Lewis's *O'Neill. The German Reception of America's First Dramatist*;[2] yet others have attempted to offer annotated editions of Eugene O'Neill's letters and manuscripts. In this category, one can list Virginia Floyd's *Eugene O'Neill at Work. Newly Released Ideas for the Theatre*,[3] Judith E. Barlow's *Final Acts. The Creation of Three Late O'Neill Plays*;[4] and most recently, Travis Bogard's *The Unknown O'Neill*, Travis Bogard's and Jackson Bryer's *Selected Letters of Eugene O'Neill* and Virginia Floyd's *Eugene O'Neill. The Unfinished Plays*.[5] These studies offer evidence to support the view of O'Neill as one of the primary creators of the dramatic forms of our century. However, they do not explore O'Neill's relationship with the American Literary tradition.

Hitherto, critics have mentioned the playwright's link with the "American Renaissance" in passing only. The reason for such neglect may originate in the larger disdain that American academic circles have always felt for American drama as an independent discipline. As Susan Harris Smith has indicated in an article published in *American Quarterly*, even recent histories of American literature do tend to gloss over American drama.[6] In other words, American scholars have refused, along the lines of Robert Brustein, to regard American Drama as serious literature.[7] As for the theatre of O'Neill, being so devoid of literary qualities, it could of course in no way be compared to the masterful achievements of Emerson, Thoreau, Melville, or Whitman. Such view still affects O'Neill scholarship today. Indeed, in his introduction to a recent collection of essays on O'Neill, Harold Bloom affirms that "O'Neill's ancestry has little to do with American tradition."[8] Without denying the paramount influence that European writers have exerted on O'Neill, I would wish to point in this study to the possibility of viewing him in an American context. I shall first seek to suggest his affinities with American culture, with American drama and theater, as well as with nineteenth century American writers. In this fashion, an examination of the O'Neill–Melville connection will appear more plausible.

A

O'Neill's life-long struggle to interpret the essential characteristics of American culture should have reached its culmination in his "cycle plays," a sequence of eleven dramatic pieces that would have constituted "A Tale of Possessors Self-Dispossessed." Of this projected cycle, O'Neill was able to complete only one part: *Touch*. Its sequel, *Mansions*, was shortened from the playwright's manuscript by Donald C. Gallup and Karl Ragnar Gierow—and only recently published in its original form by Martha Bower,[9] while yet another play, *Capricorn*, was developed from the dramatist's scenario by Donald C. Gallup a few years ago only.[10] In this series of plays, O'Neill wished to portray the process of degeneration of American society through materialism in the individual lives of the Harford family of Massachusetts. The playwright's workshop indicates that he carefully documented his studies before starting to write these plays. The notes housed in the O'Neill collection of the Beinecke reveal interesting details on O'Neill's fascination with American culture. He read studies on American history and economy in the hope of providing a realistic basis to his historical project. In a letter to Kenneth Macgowan dated March 29, 1921, he mentions John Fiske's *Discovery of America*.[11] In this romantic survey of American history, the playwright found material for several of his plays, such as his sentimental *Fountain*, *Marco*, and those intended for "A Tale of Possessors Self-Dispossessed." O'Neill was also familiar with Carl Russell Fish's *The Rise of Common Man. 1830–1851*.[12] Fish devotes chapters to Emerson, Poe, arts and sciences in the first half of the American nineteenth century, which might have served O'Neill for his cycle plays. Van Wyck Brook's *The Life of Emerson* and *The Flowering of New England*[13] may have influenced O'Neill's portrayal of Simon Harford as a Transcendentalist poet. On the other hand, his depiction of American materialism could have found its source in Matthew Josephson's *The Robber Barons. The Great American Capitalists, 1861–1901*.[14] Moreover, O'Neill also appeared interested in specific economic issues and read Frances Little's *Early American Textiles*.[15] Further, the dramatist did research on clipper ships, probably with regard to his scenario for *Capricorn*. He refers in his notes to Clark's *The Cliper Ship Era* and to Richard C. McKay's *Some Famous Sailing Ships and their Builder Donald McKay*.[16] Many other historical or economic studies on the United States are included in O'Neill's notes or housed in his private library. The reader will find a list of those books in a note, as space prohibits to include them in the main body of this text. This indicates that O'Neill was profoundly interested in American culture, and especially in the America of the eighteenth and nineteenth century.[17]

In addition, O'Neill made extant notes on subjects relating to American culture, without reference to his sources. He paraphrased lines from speeches on America delivered by well-known native speakers; he read material on the social conditions in the United States in the first half of the nineteenth century, more specifically labor conditions and the laws against the slave trade. Shays's rebellion appears to have aroused his attention at some point.[18] Finally, he recorded dates important for the development of commerce between the United States and China at the end of the eighteenth century. Again, these documents may have served him in the writing of his "American" cycle.[19]

Moreover, O'Neill's notebooks throw light on his ideas for potential plays. Among his scenarios, a few are concerned with American topics. He planned to write a play staging an Emersonian Transcendentalist. In this work, he would have shown the different layers of American society and would have examined its racial components in a historical perspective. He also intended to write a play entitled "Thomas Jefferson Play," in which he would have dramatized the corruption of twentieth century American politics. The scenario opens with a speech delivered by a contemporary president on the 4th of July. The lines are meant to reflect the corrupt and opportunistic nature of that president. In the following scenes, O'Neill would have included a speech by Jefferson, to which the crowd would have responded enthusiastically in awareness of their rights and responsibilities as voters. A coda would have reverted to the figure of the twentieth century president invoking Jefferson's name in vain. All these factors indicate O'Neill's fascination with the nature of the society in which he lived, indeed with the culture inherited from eighteenth century America.[20]

B

O'Neill was also interested, as a number of critics have ventured to demonstrate, in the American drama of the nineteenth century. O'Neill's art can indeed be seen as the continuation of the themes explored by such dramatists as Royall Tyler, William Vaughn Moody, and James A. Herne.[21] Critics generally agree that American drama was born in 1916, with the first production of O'Neill's *Cardiff* by the Provincetown Players. Prior to O'Neill, American theater was only a matter of business. Thus Whitman commented in his 1871 *Democratic Vistas*: "Of what is called the drama or dramatic presentation in the

United States, as now put forth in the theaters, I should say it deserves to be treated with the same gravity, and on a pair with the questions of ornamental confectionery at public dinners, or the arrangement of curtains and hangings in a ballroom—nor more, nor less."[22] At the dawn of the twentieth century, a similar situation was still prevailing. However, the European "Little Theater" movement provided models necessary to release the American theater from its commercial defects. Under the influence of such theaters as André Antoine's "Théâtre Libre," Otto Brahm's *Freie Bühne*, the Moscow Art Theatre, and the Abbey Theater, a spirit of renewal began to develop in America as manifested in the founding of the Chicago Little Theater in 1910, the Boston Toy Theater in 1912, and the Washington Square Players in 1915. In the same year, the Provincetown Players were founded by George Cram Cook and his wife Susan Glaspell. Their amateur qualities provided O'Neill with the possibility to experiment away from the constraints of commercial Broadway theater. When the American "Little Theater" movement merged with Broadway in the early twenties, after the Provincetown Players had disbanded, O'Neill wrote the first masterpieces of American drama.[23]

However different from eighteenth and nineteenth century American drama, O'Neill's plays nevertheless reveal affinities with the early melodramatic works of native American playwrights. They refine and amplify some of the themes with which these early dramatic experiments dealt, i.e., the quality of life in the New World. Thus, O'Neill's plays must be studied in connection with the European "Little Theater" movement and in connection with the American dramatic tradition as well: O'Neill synthesized some of the characteristics of these two backgrounds. It is necessary therefore, to show, through a brief historical survey, the slow refinement of the themes of American drama since its beginnings, which eventually led to the artistry of Eugene O'Neill.[24]

The early American drama in many ways recalls European dramatic traditions and stage conventions. For instance, Thomas Godfrey's *The Prince of Parthia* (1767) reflects the influence of works by Francis Beaumont and John Fletcher and if Royall Tyler's *The Contrast* (1787) constitutes the first successful American comedy of manners, it is nonetheless based on a British model. Consequently, it remains divorced from the New World experience. Further, in William Dunlap's *André* (1798), which dramatizes the theme of the Revolutionary War, the conflict opposes two men: the American officer Bland

and his English friend André. In other words, the melodramatic action revolves around the black and white contrast between two *dramatis personae*.

Plays written during the first half of the nineteenth century show little improvement over these early attempts. They develop, however, the theme of the New World vision and focus on specific issues of American life. Such is John Augustus Stone's *Metamora* (1829), which constitutes a rhetorical and melodramatic treatment of the noble savage theme. It deals with the predicament of the American Indian from a rather sentimental viewpoint. In *The Gladiator* (1830–1831), Robert Montgomery Bird explores the various social layers of American society and suggests the elimination of discriminatory practices against European immigrants. More complex in theme is Anna Cora Mowatt Ritchie's *Fashion* (1845), a satirical comedy using techniques derived from Restoration Theater. In her protagonist, Mrs. Tiffany, the dramatist reflects an American society in transition. Mrs. Ritchie criticizes the adherence to European social conventions in an American setting.

During the second half of the nineteenth century, dramatists continue to examine facets of the New World experience and resort to more appropriate techniques to articulate this motif. Dion Boucicault's *The Octoroon* (1859) is an adaptation of Harriet Beecher Stowe's novel *Uncle Tom's Cabin* (1852). In dealing with the issue of slavery in America, Boucicault foreshadows those who towards the end of the century would also be concerned with the interpretation of American life. One of these writers is James A. Herne with two excellent plays: *Margaret Fleming* (1890) and *Shore Acres* (1893). In the former, the dramatist analyzes the moral obligations of the individual on the new continent and concludes by asserting the supremacy of personal decision in ethical matters. In the latter work, Herne praises the value of the family in American society. O'Neill would later develop similar themes from a more pessimistic viewpoint.

An immediate ancestor of O'Neill in the field of drama, at the dawn of the twentieth century, is perhaps WilliamVaughn Moody. In *The Great Divide* (1906), that playwright investigates the intricacies of moral life in America and effects a dichotomy between the Eastern and Western parts of the country. In *The Faith Healer* (1909), Moody offers the first example of the poetic form that all American playwrights would subsequently use. Both O'Neill and Tennessee Williams composed in ways reminiscent of Moody's realistic style, and more recent dramatists such as Edward Albee, Sam Shepard, David Mamet, and

Lanford Wilson still work in that form. From this brief survey, it is clear that in his work, O'Neill illustrated themes that had haunted the imaginations of his predecessors in American drama. But he was able to reach beyond the level of sheer melodrama in his presentation of the conflicts of the American individual by drawing from the techniques of European playwrigts. As Esther M. Jackson has remarked, the dramas of Eugene O'Neill, like those of eighteenth and nineteenth century native writers, focus on typically American issues, which are: the search for identity in the New World; social equality in a heterogeneous society; the challenge of social justice in a democracy, and the impact of the idea of freedom on human character.25

Not only does O'Neill present affinities with native American playwrights, he also shares characteristics with the American popular stage tradition. In this respect, his father played a role of paramount importance. James O'Neill was a famous actor in the second half of the nineteenth century. He came to be identified in the minds of American spectators with one single role, namely the leading part of Fechter's *The Count of Monte Cristo*, in which he starred throughout his life. O'Neill repeatedly articulated his contempt for the theatre represented by his father. But as John Henry Raleigh has demonstrated, he was profoundly influenced by this melodramatic play and his work must therefore be studied in connection with it.26 Raleigh successfully argues that plays such as *Abortion*, *Sniper*, *Rope*, *Emperor*, *Desire*, *Brown*, and *Electra* were modelled on *The Count of Monte Cristo* to which they owe their melodramatic nature. Raleigh further affirms that O'Neill did not easily escape from the "Château d'If." In other words, he did not manage to free himself from the conventions of nineteenth century popular drama until he started to write his late masterpieces: *Journey*, *Iceman*, *Hughie*, and *Misbegotten*. O'Neill's double indebtedness to American drama and theater clearly reveals his infatuation with his national literary heritage.

C

It is not surprising therefore that, being fascinated by these two traditions, he would also have been conversant with the masterpieces of nineteenth century American literature, especially those of the American Renaissance. The list of American writers with whom O'Neill was familiar is very long indeed, and some of these literary relationships have been documented, albeit in a superficial manner. I wish to concentrate mainly on O'Neill's link with four writers of the nineteenth century: Emerson, Thoreau, Hawthorne, and Whitman. Indeed, these four patterns of confluence contain elements also representative of the nature of the O'Neill–Melville connection.

The kinship between O'Neill and the American poet and essayist Ralph Waldo Emerson may be difficult to discern. Emerson (1803–1882) is generally regarded as a fundamentally optimistic writer in his praise of the new possibilities of life in America. Yet, one can detect in several of Emerson's essays a pessimistic counterpoint foreshadowing the dark vision of O'Neill. Emerson at times envisioned life as a series of irreconcilable polarities.[27] It is probably that bleak component to which O'Neill was attracted in his reading of Emerson's essays. Arthur and Barbara Gelb, the playwright's biographers, indicate in their study that O'Neill's private library contained a copy of Emerson's *Essays*.[28] The O'Neill papers collected at the Beinecke further illuminate the dramatist's relationship with his American forebear. In his notes, the artist refers to "Choice" and "Compensation;"[29] in his outline for his play *Touch*, he explicitly compares his character Simon Harford to Emerson.[30] In other notebooks, he planned to write a play about an Emersonian transcendentalist;[31] he was familiar with Van Wyck Brook's *The Life of Emerson*, a sentimental biography of the philosopher;[32] finally, James A. Robinson convincingly argues that O'Neill discovered Oriental philosophies partly through his reading of Emerson. Indeed, the latter's concept of the "Over-Soul" and his neoplatonism offer parallels with Vedantic principles. If O'Neill's vision differed from Eastern systems of thought, it is precisely in his Emersonian focus on the self, i.e., "Self-Reliance."[33]

The dramatist was also fully cognizant of the works of Emerson's disciple, Henry David Thoreau (1817–1862). When the playwright lived isolated in a Coast Guard Station on Cape Cod, away from normal human civilization, he almost appeared as a latter-day Thoreau.[34] And indeed, the playwright's papers collected at the Beinecke indicate that he admired the works of Thoreau. His private library contained an edition of "Winter," a selection from *Walden*. His notes reveal that he had Thoreau in mind in his characterization of Simon Harford in *Touch*.[35] He was familiar with *The Heart of Thoreau's Journals*;[36] and James A. Robinson further speculates that the playwright knew such studies as Henry Seidel Canby's *Thoreau*,[37] which complemented his reading of *Life*

Without Principle, Walden, and *The Writings of Henry David Thoreau.*[38]

Third, O'Neill undoubtedly admired Walt Whitman (1819–1892). In *Journey*, the library of the Tyrones, the dramatist carefully indicates, contains a volume of Whitman's poems.[39] One would be tempted to believe, owing to the autobiographical nature of the play, that this mention reflects the literary tastes of the author. And indeed, Jean Chothia affirms that O'Neill had read *Leaves of Grass* by 1912.[40] A copy of the latter can be found in his private library[41] and in an hitherto unpublished introduction to Hart Crane's volume of poems *White Buildings*, O'Neill acknowledged Whitman:

> Most of it [...] he undoubtedly gets from Whitman. Whitman's range was possible in an America of prophecy. Crane's America is materially the same, but it approaches a balance of forces; it is a realization, and the poet, confronted with a complex present experience, gains in intensity what he loses in range. Morally considered, Crane's poetry is a concentration of the Whitman substance.[42]

This introduction reveals that Whitman's vision of America intrigued O'Neill. The latter, like the American poet, recorded the contradictions inherent in American civilization, in particular the opposition between the individual and society.

Nathaniel Hawthorne's (1804–1864) vision of Puritanism unmistakably presents similarities with Eugene O'Neill's reflections on the harsh religious beliefs of New England. The dramatist knew the works of his predecessor: his private library contained a copy of *The House of the Seven Gables, Mosses from an Old Manse,* and *The Scarlet Letter.*[43] Moreover, the critics Joyce D. Kennedy and James Mathews have shown how O'Neill used *The House of the Seven Gables* in *Electra.*[44] Parallels can be detected between the Greek dramatists' use of a temple facade, Hawthorne's Seven Gables, and O'Neill's Mannon House in the symbolic function of the architecture. Resemblances can also be traced in the portraits of Colonel Pyncheon and Ezra Mannon, which reflect the evil passions of their respective families and the capitalistic greed to which their relatives have fallen victims. Owing to these characteristics, it is possible to submit that in *Electra,* O'Neill was directly influenced by Hawthorne.

In addition to these four major American writers, O'Neill exhibited affinities with a myriad of others, who deserve to be briefly noted here. The similarities existing between O'Neill and Henry Adams (1838–1918) are extremely interesting to study. John Henry Raleigh has described them remarkably well.[45] The works of Adams and O'Neill coincide, according to this critic, with the theme of the doubleness of life in New England and with that of the dynamo. In *The Education of Henry Adams*, the author envisions life as a "double thing." That notion of polarities, dear to both Adams and Emerson, is found in the motif of the dynamo, of the electrical power which he had observed at the exhibition of the dynamos in Chicago in 1900. To him as to O'Neill, in the play entitled *Dynamo*, that machine was synonymous with gentleness and strength.

Arthur and Barbara Gelb note that O'Neill liked the works of Edgar Allan Poe (1809–1849) and that his favorite story by the writer was "The Imp of the Perverse."[46] In his projected introduction to Crane's *White Buildings*, already mentioned, O'Neill refers to Poe: "I do not know whether he has mastered Poe's criticism, yet some of his conviction that the artist should be intensely local must stem from Poe."[47] Esther Timar in an article entitled "Possible Sources for Two O'Neill One-Acts" suggests that O'Neill was influenced by Poe's "The Oblong Box" in composing *Zone*, as both works reveal a similar melodramatic quality.[48] It would appear that O'Neill's love for the morbid is derived from Poe: the grotesque quality of stories such as "The Fall of the House of Usher" finds an equivalent in the morbid and sometimes extravagant style of *Mansions*.

O'Neill's affinities with a New England poet such as Emily Dickinson have been examined by Joyce D. Kennedy in her article: "O'Neill's Lavinia Mannon and the Dickinson Legend."[49] She suggests that O'Neill's protagonist is patterned on the figure of Emily Dickinson. Lavinia Mannon, like the poet, is depicted as a "white-clothed stranger" and functions as a symbol of repressed Puritanism. Biographies of Emily Dickinson were extremely popular in the 1920's and O'Neill, according to the critic, might have had access to one of those while composing the first draft of *Electra*.

With Mark Twain, O'Neill shares a bold urge to transcribe in literature the language of the common man of America. Samuel Langhorne Clemens (1835–1910) atempted to record in *Huckleberry Finn* the spoken dialect of New World citizens. This linguistic experiment receives an equivalent in the sailors' vernacular in O'Neill's *Cardiff* and in the reproduction of the New York slang in *Iceman*. O'Neill's constant efforts to devise new forms and modes of language also present analogies with the novelistic techniques of Henry James (1843–1916). In his epic play *Strange Interlude*, O'Neill attempted to introduce into drama a "stream of consciousness" technique akin to that used by Henry James in *The Portrait of a Lady*.[50] Jean Chothia and Peter Egri have mentioned the link between O'Neill and Stephen Crane (1871–1900), particularly in the parallel discussions of war in *The Red Badge of Courage* and *Electra*.[51] Critics have not failed to notice the affinities existing between O'Neill and Theodore Dreiser's (1871–1945) brand of naturalism. Both *The Web* and *Sister Carrie* present characters trapped by their environment.[52] Sherwood Anderson (1876–1941) also appears to have fascinated O'Neill, as Jean Chothia notes.[53] Anderson might have influenced the playwright in the Christ symbolism of *Anna Christie*. In his last letter to Beatrice Ashe, O'Neill reveals his deep knowledge of the poems of Carl Sandburg (1878–1967) by quoting "Choices" in full.[54] He applies the theme of this poem to his own career and declares having reached a decision: "I want to be an artist or nothing." The dramatist was a contemporary of Sinclair Lewis (1885–1951), with whom he shared a satirical view of the small-town American bourgeoisie. When O'Neill obtained the Nobel Prize, Lewis sent him a letter of congratulation preserved in the records of the Beinecke. In recent studies, Susan Tuck has convincingly demonstrated the relationship existing between the works of O'Neill and William Faulkner (1897–1962) especially in their treatment of the black character.[55] Finally, one should mention that O'Neill knew the poet Hart Crane (1899–1932) whom he admired so much that he recommended his works to be published by Liveright. From this rapid overview, it is manifest that O'Neill shared resemblances with an impressive number of American writers.

D

I would now wish to concentrate more specifically on O'Neill's relationship with Herman Melville. Although that phenomenon has not attracted much critical attention hitherto, several scholars have discussed that aspect of O'Neill's artistry.

Travis Bogard, Frank R. Cunningham, and Marleen Lowel have remarked in passing on a few analogies between the two writers.[56] On the whole, these scholars have studied the points of confluence linking O'Neill and Melville in a fragmentary fashion, either confining themselves to generalizations or focusing on details. While O'Neill's affinities with Melville are generally taken for granted, the details of this literary relationship have remained rather obscure. The best critical analysis of the O'Neill-Melville connection to date can be found in John Henry Raleigh's *The Plays of Eugene O'Neill*,[57] in which a chapter on O'Neill and American writers is inserted. Raleigh lists a number of elements of confluence between the novelist and the dramatist. His examination leaves room, however, for further investigation. Raleigh mentions the similarities between O'Neill's and Melville's sea symbolism: the ship as a microcosm of human life; variations on Ahab-like figures; contradictory range of meanings attributed to the ocean; the image of the dying sailor. Furthermore, Raleigh argues, the two American artists present the city as hell and rely heavily on the use of masks; both are fascinated by the power of electricity. As writers of prose, they evince three contradictory impulses: the desire to fathom the individual consciousness; the attempt to compose in a variety of styles; and, a tendency to resort to hyperboles. Their characters function either as allegories or multicharacters and feel invariably torn between the wish to dwell in solitude or to communicate with the outside universe. Raleigh's intelligent study possesses the great merit of suggesting that O'Neill's relationship with Melville extends beyond sea symbolism.

If Raleigh does not try to prove the influence of Melville on O'Neill, Joyce D. Kennedy attempts to do so in "*Pierre*'s Progeny: O'Neill and the Melville Revival."[58] She argues that in *Electra*, O'Neill stood under the influence of Melville's novel *Pierre*. The two works reveal patently similar dramatic patterns: both trace the doom of a fated family and attribute the origin of incest to the Puritan sources of the American character. In *Pierre*, O'Neill might have found his inspiration for the sister-brother incest motif that emerges in *Electra*. O'Neill's and Melville protagonists, Kennedy notes, long to dwell with their sister in a paradise of peace and darkness. Finally, *Pierre* and *Electra* deal with similar aspects of American history such as the loss of innocence in the New World. In this article, the critic has provided a specific example of Melville's legacy to O'Neill's plays.

Ronald T. Curran in "Insular Typees: Puritanism and Primitivism in *Mourning Becomes Electra*," considers some of parallels between O'Neill's and Melville's thematic concerns.[59] In *Electra*, O'Neill depicts the collapse of the Puritan theological basis for New England Protestantism. In referring to

Melville's Rousseau-like dream, O'Neill interprets the failure of Primitivism in the light of our modern psychological insights. As in *Typee*, Curran explains, the characters of O'Neill's trilogy possess an imaginary island, representing the repressed hopes of sexual freedom in New England Puritan society. This desire to revert to a prelapsarian world has no chance of survival in the universe of the Mannons: Brant, the figure of renewal, is eventually murdered. According to Ronald Curran, O'Neill uses quotations from *Typee* to dramatize the gradual disappearance of Rousseau-like ideals in nineteenth century New England. This article, along the lines of Raleigh, examines a topical instance of confluence between the works of Melville and the plays of O'Neill.

Articles published hitherto indicate that critics have sensed the existence of a relationship uniting the dramatist and the novelist, for which they have felt unable to account completely. That phenomenon may be due in part to the fact that the playwright only rarely acknowledged his indebtedness to Herman Melville. If proofs of factual influence are difficult to discern, they nonetheless deserve to be mentioned in this introduction.

The very existence of Eugene O'Neill's sea plays suggests that he had been impressed by Melville's romances early in his career. Whether he knew Melville by the time he wrote *Cardiff* (1914) is still uncertain. And yet, Jean Chothia asserts that he had read *Moby Dick* and Melville's short stories at school and in college, before 1912.[60]

In a private communication, Louis Sheaffer, whom many consider to be the best biographer of O'Neill, informed me that Agnes Boulton, O'Neill's second wife, confirmed her husband's admiration for *Moby Dick*. This indicates that, after 1917, O'Neill may have been familiar with the works of Melville. Indeed, as Louis Sheaffer records, Agnes first met O'Neill in the fall of 1917 and became his wife on April 12, 1918.[61] It is likely, then, that the dramatist might have been infuenced by Melville in his sea one-acts: *Caribbees*, *Long Voyage*, *Zone*, and *Ile* were written in 1917, while *Cross* was completed in 1918.

Commenting on his play *Diff'rent*, written in 1920, O'Neill publicly acknowledged *Moby Dick*:

As for Caleb, he dies because it is not in him to compromise. He belongs to the old iron school of Nantucket-New Bedford whalemen whose slogan was "A dead whale or a stove boat." The whale in this case is transformed suddenly into a malignant Moby Dick who has sounded to depths forever out of reach. Caleb's boat is stove, his quest is ended. He goes with his ship.[62]

In view of this quotation, one can conjecture that O'Neill patterned his early play on Melville's novel. Moreover, the playwright appears to have been aware of the metaphysical ramifications of *Moby Dick*, as he says, "depths forever out of reach," thereby pointing to the Absolute with which the white whale is associated. To O'Neill, Moby Dick is also "malignant," which suggests that, himself obsessed with religious issues, he identified with Ahab's idea of the whale/God as a terrible divinity, punishing man with cruelty. Third, his reference to the "iron school" of Nantucket exhibits his familiarity with the type of character epitomized by Ahab, i.e., the self-centered captain of the "Pequod."

In the draft of his foreword to Crane's *White Buildings*, O'Neill further alludes to the nineteenth century American novelist. Louis Sheaffer tells us briefly the genesis of this aborted attempt at critical writing.[63] Having granted the playwright's request to publish some of Crane's poems, Liveright required that O'Neill should write a preface to the volume. The latter tried to comply in the course of 1926 but failed in his endeavors. Allen Tate eventually wrote these prefatory comments although their published form retained O'Neill's signature. The first version of the introduction written by O'Neill, preserved in the Berg Collection of the New York Public Library, nonetheless clarifies his link to Melville:

> [...] (Hart) Crane is the most interesting poet I have read since Robinson, Pound, Sandburg, Eliot [...]. It is an American poetry [...]. Themes [...] are definitely confined to an experience of the American scene [...]. Melville and Whitman are his avowed masters. In Crane's sea poems [...] there is something of Melville's intense brooding on the mystery of 'the high interiors of the sea.'[64]

In this quotation, O'Neill again stands in admiration for the metaphysical quality of Melville's literary ocean as his quotation: "the high interiors of the sea" suggests. It should also be noticed that Crane's poems, with which the dramatist was undoubtedly conversant, include six pieces entitled *Voyages*. O'Neill might have felt attracted by the sea symbolism of these lyrics, the last of which, "At Melville's Tomb," is unmistakably reminiscent of the author of *Moby Dick*. In this poem, Crane presents the American novelist as a haunting shadow of the sea. It is conceivable that in reading Crane, O'Neill felt prompted to discover Melville.[65]

In addition, one finds, in O'Neill's private library, a copy of Melville's *Israël*. If the dramatist actually read that novel, he certainly was spell-bound but its sea imagery, which offers the reader a dark vision of the North Seas, akin to the one found in *Long Voyage*.[66]

Further, Joyce D. Kennedy speculates that the dramatist might have been introduced to the novel *Pierre* by Carl van Vechten, one of his best friends, who was extremely influential in the Melville revival of the early twenties. Moreover, O'Neill could have known van Vechten's article "The later Works of Herman Melville," published in *Double Dealer* in 1922.[67]

O'Neill surely had Melville in mind when he was writing *Electra*. In this important play, Orin declares to Christine:

> ORIN: [...] Have you ever read a book called "Typee"—about the South Sea Islands? [...]. Someone loaned me the book. I read it and reread it until finally those islands came to mean everything that was peace and warmth and serenity. I used to dream I was there. And later on all the time I was out of my head I seemed really to be there. There was no one there but you and me. And yet I never saw you, that's the funny part. I only felt you all around me. The breaking of the waves your voice [...]. The whole island was you. (*The Hunted*, p. 776)[68]

Typee, all critics agree, remained Melville's most popular novel until the 1920's. It is in *Electra*, then, that one detects O'Neill's most overt reference to Melville and in the first draft of the play, the allusion is even more precise. Indeed, Orin says, "[...] Did you ever read a book by Herman Melville called 'Typee'—about the South Sea island he lived on for a time [...]."[69] In view of these elements, it seems apparent to me that O'Neill's dramatic canon was indeed influenced by Melville. The latter's imprints are most evident in the first part of the playwright's life, i.e., between 1912, the date of the composition of his first sea play, and approximately 1930, as he was working on *Electra*.

E

My study necessitates the use of methods derived essentially from comparative literature. This field was often regarded as the mere determination of influences between foreign authors. René Wellek in "The Crisis of Comparative Literature" reacted against this narrow definition in the following terms:

> [...] Van Tieghem, his precursors and followers conceive of literary study in terms of nineteenth-century positivistic factualism, as a study of sources and influences [...]. Works of art, however, are not simply sums of sources and influences: they are wholes in which raw materials derived from elsewhere cease to be inert and are assimilated into a new structure.[70]

Accordingly, I shall not seek to list all the possible examples of Melville's influence on the plays of O'Neill. Rather, I shall concentrate on instances of confluence between the vision of the novelist and the playwright. If some of their parallel themes cannot always be attributed to a direct borrowing, the resemblances affecting some of their works deserve consideration. O'Neill may not have needed a literary model in order to create his sea symbolism. The latter can, however, be compared to that of Melville on the basis of internal, textual evidence. In most cases, the two writers appear to have undergone analogous developments. It could be argued therefore that O'Neill unconsciously translated themes and techniques which had been developed earlier by Melville.

In his study *Faulkner and Dostoevsky. Influence and Confluence*,[71] Jean Weisgerber has examined the link between Faulkner and Dostoevsky with the help of a method I shall also use in this study: I shall attempt to explain the plays of O'Neill in the light of Melville's novels. The latter will constitute as it were a vantage point from which to analyze the American roots of the dramatist. I plan to draw as complete as possible a list of the elements of confluence between both writers for it is only when this task has been accomplished that instances of influence will be determined. Accidental or even superficial similarities need to be considered side by side with acknowledged references or convergent patterns of a broader significance in the hope of delineating the nature of the link between the two authors in a more accurate mode. As Wellek pointed out, a source is modified when a writer integrates it in a new structure. And indeed, O'Neill differs from Melville in ways that are as important to examine as the exact parallels. In other words, he seems to have been impregnated with the Melville substance and to have borrowed motifs and themes subsequently assimilated in his plays in various and subtle ways such as ironic counterpoint and satirical distance.

The method I have described will also contribute to a better evaluation of O'Neill's skills as a playwright. In "Le Jugement de Valeur en Littérature Comparée: Le Comparatisme au Service de l'Evaluation Artistique," Jean Weisberger analyzes the implications of comparative literature in the case of literary evaluation.[72] If two writers treat comparable motifs, the critic argues, the writer having achieved a better integration of this theme in the overall structure of his work will have composed a more subtly balanced novel, poem or play. Owing to this characteristic, the evaluation of the work of such writer will be positive. As for O'Neill, the comparison of his plays with the novels of Melville will enable me to show the playwright's capacity to fuse motifs derived from two traditions, the European and the American. This feature will testify to the richness of his plays.

My comparison will serve another and more essential purpose, that of illuminating the nature of O'Neill's American literary roots. While O'Neill shares analogies with writers of the American Renaissance other than Melville, these parallels are limited in scope: like Emerson, the dramatist envisions the world as polar; like Thoreau, he satirizes American materialism; like Whitman, he focuses on the pursuit of happiness; and like Hawthorne, he rejects Puritan morality. Melville, however, synthesizes all these characteristics in his novels and, like O'Neill, adopts a pessimistic viewpoint towards the conditions of life in America. The works of Melville therefore offer the most encompassing observation post from which to clarify O'Neill's perception of the New World.

Like Melville, O'Neill is a creator of cosmologies: he seeks to describe the new continent to which his forebears have migrated while simultaneously defining the role of the individual in that new society. For both writers, this anxiety about the nature of the American environment culminates in their wish to determine spatial reality at large. Thornton Wilder has underlined the American quality of this search for the identification of the setting as follows: "(The European) [...] environment is so thickly woven, that the growing boy and girl will have something to kick against. The American, on the other hand, is at sea—disconnected from place." (p. 35)[73] In order to compensate for this natural uncertainty about the stability of their setting, American writers, and particularly O'Neill and Melville, attempt to generate unity through the medium of literature, through kindred artistic forms.

One cannot, of course, always determine to what extent O'Neill and Melville consciously comment on the nature of the American experience and environment, although, to a modern critic, their works, viewed in that perspective, gain considerable significance. Their vision of America serves as it were as a departure point from which to formulate a universal statement about the plight of mankind.

Throughout my study, the term "American" will cover several shades of meaning: first, it will refer to both writers' depiction of life in the New World. Certain of the features that they envision as typically American are thus only by degree, existing as they do in a more forcible way in the New World; second, it will designate the literary tradition in which they are working; and third, it will point to their tendency to focus on democratic issues, such as the predicament of ordinary persons, even in settings divorced from the American continent. My study cannot examine every single work written by O'Neill and Melville. Only representative instances of my thesis will be provided, so as to prevent this book from degenerating into a mere "catalogue" of the analogies linking O'Neill and Melville.

Naturally, O'Neill's and Melville's views on American experience always remained intensely personal. This study reflects the subjectivity of their vision. In other words, my style often penetrates directly into their imaginary universes and only seemingly adheres to their beliefs. In the following chapters, retracing the writers' complex journey from sea to land, the reader will progressively discover the kinship of their songs of American experience.

CHAPTER II. AUTOBIOGRAPHICAL JOURNEYS

> I celebrate myself, and sing myself,
> And what I assume you shall assume,
> For every atom belonging to me as good
> belongs to you.
>
> Walt Whitman, from *Songs of Myself*
> in *Leaves of Grass*

Melville and O'Neill, perhaps more than any other American writers, constantly integrate events drawn from experience into the fabric of their novels and plays. They offer highly sophisticated records of personal life, in which autobiographical sources are often difficult to discern for they are blended with elements of mythic and symbolic significance. To both of them, the autobiographical tendency proceeds from the imagination: it serves to structure their lives along the guidelines of artistic inspiration. They are, in other words, preoccupied with the possibility to pattern one's past through the medium of language and to reconcile in this fashion otherwise fragmented aspects of one's self.[1] Not only does this characteristic refer to the fundamentally American doubt about the nature of one's personal identity that Thornton Wilder diagnosed, it also reveals a deep anxiety about the quality of the American setting, which emerges clearly in the writers' vision of the land/sea dichotomy as source of tragic tension.

Naturally, it would be difficult to speak of straightforward "autobiography" with either Melville or O'Neill, for none of them really intended their works to be real autobiographies at the outset, but essentially fiction or drama. Nonetheless, these novels and plays are so often replete with elements of an autobiographical nature that one can indeed regard them as thinly disguised autobiographies. One could argue, in any case, that O'Neill and Melville introduced patterns typical of the autobiographical genre into their works and fused them with more purely artistic elements. As far as sea memories are concerned, their modification of autobiography underwent a comparable pattern of development: beginning with romantic works such as *Typee* or *Cardiff*, they progressively refined their techniques in *Moby Dick* and *Journey*, which combine personal reminiscences with themes of a symbolic and mythic import. In a third phase of his career, O'Neill appeared to replace private memories in existential contexts analogous to those of Melville's *Billy Budd* or *Clarel*. The concerns of plays such as *Iceman* and *Journey*, works envisaging a nihilistic universe, are by and large of a humanistic nature. In these late dramas, man must learn to cope with an uncongenial environment from which the shadow of god has totally vanished. In short, the two artists insert sea memories into contexts charged with either romantic, metaphysical, or existential resonances. Such a constant would tend to suggest the progressive darkening of O'Neill's and Melville's autobiographical vision of the sea motif. Both artists were fascinated by the sea, on which they had sailed in early manhood. They often recorded, in their novels and plays, the various facets of the ocean with which they had been confronted.

Similarly, their vision of the land is not entirely divested of autobiographical connotations. In the case of these autobiographical remembrances, however, the pattern of love/hate tension tends to prevail, as I shall demonstrate below. I do not wish to devote in this section lengthy passages to an analysis of the direct link between the authors' biographies and their works, although some background information is necessary. The biographical connections have been sufficiently established by Louis Sheaffer and Edwin Miller, to whom I shall refer in my survey.[2] My brief consideration of O'Neill's and Melville's autobiographical vision of the land will form a prelude to my more thorough examination of their sea motif.

A. The Land as Autobiography

Focusing on their reminiscences of the land, of society, both O'Neill and Melville were deeply affected by the disintegration of the American family unit. While they had experienced that phenomenon directly in their childhood and adolescence, they transposed it in novelistic and dramatic forms by emphasizing the love/hate tensions existing in the relationships between members of the family. This accentuated the dramatic poignancy of their works, but unfortunately often made them verge on melodrama. Needless to say, these tensions are endowed with Freudian overtones, particularly in the case of O'Neill, who was imbued with psychoanalytical theories. Naturally, these Freudian allusions are superficial and no exact clinical correspondence between O'Neill's and Melville's descriptions and Freud's tenets should be attempted. Nonetheless, in both O'Neill and Melville, brothers, fathers, mothers, and sons are the protagonists of a drama, the dynamics of which often remain hidden in the characters' unconscious.

I

Gansevoort Melville, Herman's brother, was extremely gifted and intelligent and his parents preferred him to homely Herman. As a result, the young novelist envied his sibling and constantly emulated him. Gansevoort was a charismatic figure and so successful in public that he finally went into politics. Nevertheless, toward the end of 1837, Gansevoort injured his ankle and took to bed. He subsequently suffered from a kind of nervous breakdown. Herman developed mixed feelings of love and hate towards this brother figure, feelings which took their roots in an ambivalent attitude of admiration and jealousy. Although Melville never directly portrayed his brother in his works, he alluded to him in at least two instances. The first of these instances indicates Herman's hidden emotion of hate towards the brother figure, as he focuses on Gansevoort's physical ailment. In *Typee* (1846), Edwin Haviland Miller argues, Tommo's mysterious leg injury recalls Gansevoort's illness.[3] On the contrary, Edwin Haviland Miller continues, feelings of love towards the brother figure dominate in *White-Jacket*. In this novel, the narrator alludes to a brother who "is at liberty to call personally upon the President of the United States, and express his disapprobation of the whole national administration" while the hero is "subject to the cut-throat martial law!"[4] While the brother motif is but embryonic in the works of Melville, it acquires larger dimensions in the plays of O'Neill. Still, it revolves around the love/hate tension, as in the works of the novelist.

Like Melville, O'Neill felt linked to his brother Jamie through bonds of unusual intensity. Jamie O'Neill, Sheaffer tells us, was an extremely gifted youth whom Eugene rivaled. Jamie introduced his younger brother to poetry and almost started his literary career. He also initiated him to alcohol and sexuality.[5] Eugene, however, felt jealous of the love his mother conferred upon Jamie. Like Melville, he appears to have experienced an ambivalent attitude of love/hate and admiration/jealousy towards his brother. Moreover, he felt compelled, much in the manner of Melville, to integrate reminiscences of Jamie into the texture of his dramas. In *Journey* (1941), the love/hate tension serves to illustrate the Freudian conflicts existing between the two young men. O'Neill makes it clear that Jamie and Edmund like each other: "JAMIE: [...] We've been more than brothers. You're the only pal I've ever had. I love your guts. I'd do anything for you. EDMUND: (reaches out and pats his arm). I know that, Jamie." (p. 143) When Jamie sardonically describes his mother as Ophelia, however, the hostility between the two brothers is evident: "JAMIE: [...] The Mad Scene. Enter Ophelia! [...] Edmund [...] slaps Jamie across the mouth with the back of his hand." (p. 151) In *Misbegotten* (1943), O'Neill attempts to overcome his conflict with Jamie and tries to sympathize with his predicament. In this play, Jamie confesses his guilt to a benevolent heroine named Josie Hogan:

> TYRONE: I had to bring her (his mother's) body East to be buried beside the Old Man. I took a drawing room and hid in it with a case of booze. She was in her coffin in the baggage car...I found I couldn't stay alone in the drawing room [...]. I was going crazy [...]. I'd spotted one passenger [...]. She had parlor house written all over her—a blonde pig who looked more like a whore than twenty-five whores. (pp. 96–97)[6]

When at the end of the play, Josie forgives Tyrone, the reader senses that she is giving him the blessing that O'Neill would have wished to grant his relative. Although O'Neill eventually appears willing to transcend the love/hate relationship that fettered him to his brother, this emotional tension nonetheless runs through *Journey*, where it receives Melvillean connotations.

II

Allan Melville died when his son Herman was only twelve. He had been a dogmatic father and had always plainly demonstrated his preference for his elder son, Gansevoort. Because he had failed in business, his family was forced to pay his debts after his death. Consequently, Melville constantly felt the need to search for a father surrogate. In a number of his works, feelings of love/hate towards the father image can be detected: the writer longed for the protection of paternal love while simultaneously resenting his father's inability to bring him security and affection.[7] In *Redburn* (1849), the father figure is associated with the happiness of childhood. Redburn confesses: "I must not think of those delightful days before my father became a bankrupt, and died, and we removed from the City; for when I think of those days, something rises up in my throat and almost strangles me." (p. 82)[8] In *Moby Dick*, however, it is anger that influences Melville's characterization of Ahab as a negligent father. The Captain sacrifices his child in order to pursue selfish goals and does not listen to Starbuck's plea to return home. The two facets of love and hate are united in *White-Jacket* (1850). As Miller argues, the sailor Jack Chase represents a father surrogate, a latter-day Apollo, a symbol of purity to whom the crew must look up.[9] But the hero's sense of jealousy towards this disguised father figure eventually supersedes his admiration. He debunks Jack Chase by having him profer enthusiastic but exaggerated assertions:

> How many great men have been sailors, White Jacket! They say Homer himself was once a tar, even as his hero, Ulysses, was both sailor and shipwright. I'll swear Shakespeare was once a captain of the forecastle. Do you mind the first scene in *The Tempest*, White Jacket? And the world-finder, Christopher Columbus, was a sailor! And so was Camoëns, who went to sea with Gama, else we had never had *The Lusiad* [...]. Old Noah was the first sailor [...]. There's Shelley, he was quite a sailor. Shelley—poor lad! a Percy, too—but they ought to have let him sleep in his sailor's grave—he was drowned in the Mediterranean, you know [...]. And was not Byron a sailor [...]. There never was a very great man yet who spent all his life inland. (pp. 254–255)

Earlier, the narrator had already observed that the noble Jack Chase was "[...] a little bit of a dictator [...]. Intent on egotistically mending our manners and improving our tastes, so that we might reflect credit upon our tutor." (p.18) A comparable love/hate tension marks O'Neill's vision of his father.

During his youth, the dramatist used to run down his father; he complained to friends of his being miserly; he despised the theatre in which he worked. In the 1920's, as he wrote to a friend, he experienced a change of heart: "[...] Father's death leaves a big hole in my life. He and I had become great pals in the last two years."[10] In the O'Neill Collection of the Beinecke, one finds a diagram drawn by the playwright as a child, illustrating the nature of his relationship with the various members of his family. It indicates, among other things, that O'Neill hated his father for having sent him away to boarding school at the age of seven, thereby depriving him of the maternal presence.[11] This ambiguous stance towards the father reappears in a number of plays. In *Cross* (1918), O'Neill offers a negative view of the father figure by presenting Captain Bartlett as a hard man. In *Wilderness* (1932), on the contrary, he introduces a sentimental and idealized portrait of James O'Neill. These two images are juxtaposed in *Journey*. On the one hand, Edmund/O'Neill hates his father for sending him to a cheap sanatorium, where his chances of recovery from tuberculosis are slight: "[...] But to think when it's a question of your son having consumption you can show yourself up [...] as such a stinking old tightwad!" (p. 126) A few moments later, James explains how he had to struggle to survive during his miserable childhood. At that point, one feels that O'Neill voices his sympathy for the sufferings his father had to endure:

> TYRONE: [...] My mother was left, a stranger in a strange land, with four small children, me and a sister a little older and two younger than me. My two older brothers had moved to other parts. They couldn't help. They were hard put to it to keep themselves alive. There was no damned romance in our poverty. Twice we were evicted from the miserable hovel we called home, with my mother's few sticks of furniture thrown out in the street, and my mother and sisters crying. I cried, too, though I tried hard not to, because I was the man of the family. At ten years old! There was no more school for me [...]. (pp. 128–129)

In his most autobiographical play, then, O'Neill offers a refined version of the father/son conflict which he had already treated in *Cross* and *Wilderness*. Like Melville, he creates his play by heightening the love/hate tensions hidden under the surface of reality.

III

Throughout her life, Maria Melville suffered periods of nervous breakdowns. As her health deteriorated rapidly, Allan Melville constantly referred to her "delicate" condition. In order to compensate for her sense of insecurity, she tended to adopt a commanding tone towards other members of the household. The novelist loved this neurotic mother but at the same time could only disapprove of her authoritarian attitude. In two of his works, he expressed these ambivalent feelings.[12]

In *Moby Dick* (1851), he associates the maternal symbol with love. After the sinking of the "Pequod," the writer records Ishmaël's rescue in the following terms: "On the second day, a sail drew near, nearer, and picked me up at last. It was the devious-cruising Rachel, that in her retracing search after her missing children, only found another orphan." (p. 687)[13] It is through maternal care that Ishmaël is saved after having been attacked by the masculine power of the white whale. In *Pierre* (1852), however, the novelist describes the mother as a possessive being. Mrs. Glendinning manipulates her son so that "he remain all docility" to her (p. 26).[14] O'Neill resorts to comparable strategies in order to present the mother figure as either endearing or despicable.

After the birth of Eugene, Ella Quinlan O'Neill rapidly became drug-addicted. Indeed, during her pregnancy, she had taken much morphine in order temporarily to relieve her pain. She subsequently underwent periods of depression and retired in isolation.[15] Although O'Neill resented her behavior, he adored his mother as much as she loved him, an emotional ambiguity which can be traced in *Desire* (1924) and *Wilderness*. In the former, O'Neill dramatizes the effects of a "sinister maternity" whereas in the latter, he idealizes the mother figure. These two facets recur in *Journey*, in which Edmund accuses his mother of having caused the disintegration of the family unit through her addiction. His lines reveal an underlying sense of anger:

EDMUND: [...] It was right after that papa and Jamie decided they couldn't hide it (Mary's addiction) from me any more. Jamie told me. I called him a liar, I tried to punch him in the nose [...]. God! It made everything seem so rotten [...]. I'm going to tell you whether you want to hear it or not. I've got to go to a sanatorium.

MARY: [...] Go away? No! I won't have it! How dare Doctor Hardy advise such a thing without consulting me! How dare your father allow him! What right has he? You are my baby! (p.103)

In this dialogue, critics generally agree, O'Neill indirectly presents his mother as a possessive figure, comparable to Melville's own mother. Towards the end of the work, however, O'Neill sympathizes with Mary Tyrone's (his mother surrogate) ordeal. As she enters the room in the final scene after taking an unusual dose of medecine, she evokes youthful memories: "[...] I had a talk with mother Elizabeth [...]. I told her I wanted to be a nun [...]. Then in the spring something happened to me. Yes, I remember. I fell in love with James Tyrone and was so happy for a time." (pp. 155–156) Transposing art into reality, the spectator cannot help but being moved by the fate of O'Neill's beloved mother for, like Melville, the playwright patterns autobiographical material of a quasi-Freudian nature into dramatic art through emotional tensions.

Depicting the American family through kindred artistic forms, O'Neill and Melville explore aspects of the status of the individual in the New World. Indeed, in analyzing family feuds, they wish to elucidate the identity of the self by opposition to brother, father, and mother. Such quest lends a genuine emotional quality to some of their best novels and plays.

B. The Sea as Autobiography

I

On June 5, 1839, Melville sailed aboard the "St Lawrence" and, after a short stay in Liverpool, came back to the United States on September 30, 1839. Two years later, he felt tempted to sail again. He boarded the whaler "Acushnet," which was headed for the Pacific, via Cape Horn, on January 3, 1841. In June, 1842, his ship reached Nukahiva in the Marquesas Islands and on July 9, Melville deserted with a friend. After living for a month among the natives, he escaped on an Australian whaler, the "Lucy Ann," which took him to Tahiti in September. There he was imprisoned by the British consul for having refused to pay duty. With the help of a few companions, Melville managed to flee to the island of Moorea. From there, he shipped as a boat-steerer on the Nantucket whaler "Charles and Henry" to be discharged in Hawaii in April, 1843. He spent nearly half a year in Honolulu and on August 17, 1843, he enlisted in the U.S. Navy as an ordinary seaman aboard the frigate "United States." On October 14, 1844, Melville reached Boston and was reunited with his family at Lansingburgh. He subsequently decided to write novels, but nevertheless went to sea a few more times. In 1849, he sailed to Europe in order to sell proof sheets of his novel, *White Jacket*, to an English publisher. After a brief tour to Paris and to Rhineland, he returned to New York in February, 1850. A few years later, urged by his family, in October, 1856, he began a leisurely trip to England—where he visited Hawthorne—, the Mediterranean and the Holy Land. Finally, in 1860, he undertook a voyage to San Francisco aboard the clipper "Meteor" under the command of his young brother Tom. Although he had intended to sail round the world from San Francisco, he hurried back home by steamer. Until his death in 1891, Melville never went to sea again, although his late works continued to mirror his passion for the ocean.[16]

Through his various voyages, O'Neill, like Melville, explored the North and South Seas of the world. Although he never sailed on the South Pacific, he was exposed to the sensuousness of the Caribbean, and visited the enchanted islands of the Far East. In addition, he crossed the Atlantic several times on his way to Europe and thus experienced the bleakness of the North Seas.[17]

Upon Coming back to the United States after his trip to Central America, O'Neill felt increasingly bored with bourgeois life. He decided to embark on another trip to far-off confines of the earth. He signed up on board the "Charles Racine," a windjammer, headed towards Buenos Aires and commanded by Captain Waage. O'Neill was accepted as a semi-passenger: he paid $ 75 for his passage and was expected to perform minor duties on deck. After having to anchor for two days near the harbor because of heavy fogs, the ship finally left for Buenos Aires on June 8, 1910. Between Boston and Buenos Aires, the

"Racine" was assailed by headwinds and storms, and the voyage took fifty-seven days. She arrived in Buenos Aires on August 4. A few days later, the dramatist went to work in a Singer Sewing Machine plant for five pesos a day. While he stayed at the hotel Continental for several weeks, O'Neill also frequented the Sailor's Opera and other cafés. He subsequently managed to obtain a position with the local branch of the United States Electrical Supplies Company by posing as a draftsman. He continued, however, to feel restless. It is even alleged that during his stay in Argentina, he made a quick trip to South Africa, tending mules on a British cattle steamer. Today, critics tend to consider this African passage as purely fictitious. Finally, the young playwright went home on the "S.S. Ikala," on which he signed up on March 20, 1911, for the nominal pay of one shilling a month. He had to do his full share of the work, i.e., scrubbing deck, chipping crust, and painting. En route to New York, the "S.S. Ikala" stopped for several days at Port of Spain to load bunker coal and Trinidad cocoanuts. O'Neill remained on the "S.S. Ikala" less than a month and arrived in New York on the night of April 15, 1911. There he began to lead a dissolute life on the waterfront and became one of the *habitués* of "Jimmy the Priest's," a bar located on Fulton Street. A few months after his return, he sailed again, this time to Europe. On July 22, 1911, he boarded the "S.S. New York" as an ordinary seaman. This luxury liner of the American line was headed for Southampton. When O'Neill arrived in England, a general strike paralyzed the harbors of the British Isles, an episode later called the Great General Strike of 1911. He came back from Southampton on August 19, 1911, on the "Philadelphia" as an able-bodied seaman. At that point, he had become familiar with the ship's nomenclature; he could tie all the standard knots and use the compass. After that trip, O'Neill never went back to sea as a sailor. In 1928, having abandoned his second wife Agnes Boulton, he nevertheless undertook a long voyage to the Far East with his third wife, Carlotta Monterey. It is conceivable that, drawing from his past experience, O'Neill behaved as an observer more perceptive than others. He and Carlotta left with the "S.S. André Lebon" in Marseille on October 5, 1928. The playwright celebrated his 40th birthday while sailing through the Red Sea (on October 16). The ship stopped at Djibouti, Colombo, Singapore, and Saigon. O'Neill suffered from a sunstroke in Singapore and succumbed to gambling fever in Saigon. The couple subsequently moved to Hong Kong, Shanghai and Manila. After a quarrel, they sailed back to Europe on different ships: the playwright on the "Coblenz" and the actress on the "President Monroe." When the two vessels anchored at Port Saïd, they were reconciled and continued their journey together to Genoa. In the course of his career, O'Neill embarked on several other voyages. At one point, he sailed back and forth between New York and the Bermudas where he lived for a while with Agnes. These trips, however, do not seem to have had any lasting impact on his creative imagination. His voyages to South America, Europe, and the Far East confronted him with the two facets of the sea—the dark North Seas and the idyllic South Seas—of which Melville constantly spoke in his novels.

II

In the South Seas romance *Typee*, Melville records episodes of his voyage to the Pacific, as a summary of the plot suggests. The young heroes, Tommo and Toby, weary and bored after fifteen months on the whaler "Dolly" commanded by Captain Vaugs, suddenly desert the ship in order to explore the hills of Nukahiva. They set off in search of the Happars, a peace-loving tribe. However, as Tommo is injured on the way, the two companions are forced to take refuge in the idyllic valley of the Typees, a tribe of cannibals. The natives take good care of the young men. But after the mysterious disappearance of his friend Toby, Tommo, the hero, prefers to escape from the Typee valley. Tommo violently strikes the chieftain Mow-Mow on his way to the vessel "Julia." His cruel gesture allows him to run away from the false paradise of the South Seas. The autobiographical nature of this narrative is evident in the profusion of realistic details that Melville offers about the daily life of the Typees. And yet, it would seem that the novelist blends facts with elements of a more literary quality: he presents actual experience through the filter of individual memory. It could be argued that, in the process of composition, Melville relies both on personal reminiscences and on documentary works on the Pacific scene or travel narratives. The best instance of that phenomenon of romantic—in the sense of lyrical and sentimental—idealization undoubtedly resides in Tommo's relationship with Fayaway, a nymph evoking the pastoral overtones of exotic tales of far-away voyages. The heroine looks unreal and, from the start, represents perfection:

Her free pliant figure was the very perfection of female grace and beauty. Her complexion was a rich and mantling olive, and when watching the glow upon her cheeks, I could almost swear that beneath the transparent medium there lurked the blushes of a faint vermilion. [...] Her hair of the deepest brown, parted irregularly in the middle, flowed in natural ringlets over her shoulders, and whenever she chanced to stoop, fell over and hid from view her lovely bosom [...]. The skin of this young creature, from continual ablutions and the use of mollifying ointments, was inconceivably smooth and soft [...]. (pp. 133–134)[18]

Melville resorts to a language replete with adjectives suggestive of idealistic beauty. As a result, he fails to present us with an authentic portrait of the female native of the Marquesas and betrays his indebtedness to romantic travel literature. A similar mood pervades Melville's vision of the sea, steeped as it is in biography, in *Omoo*, *Mardi*, *Redburn*, and *White-Jacket*.

While in works written between 1846 and 1850, the novelist draws from personal and lyrical reminiscences in order to structure his literary creations, in his masterpiece *Moby Dick*, his fictionalized autobiography betrays metaphysical concerns, through an interest in the existence of a ruling deity. Certainly, *Moby Dick* constitutes the culminating point of an evolution that led the author away from a purely sentimental vision. He seemed able here to conceal his sources so craftily that the exact correspondence of the voyage of the "Pequod" with his personal biography is somewhat difficult to discern. One of the most evident aspects of symbolism in *Moby Dick* resides in Melville's innovative view of the sea: the ocean elicits an ambivalent response from the sailor confronted with its power. While man can acquire nobility in trying to conquer the sea, he will undoubtedly be repelled by the treacherousness of the deep. The ocean possesses a divine nature, for it is "shoreless, indefinite as God." (p. 203) But the power of Melville's oceanic deity, epitomized by the white whale, is intent on destroying mankind: "wonder ye then at the fiery hunt?" (p. 296) From these short quotations, it is clear that, in *Moby Dick*, Melville deserts the sentimental strain inherent in his earlier novels. His modified techniques affect more than his sea symbolism: they also serve to enhance characterization.

The main protagonist of *Moby Dick*, Captain Ahab, is both a real and mythical figure. In attempting to transform Ahab into a symbol of human pride,

Melville enlists the aid of patterns belonging to classical mythology. Critics have not failed to note the parallel between Ahab and Prometheus and have interpreted his fire grabbing gesture in "The Candles" as a modern equivalent of the Greek hero's stealing of the fire.[19] Unable to understand the evil nature of his pride, Ahab resembles Oedipus; he also recalls Narcissus when in "The Doubloon" he admires his own reflection in the mysterious coin. Melville equally endows Ishmaël with mythical overtones. The latter serves, not unlike his Biblical counterpart, as a symbol of the outcast. Moreover, towards the end of the novel, he is compared to Ixion, revolving for a while in the whirlpool of Ahab's madness but eventually escaping total destruction. These mythical allusions contribute to heightening the universality of Melville's metaphysical probings.

In his late career, Melville continues to admire the sea but transmutes reminiscences of his sailor days through methods diverging from those to which he had resorted in his early and middle years. In 1876, he publishes *Clarel. A Poem and Pilgrimage to the Holy Land*, which possesses clear roots in his biography inasmuch as it is inspired by his 1856 trip to Europe and the Holy Land. In this long epic poem, Melville refers to the Dead Sea as a background to the philosophical discussions held by his characters. The Dead Sea symbolizes the sterility of a contemporary world forgotten by God. While the writer no longer places the sea in a mythic context as in *Moby Dick*, he suffuses *Clarel* with existential connotations, such as man's attitude towards the absurdity of life.

My concept of "the absurd" and "existentialism," which will recur in this and other chapters, is derived from Albert Camus's *The Myth of Sisyphus and Other Essays*.[20] Camus claims that the absurd is located in the disjunction between man and the universe. In such a world, man is deprived of the help of faith: "[…] in a universe suddenly divested of illusions and lights, man feels an alien, a stranger. His exile is without remedy since he is deprived of the memory of a lost home or the hope of a promised land." (p. 5) Camus sees the absurd as the condition of tragedy and its joy: "All Sisyphus's silent joy is contained therein. His fate belongs to him. His rock is his thing. Likewise, the absurd man, when he contemplates his torment, silences all the idols […]. The absurd man says yes and his effort will henceforth be unceasing […]. Sisyphus teaches the higher fidelity that negates the gods and raises rocks […]. The struggle itself towards the heights is enough to fill a man's heart. One must imagine Sisyphus happy." (pp. 90–91) In this passage, Camus develops a philosophy related to O'Neill's and Melville's late works in its praise of man's courageous acceptance of an apparently godless universe. Although Camus's existential philosophy has clear roots in the works of Kierkegaard, Nietzsche and Sartre, I have chosen to focus in this study on *The Myth of Sisyphus* because it sets forth the precepts of existentialism in unsystematic and quasi-artistic modes which can be more readily applied to the examination of O'Neill's and Melville's works.

In *Clarel*, then, the physical presence of the sea has lost its impact but nonetheless serves to stress the didactic considerations of the novelist. Time and again in the course of this epic poem, the hero is exhorted to be concerned only with intellectual and humanistic issues. Although O'Neill was obviously closer to Camus than Melville is in *Clarel*, in which one can also see what some critics have called a "religious conversion to life,"[21] the protagonist's bold facing of the limitations of existence nonetheless foreshadows the thinkings of later existentialist writers.

Billy Budd, published only in 1924, also deals with our perception of a universe from which divine justice has seemingly disappeared. In this short novel, the writer relegates sea-faring memories to the background in order to voice an existential comment on the nature of the human predicament. In condemning the hero of the story to death, Captain Vere punishes the young sailor in excess of his guilt. Although Billy Budd actually committed murder, his gesture was not motivated by vice but rather, constituted a direct consequence of his ignorance of evil. God, Melville suggests, strips man of all hope in a universe that holds no possibility of redemption. In that world, brutality renders goodness ineffectual. As Billy is about to be executed, Melville obliquely compares him to "the Lamb of God seen in mystical vision." (pp. 400–401)[22] But in showing how his hero fails to *resurrect*, the novelist implies that mankind is deprived of any Savior and can only achieve grandeur in resisting the absurdity of existence.

Romantic vision, metaphysical considerations, existential themes: these are the three factors which lend a literary form to Melville's reminiscences of the South and North Seas. Melville evolved through these three stages in a neat chronogical sequence. Moreover, he used the autobiographical mode in order to express and exorcise typically American anxieties about the identity of the self and the setting.

The narrators of his tales—in fact, disguised versions of himself—are in many ways questing heroes, who seek to define their situation in the universe. In

Typee, the protagonist has learned the essence of evil through his stay in the cannibal island; in *Moby Dick*, Ishmaël musters the courage to bear his own human limitations after witnessing the tragedy of Ahab. In *Clarel* and *Billy Budd*, Melville appears to have lost faith in the possibilities of self-fulfillment in this world. Man's efforts at self definition are crushed by the annihilation of death.

Further, Melville introduces in his autobiographical works a certain feeling of doubt about the stability of the human setting, a concern that extends beyond the self. Like many other American writers, he comments on the New World environment, often regarded as threatening.[23] It is not surprising therefore to note that Melville's heroes often embark on a voyage, during which they try to discover the meaning of their milieu. They never seem able to find a final haven until they have achieved the goal of their quest. Melville's journeys combine actual and metaphorical levels of significance: in *Moby Dick*, the sailors of the "Pequod" pursue the godly whale. At the end of their search, however, the protagonists often fail to experience any sense of continuity in space. Like Ishmaël, they cannot belong in any specific setting. Their psychological restlessness thus finds a correlative in their spatial instability. Like Melville, Eugene O'Neill seeks, however vainly, to exorcise deeply-rooted fears about the self and the environment through the medium of autobiographical literature.

III

In his first works about the sea, O'Neill, like Melville, confers sentimental and nostalgic overtones upon private recollections. Louis Sheaffer believes that in composing *Cardiff* (1914), O'Neill took the "S.S. Ikala," on which he had sailed back from Argentina, as a model.[24] Sheaffer details the sources for O'Neill's *dramatis personae* to reach identical conclusions. On his way back to the United States from Europe in August 1911, the dramatist encountered a Liverpool Irishman named Driscoll, whom he later described in the following terms:

Five feet seven, in his early thirties, built rather like an unpended anchor, with massive arms and shoulders overarching a sturdy body, he was, O'Neill said, a "giant of a man, and absurdly strong. He thought a whole lot of himself, was a determined individualist. He was very

proud of his strength, his capacity for grueling work. It seemed to give
him mental poise to be able to dominate the stokehold, to do more than
any of his mates."[25]

In *Cardiff*, the critic maintains, O'Neill endowed his two protagonists with some
of the characteristics he had observed in this Irishman. But his one-act is more
than a mere record of facts. Yank, the dying sailor, remembers his past life in a
long interior monologue. Although Yank experienced some degree of happiness
during his various voyages around the earth, he nonetheless had to suffer from
the poor living conditions aboard ship: "This sailor life ain't much to cry about
leavin'—just one ship after another, hard work, small pay, and bum grub [...]."
(p. 46)[26] O'Neill clearly wishes us to sympathize with Yank's laments and
suffuses the portrayal of his character with heavily idealistic touches in an attempt
to move the audience. In this respect, his romantic method resembles that adopted
by Melville in *Typee, Mardi, Omoo,* and *White Jacket.*[27] In other plays
written during his early career, such as *Caribbees, Zone, Long Voyage,
Cross, Anna,* and *Ape,* O'Neill modified memories of the sea along
comparable lines, i.e., in a marked romantic fashion.

In his trilogy *Electra* (1931), O'Neill inserts the sea motif in a thematic
context dealing with metaphysical issues. Like Melville in *Moby Dick,* he utilizes
intensely private reminiscences in order to illustrate the conflict between man and
the justice of God. His ocean, it is true, contrary to that of the novelist, is
relegated to the background while the action takes place on the continent, in New
England. The South Seas Islands to which the characters of the play allude
symbolize a desire to avoid the revenge of the divinity whereas in *Moby Dick,* a
violent confrontation occurs directly on the deep. The sea imagery of Electra is
in sharp contrast to the fate that crushes the Mannons, and the "Blessed Isles"
represent Edenic innocence: "BRANT: [...] I told you of the islands in the South
Seas where I was shipwrecked my first voyage at sea [...]. They (the natives) live
as near the Garden of Paradise before sin was discovered as you'll find on this
earth [...]. You can forget there all men's dirty dreams of greed and power!" (p.
706)[28] Throughout the drama, one gathers the impression that a fierce deity
forces the Mannons to atone for their crimes. In Act V of *The Hunted,* Christine
says: "Now I know there is only hell" (p. 805) as she apparently feels mentally
exhausted with the burden of remorse. Like Melville, O'Neill universalizes the

conflict between mankind and the avenging deity through mythical references. It is the story of Orestes that underlies the structure of *Electra* and lends a measure of coherence to its metaphysical underpinnings. This pattern, along with the image of the islands as a Biblical paradise, offers O'Neill the opportunity to modify experience into dramatic art.[29]

In a third phase of his career, O'Neill replaces sea memories in existential contexts. *Iceman* (1939) divulges the impressions that O'Neill recorded during his stay at "Jimmy the Priest's" in 1911, after his return from Argentina. In this late masterpiece, he stresses the harrowing possibility that only false saviors exist in our universe. Larry Slade powerfully expresses his bleak philosophy in the last moments of the play when, persuaded that no divinity could rescue man, he reveals a profound yearning for death: "[...] Be God, I'm the only real convert to death Hickey made here. From the bottom of my coward's heart I mean that now!" (p. 258) [30]Lurking in the background of this desolate world, the image of the sea serves to heighten the sense of despair. Larry ironically describes the bar as "[...] the No Chance Saloon. It's bedrock bar, The End of the Line Café, The bottom of the Sea Rathskeller! Don't you notice the beautiful calm in the atmosphere? That's because it's the last harbor [...]." (p. 25) Thus, in *Iceman*, O'Neill's autobiographical sea motif confers more authenticity upon his existential considerations on human life.

In *Journey*, he explores related issues within the narrower context of the American family. The factual underpinnings of this play have been repeatedly underlined.[31] Edmund Tyrone has been associated with the playwright's self-portrait and the scenes recording his sea adventures rank among the best of the entire drama. Edmund's father explains his son's distraught state in religious terms. Accusing him of reading atheistic novels, he comments indignantly: "[...] You've [...] flouted the faith you were born and brought up in—the one true faith of the Catholic church—and your denial has brought nothing but self-destruction." (p. 66) It is in a context dealing with man's loss of faith and the absence of God that sea imagery emerges. Edmund's daydreams suggest that the only solution open to mankind consists in a mystical union with nature: "[...] I was set free! I dissolved in the sea, became white sails and flying spray, became beauty and rhythm, became moonlight and the ship and the high dim-starred sky!" (p. 134) However, Edmund's visions can only provide a temporary sense of relief. In the end, man will be confronted with the shattering reality of death. In skillfully weaving the sea-motif into the existential and psychological framework of his play, O'Neill manages to reap artistic effects analogous to those devised by Melville in *Billy Budd* and *Clarel*.[32]

The sea held such a strong fascination for both O'Neill and Melville that, as young men, they left their families to become sailors. Not only is the *bios*, i.e., the factual, component of their autobiographical works strikingly similar, their literary response towards experience translated itself into a nearly identical use of stylistic realism.[33] Indeed, I have made clear that both writers inserted their sea memories into progressively darker contexts charged with either romantic, metaphysical, or existential resonances.[34] Likewise, when dealing with the family, they concentrate on similar tensions of love and hate. A further point of confluence between the technical aspect, i.e., *graphein*, of their autobiography-slanted works deserves examination. Both are pursuing in these novels and plays the same goal: that of defining the self and commenting obliquely on anxieties inherent in the American psyche, more specifically on the American doubt about the nature of the human environment.

In the early one-act plays of Eugene O'Neill, the main protagonists, like those of Herman Melville, are tortured by self-doubts. In *Cardiff*, Yank remembers his past life before dying and in doing so, seeks to obliterate the thought of death. In addition, his attempts allow him to consolidate his sense of identity by determining his position in the universe. In *Electra*, the characters intensely yearn to understand the nature of their link with God. Finally, in *Iceman* and *Journey*, the anti-heroes engage in a search for psychological strength in order to withstand the painful reality of the death of God, a fact threatening to fragment the self.

If a stable definition of the self needs to be arrived at, the setting also requires thorough identification. In O'Neill's early sea plays, as in Melville's early romances, the heroes embark on quests that take the shape of a physical voyage. In the course of these seemingly endless journeys, man appears unable to find the security of the land. In *Cardiff*, Yank dies before reaching England; in *Electra*, the Mannons can reach happiness neither in New England nor in the South Seas Islands; in *Journey*, Edmund cannot feel at home in Connecticut: the vastness of the ocean, on the contrary, renders his life meaningful; finally, in *Iceman*, Harry Hope's bar functions as a last harbor of peace to all those who have failed to experience human warmth in the outside world. In other words, O'Neill's alienated heroes are generally dismayed at the discontinuity of the American setting.

If Melville's and O'Neill's autobiographical tendencies displayed a wish to establish a self and to endow their environment with meaningful unity, the bitter fate of which their protagonists eventually become the victims indicates that the two authors slowly came to regard their initial purpose as impossible to achieve. Critics have often remarked that American autobiographies served to exorcise painful memories, either personal or cultural in essence.[35] In the case of O'Neill and Melville, however, a significant departure from that model can be traced: it could be argued that, in some measure, both writers were writing in a mode that could be loosely defined as "ironic autobiography."

C. "Songs of Myself."

That critics should have taken O'Neill's affinities to Melville for granted is not surprising. In this chapter, I have delineated some artistic factors tending to establish the validity of that concept. It is perhaps owing to the similarity between their biographical sources that O'Neill's and Melville's literary outputs reveal so many resemblances. Their autobiographical journeys thus determine the parallels existing between the shape of their career, the "Gestalt" of their fiction and drama. These traces of confluence alone would not justify an examination of O'Neill's kinship with Melville, were they not borne out by more specific similarities, such as those that I shall explore in the following chapters. The latter, however, will gain significance if they can be placed in the larger context of Melville's and O'Neill's autobiographical concerns. In many ways, the two men of letters are working—perhaps unconsciously—in the tradition of Walt Whitman's "Song of Myself." Like the poet, they celebrate the self, the source of autobiographical literature, but do so in different genres: the novel and the drama. Like him, they use autobiographical techniques to reconcile the self with its environment. In the end, through their kindred ironic vision, they contribute, albeit obliquely, to the development of American autobiography.

CHAPTER III. MARINERS AND MYSTICS

In cabin'd ships at sea,

The boundless blue on every side expanding,

With whistling winds and music of the waves,

the large imperious waves,

Or some lone bark buoy'd on the dense marine,

Where joyous full of faith, spreading white sails,

She cleaves the ether mid the sparkle and the foam

of day, or under many a star at night,

By sailors young and old haply will I, a reminiscence of the land, be read,

In full rapport at last.

Walt Whitman, "In Cabin'd Ships at Sea"[1]

O'Neill's and Melville's strikingly convergent visions of sea imagery prompted them to regard oceans as a source of mystical experience. Drawing from their personal reminiscences, Melville and O'Neill described the ocean from their perspective as New World observers: they were fascinated by both the mystery and the freedom it offered. In their works, one detects a multifaceted and romantic vision of the sea, which exhibits correspondences to Whitman's "Sea-Drift." If, like Whitman, the two authors celebrate the beauty of the boundless oceans, they nonetheless adopt a more pessimistic viewpoint than the poet. They record the cruel power of the sea while extolling the metaphysical vistas it opens to mankind. In this chapter, besides many instances of confluence, I shall focus on parallels at times so evident that it will be possible to interpret them in terms of influence. First, I shall review O'Neill's and Melville's portrait gallery of outcast mariners (*Moby Dick, Ile, Electra*) or dreamy mystics (*Moby Dick, Journey*).

At the outset, it may seem surprising to compare O'Neill's sea symbolism with that of Melville. Indeed, critics have repeatedly asserted that the playwright's plays stood under the direct influence of Joseph Conrad. While the imprints of the British writer are at times unmistakable, O'Neill modifies his model in several respects.2

Whereas Conrad in *The Nigger of the Narcissus* is concerned with allegory and morality, in *Cardiff* O'Neill explores the metaphysical implications of the predicament of a dying sailor. A major element of divergence between the two writers lies in their opposed concepts of the sea as a symbol of God. Conrad writes:

> The true peace of God begins at any spot a thousand miles from the nearest land; and when He sends there the messengers of His might it is not in terrible wrath against crime, presumption and folly, but paternally, to chasten simple hearts—ignorant hearts that know nothing of life, and beat undisturbed by envy or greed.3

If Conrad's deity is a benevolent one that punishes "paternally," O'Neill's God manifests a more cruel behavior. In *Cardiff*, Yank is abandoned by his creator in a terrible universe. In this respect, the playwright's notion of the divinity governing the seas offers more similarities with that of Melville in *Moby Dick*.

Secondly, O'Neill and Conrad differ in their presentation of sea creatures. While in *The Nigger of the Narcissus*, the novelist delineates his sailors as "simple hearts," O'Neill distances himself from such a poetic view. Having at first entitled his one-act "Children of the sea," perhaps as a token of admiration for Conrad, he subsequently adopted the title *Cardiff*. One may detect in this change a desire to avoid the tone in which Conrad depicts his characters.4 O'Neill's sailors are not naive creatures: on the contrary, they have experienced evil, since in *Cardiff*, Yank confesses once committing a murder in the course of his voyages. O'Neill devises a personal realistic style contrasting with Conrad's presentation of James Wait as an allegory of death. Yank, unlike Wait, does not symbolize death: he is merely crushed by it. In Conrad's novel, Wait epitomizes the fearful symbol of physical destruction which terrifies the sailors: "Donkin, as if fascinated by the dumb eloquence and anger of that *black phantom*, approached [...] and it seemed to him suddenly that he was only the shadow of a man crouching high in the bunk on the level with his eyes [...] 'Yer black, rotten *incumbrance* [...] you corpse!'" (p. 127, I italicize) James Wait is merely a ghost: Conrad's insistence on "rotten incumbrance" suggests that he equates his protagonist with death. Thus Conrad's and O'Neill's sea motifs constitute images of two widely opposed universes, in which the characters and their metaphysical environment belong to such different literary traditions as the European and the American.

I will not try to refute the thesis of those critics having analyzed O'Neill's relationship with Conrad. I do agree with Paul Voelker's splendid examination of O'Neill's indebtedness to Conrad in *Cardiff*.[5] But although *Cardiff* has been influenced by *The Nigger of the Narcissus*, I do claim that the dramatist modifies his model along lines similar to those adopted by Melville in his sea works. It is worthwhile in this respect to note that the similarities between O'Neill, Conrad and Melville may find justification in a phenomenon of indirect influence. Indeed, one could argue that O'Neill partly rediscovered Melville through Conrad. Critics such as Harold Beaver and Leon Seltzer have underlined the fact that Conrad might indeed have been strongly influenced by the author of *Moby Dick*.[6] In particular, Seltzer argues that Conrad owes to Melville his use of the techniques of "inscrutability." Like Melville, he offers a discouraged view of reality through kindred portraits of idealists, inverted symbols, confusing rhetoric, restricted narrative viewpoint, and an open form. But Melville's exceedingly religious nature duplicates the specifically American roots of O'Neill's metaphysical vision of the sea to a greater extent than that of Conrad. Like Melville's, O'Neill's depiction of sea dreamers corresponds to a critique of American Transcendentalism foreign to Conrad. Thus, if the origin of some sea motifs in O'Neill are at times difficult to pinpoint I submit that O'Neill's sea symbolism gains added significance when studied against the background of American sea literature, of which *Moby Dick* forms a prominent example.

Moreover, it is reasonable to assume that both Melville and O'Neill, in their rendition of sea imagery, share a common ancestor. They had read and admired Samuel Taylor Coledridge, whose *Rime of the Ancient Mariner* amalgamates, as in many of Melville's and O'Neill's works, sea symbolism and metaphysical probings. Coleridge's concept of the sea as both divine and as source of redemption is mirrored by the two American writers. Merton Sealts even suggests in his study *Melville's Reading* that Melville was familiar with Coleridge's *Biographia Literaria* and *Notes and lectures upon Shakespeare*.[7] O'Neill, on the other hand, even went so far as to dramatize Coleridge's work. The manuscript of that play, entitled *The Ancient Mariner*, is preserved at the Museum of the City of New York.[8] This element of similar ancestry reinforces the link between the novelist and playwright.

In order to examine adequately the romantic nature of O'Neill's and Melville's sea symbol, I have most often relied on Gaston Bachelard's *L'eau et les Rêves* (1942).[9] This French critic is concerned with the river symbol, although his conclusions can be applied to the study of the novelist's and the dramatist's sea. Bachelard classifies different types of literary imaginations according to material principles, i.e., fire, water, earth, and air. For the French critic, the main connotation of the water symbol is death, a view with which both Melville and O'Neill would have agreed. Bachelard suggests that in literature the water principle often becomes associated with such elements as fire, earth, and night. After commenting on the feminine and maternal qualities of the river, he briefly focuses on the ocean which he links with the image of the tempest. He stresses the importance of the human response to the violence of the sea. It can be argued that Melville's and O'Neill's works manifest the phenomenon Bachelard terms "imagination matérielle," i.e., an artistic vision based on the supremacy of the water/sea element. The profundity of a writer's "imagination matérielle/material imagination" can be gauged from the variety and ambivalence of feelings his symbols generate in the reader's mind. Such variety and ambivalence certainly typifies the works of O'Neill and Melville. Thus, Bachelard's theories offer an index to measure the authenticity of the two authors' perception of the sea setting.

A. Melville's Influence

Two novels by Melville have inspired O'Neill straightforwardly: *Typee* and *Moby Dick*. At various stages of his career, the dramatist transposed in his plays motifs borrowed from these two works. A methodological note seems warranted before I launch into this examination: my use of the term "ironic" will refer to a somewhat unusual meaning in this section. It will indicate O'Neill's deceptive, unexpected manipulation of his source, often resulting in a reversal of the significance of the original. I would wish first to concentrate on echoes of *Typee*, Melville's youthful masterpiece, in O'Neill's imaginary universe.

The structure of *Electra*, which contains an explicit reference to *Typee*, derives part of its emotional power from the dramatist's allusions to Melville's novel. Critics such as Ronald T. Curran and Joyce D. Kennedy have noted O'Neill's literary quotation but have not fully examined the implications of the playwright's borrowings.[10] The similarity between *Typee* and *Electra* resides primarily in the South Seas Islands motif, which both authors associate with sexual freedom and innocence. In other words, the "Blessed Islands" of both *Typee* and *Electra* contrast sharply with the Puritanism of New England. Critics have failed to pay attention to the context in which O'Neill's South Seas Islands motif is inserted into the play and to the way in which it is contrasted with the darkness of the North Seas. The song "Shenandoah," which works as a leitmotif in the trilogy, reflects the "brooding rhythm of the sea" (p. 688), one associated in O'Neill's universe with the fierceness of the North seas. In the stage directions of Act I, in "The Homecoming," a male voice sings: "Oh, Shenandoah, I long to hear you/A-way, my rolling river/Oh, Shenandoah, I can't get near you/Way-ay, I'm bound away/Across the wide Missouri." (p. 688) The same song is repeated in the stage directions of Act III of "The Homecoming" (p. 727), and in Act IV of "The Hunted," where it is described as a "capstan chanty," endowed with "sentimentally mournful" qualities (pp. 789–790). This song introduces reminiscences of a bleak sea while constituting an ominous prefiguration of the tragic action. It forms a foil to the South Seas Islands imagery, which the playwright develops in the various acts of the work.

The dark connotations evoked by the "Shenandoah" song are heightened by O'Neill's direct depiction of the North Seas. In Act IV of "The Hunted," a murder is performed on the wharf of East Boston harbor, which O'Neill presents as a morbid setting:

> The stern section of a clipper moored alongside a wharf in East Boston [...]. The ship is unloaded and her black side rises nine or ten feet above the level of the wharf. Below the deck the portholes show a faint light from the interior of the cabin [...]. The moon is rising above the horizon off left rear, its light accentuating the black outlines of the ship. (p. 789)

The black outlines of the ship contribute to augmenting the disquieting atmosphere of the scene. A few moments later, "Orin steps through the door and with the pistol almost against Brant's body fires twice." (p. 801) In *Electra*, the Northern Seas are the background against which the South Seas Islands display their aura of innocence, peace and harmony. In a passage quoted in Chapter II, I have indicated how, in *Typee*, Melville rejects the Puritan hatred of sex. Indeed, through his depiction of the pure nymph Fayaway, he suggests that sexual desire can be devoid of sin. Instead of patterning his image of the South Seas Islands without departing from the Melvillean model, O'Neill confers an ironic twist upon the meaning of *Typee*. He appears to be more profoundly aware than Melville of the false promises held by these islands. O'Neill distances himself from the idealistic vision of the American novelist and therefore examines, unlike Melville, various characters' vision of these "Blessed Islands." By illuminating the significance of the South Seas Islands from divergent perspectives, he indicates that they can only exist in the imagination of the protagonists and represent mere pipe-dreams, inefficient to liberate man from the pressure of Puritanism.

Through the figure of the sea Captain Adam Brant, O'Neill attempts to dramatize an aspect of the conflict between Rousseauism and Puritanism. Brant is a romantic persona, an adventurer, who, like Melville, has "sailed all over the world—he lived on a South Island once, so he says." (p. 697) O'Neill opposes this protagonist, representative of Rousseauistic ideals, to Lavinia Mannon, who epitomizes the sexual represssion of New England Puritanism:

LAVINIA: (in a dry, brittle tone). I remember your admiration for the naked native women. You said they had found the secret of happiness because they had never heard that love can be a sin.

BRANT: [...] And they live in as near the Garden of Paradise before sin was discovered as you'll find on this earth! Unless you've seen it, you can't picture the green beauty of their land set in the blue of the sea! The clouds lie down on the mountain tops, the sun drowsing in your blood, and always the surf on the barrier reef singing a croon in your ears like a lullaby! The Blessed Isles, I'd call them! You can forget there all men's dirty dreams of greed and power! (p. 706)

Brant's Melvillean description fails to move the heroine. Lavinia lives secluded in the house of the Mannons, which resembles a sepulchre: "the 'whited' one of the

Bible—pagan temple front stuck like a mask on Puritan gray ugliness!" (p. 699) In a second scene with Christine Mannon, Brant voices even more explicitly his admiration for those "Blessed Isles" by associating them with his love for Christine: "BRANT: [...] I'd take you on a honeymoon there! To China—and on the voyage back, we'd stop at the South Pacific Islands I've told you about. By God, there's the right place for love and a honeymoon! [...]." (p. 723) In a third scene, Brant eventually recognizes the elusive nature of the dream evoked by those islands. After plotting with Christine the death of Ezra Mannon, he confesses his doubts to his mistress: "BRANT: (with a bitter, hopeless yearning). Aye—the Blessed Isles—There's peace, and forgetfulness for us there—if we can ever find those islands now!" (p. 799) In the course of action, Brant is submitted to a process of corruption and painfully realizes that the "Blessed Isles" will stay confined within the narrow boundaries of his imagination. A similar evolutionary pattern can be detected in the other characters' vision of the South Seas Islands. Ezra Mannon thinks of them in terms bearing close affinities to Brant's lyrical outbursts, especially when he declares to his wife: "I've a notion if we'd leave the children and go off on a voyage together—to the other side of the world—find some island where we could be alone a while. You'll find I have changed, Christine. I'm sick of death! I want life! Maybe you could love me now! " (p. 740) As Brant's dreams are shattered, Ezra's desire to dwell on an island of love is crushed by reality: he eventually falls a victim to Christine's murderous plans. The "Blessed Islands" only appear to represent peace: their illusory nature is quickly revealed.

Alluding to the South Seas Islands, Orin Mannon makes an overt reference to Typee, in asking his mother: "Have you ever read a book called '*Typee*' about the South Sea Islands?" (p. 776) This notation was even more definite in the first draft of *The Hunted*, as I noted in Chapter I.[11] Like Brant and Ezra, Orin at first envisions these islands as a garden of Eden, and, in mentioning them, betrays an incestuous passion for his mother: "[...] I used to dream I was there [...]. I only felt you all around me. The warm sand was like your skin. The whole island was you." (p. 776) Although in an initial stage, these isles stand in sharp opposition to the moral constraints of New England, they subsequently offer but disappointment to Orin upon his return from the Pacific: "They only made me sick—and the naked women disgusted me. I guess I'm too much of a Mannon, after all, to turn into a pagan [...]." (p. 832) He even decodes the isles as emblems of mortality: "Yes! It's the way to peace—to find her again—my lost island—Death is an Island of Peace, too—Mother will be waiting for me there [...]." (p. 854) Orin again links the islands with the space in which sex can be enjoyed without fear of sin, but the death connotations attached to that motif indicate that he has progressively come to recognize the impossibility of experiencing genuine and lasting happiness there. A convergent pattern can thus be established in Brant's, Ezra's and Orin's ultimate disappointment.

O'Neill also concentrates on a fourth character's attitude towards the "Blessed Isles," i.e., Lavinia Mannon's. After travelling to the Pacific, she expresses her admiration for the innocence of the natives in terms evocative of Melville's lyrical description of *Typee*:

> I loved those Islands [...]. There was something there mysterious and beautiful—a good spirit—of love—coming out of the land and the sea. It made me forget death. There was no hereafter. There was only this world [...]. The natives dancing naked and innocent—without knowledge of sin! (pp. 833–834)

The heroine quickly realizes, however, that she will never recapture in New England the sense of a comparable harmony with the universe. Accordingly, she decides to bury herself alive in the House of the Mannons. Through Lavinia's vision of the South Seas Islands, one can detect the same darkening pattern as the one illustrated by Brant's, Ezra's, and Orin's psychological evolution. This points to the pessimistic philosophy to which O'Neill adhered in order to modify his Melvillean model.

Electra represents perhaps the clearest instance of Melville's influence on O'Neill. While critics have commented on this characteristic, they have neglected to draw attention to O'Neill's alterations of the Melvillean motif of the South Seas Islands. The dramatist has relied exclusively on Melville's lively depiction of the Typee valley and has left aside the novelist's suggestion that the South Seas paradise was already corrupted. The American Renaissance writer provides the reader with two views of his Edenic island. If it constitutes a paradise devoid of the knowledge of sexual sin, its inhabitants can nonetheless adopt a violent and cruel behavior in society. Such is the case when they want to force the hero to stay on their island through sheer violence. The playwright distances himself from Melville's idealistic presentation of the "sin of the flesh," and integrates his source into a highly personal texture. In order to achieve this purpose, he utilizes a dramatic technique based on contrasts. All the characters finally recognize the shallowness of the dream evoked by Melville's islands and remain the prisoners of New England Puritanism. In qualifying Melville's vision, O'Neill develops a theme which reappears in *Iceman*, i.e., the impossibility for man to live without pipe-dreams. In *Electra*, the pipe-dream acquires a powerful expression in the South Seas Isles symbol. The protagonists of *Electra* can only muster the courage to face the harshness of their Puritan world in wilfully identifying with the novelist's romantic but unreal islands. A comparison between O'Neill's *Electra* and Melville's *Typee* thus allows the critic to determine the extent to which the playwright depended on his characters' consciousness in order to transpose his Melvillean source into innovative dramatic forms. To Melville's "monolithic" narrative viewpoint, O'Neill substitutes a form of "exploded" angle of vision. In other words, he presents us with a cubist-like view of Melville's novel, as the multiplication of viewpoints indicates. It is to O'Neill's skillful use of contrasts in creating dramatic structure that *Electra* owes its coherence and stylistic effectiveness.

I shall show in my chapter on tragedy that *Electra* was also indebted to *Pierre, or the Ambiguities*. It could even be argued that in *Electra*, O'Neill reproduces the atmosphere of idyllic happiness pervading the initial pages of *Pierre* through the symbol of the "Blessed Islands" derived from *Typee*. In the opening chapter of *Pierre*, the hero enjoys an unmitigated harmony with his mother in Saddle Meadows, a haven of peace akin to the earthly paradise. In *Electra*, Orin talks of a similar tranquillity with Christine in Typee. That *Electra* should contain two references to various novels by Melville, points, together with their skilfully entertwined relationship, to O'Neill's complex vision of his model. As Jean Weisgerber suggests in his article "The Use of Quotation in Recent Literature," O'Neill adopts in *Electra* the attitude and composition technique of a modernist.[12] Like Woolf or Joyce, he quotes from various works of past literature, both in order to assert his link with the tradition, in this case that of his national literary heritage, and to allow the reader to decode the meaning of the work by himself, and thus to participate in the creative process. Through such modernist openness of structure, O'Neill manages to introduce comparisons between his characters and those of nineteenth century writers, thereby pointing to the continuity of human behavior through the ages. The pattern of elaborate quotations I have delineated clearly indicates that *Electra* is a far better structured work than has been recognized hitherto. It deserves to be ranked among the most innovative dramas of this century.[13]

I would now wish to proceed with an examination of the legacy of *Moby Dick* in the works of America's first playwright. O'Neill stood most likely under the direct influence of Melville's *Moby Dick* in composing several of his dramas, i.e., *Ile*, *Cross*, *Diff'rent*, *Electra* and *Journey*. Critics such as Travis Bogard and John Henry Raleigh have noted in passing the analogous situations in *Ile* and *Moby Dick*, without exploring the essence of the parallel in depth.[14] Although O'Neill did not acknowledge the influence of *Moby Dick* upon his one-act *Ile*, internal evidence suggests that the dramatist was profoundly familiar with Melville's novel by the time he wrote his early play.

Ile (1917) can be compared to *Moby Dick* in three respects, i.e., characterization, plot, and setting. If resemblances can be detected, divergences subsist between the two works. These differences can be viewed as an ironic comment on the significance of O'Neill's model. In *Ile*, he presents us with a ferocious whaling captain, not unlike Melville's Ahab in his mad quest for oil. The stern physique of Captain Keeney resembles Ahab's savageness:

> He is a man of about forty, around five-ten in height but looking much
> shorter on account of the enormous proportions of his shoulders and
> chest. His face is massive and deeply lined, with gray blue eyes of a
> bleak hardness, and a tightly clenched, thin-lipped mouth. (p. 116)[15]

Keeney's physical appearance recalls the wild portrait that Melville draws of Ahab, in the initial chapters of *Moby Dick*:

> His whole high, broad form, seemed made of solid bronze, and shaped
> in a unalterable mould, like Cellini's cast Perseus [...]. There was an
> infinity of firmest fortitude, a determinate, unsurrenderable wilfulness,
> in the fixed and fearless, forward dedication of that glance. (pp.
> 218–220)

Keeney and Ahab share a certain massiveness, a "firmest fortitude" and their glance bespeaks simultaneously harshness and a "unsurrenderable willfulness." Keeney, however, possesses more caricatural traits than Ahab, who is a "[...] good man [...] desperate moody [...]." (p. 177) While Ahab has been punished by the godly whale and has been deprived of his leg, Keeney equally seems burdened with a curse and progressively loses his senses. In *Moby Dick*, Peleg comments on his captain: "I know that on the passage home, he was a little out of his mind for a spell [...]. I know, too, that ever since he lost his leg last voyage by that accursed whale [...] he's been kind of moody [...]." (p. 177) Similarly, in *Ile*, the steward tells us of Keeney's strange behavior:

> [...] 's if it was our fault he ain't had good luck with the whales [...]. I think the man's mighty nigh losin' his senses [...]. Aye, it's the punishment o'God on him. Did you ever hear of a man who wasn't crazy do the things he does? (pp. 114–115)

Both Keeney and Ahab have not had much luck with whales and now stand under the punishment of the divinity: Keeney becomes crazy and Ahab appears moody. These various elements point to the confluence linking O'Neill's and Melville's concept of characterization.

The similarities in plot between the two works deserve consideration as well. Keeney and Ahab are engaged in a quest, of which the nature varies in *Ile* and *Moby Dick*. Whereas in Melville's novel, the quest consists in confronting the harsh divinity governing the world, O'Neill introduces the reader to a godless universe. Accordingly, the quest of *Moby Dick* acquires metaphysical overtones whereas that of *Ile* is motivated by purely materialistic reasons: "KEENEY: [...] I can't go back to Homeport with a measly four hundred barrel of ile. I'd die fust. I ain't never come back home in all my days without a full ship." (pp. 121–122) Although Keeney shares with Ahab a fierce sense of determination, he does not seek to encounter the deity which inflicted him the curse of bad luck. One can detect in this divergence a more skeptical vision than that of the universe of *Moby Dick*: the romantic ideals characterizing Ahab no longer apply in the materialistic—indeed "commercial"—American society of the turn of the century.

Another subtle distinction can be made between the opposed natures of the universes looming in the backgrounds of *Moby Dick* and *Ile*. Both Ahab and Keeney are the clear victims of destiny. Ahab sees himself as the prisoner of a "fixed fate." In other words, he has been programmed by the creator to revolt against the white whale, the power of God. The origin of that fate thus resides in the will of a deity, whatever the form that divinity may have. In *Ile*, on the contrary, Keeney is the prisoner of what O'Neill's critics have termed an "ironic fate."[16] The playwright insists to a greater extent than Melville upon the personal responsibility of the protagonist in his doom. While Ahab's demise is ordained in a large measure by a Calvinist deity, Keeney's fall is caused solely by his foolish pride. O'Neill depicts a universe devoid of any ruling presence, one which prefigures *Iceman*. Although at this early point his career, O'Neill does not yet, as he would in *Iceman*, suggest what man's behavior should be in front of the "Absurd," the world of *Ile* shows correspondences, however minimal, with the godless environment envisioned by Ishmaël's existential ethics. To O'Neill as to Ishmaël, man is trapped in a no exit situation, from which no divinity will rescue him.

In *Ile* as in *Moby Dick*, the captains sacrifice human love and friendship in order to achieve the goal of their quest. They symbolize the self-enclosed individualism against which O'Neill and Melville strongly reacted. In *Moby Dick*, Ahab threatens the revolted crew with a harpoon struck by lightning:

> But dashing the rattling lightning links to the deck, and snatching the burning harpoon, Ahab waved it like a torch among them; swearing to transfix with it the first sailor that but cast loose a rope's end. Petrified by this aspect, and still more shrinking from the fiery dart he held, the men fell back in dismay [...]. (pp. 617–618)

Conversely, in *Ile*, Keeney menaces his crew, who are on the verge of mutiny, with the fire of his pistol: "The men pull out their sheath knives and start a rush, but stop when they find themselves confronted with the revolvers of Keeney and the mate [...]." (pp. 123–124) By opposition to Ahab, who resorts to natural fire in order to subdue the sailors, Keeney uses the modern, artificial fire of his gun. The dramatist's apparent modification of the Melvillean model again originates in a pessimistic apprehension of modern realities. Keeney has lost touch with nature whereas Ahab identifies with the thunderstorm. In spite of this difference,

O'Neill and Melville express an identical statement about their captain's exaggerated idealism: in refusing to provide for the needs of their crew, Ahab and Keeney forfeit human compassion. Not only do they adopt this selfish attitude towards the sailors, but also towards their family. In *Moby Dick*, Starbuck attempts to convince Ahab to abandon his quest and to return home in order to be reunited with his family. Although Ahab is at first moved by that plea, in the end his "glance was averted." (p. 652) Ahab eventually decides to proceed with the chase and completely liberates himself from the bonds of human society. In *Ile*, O'Neill presents us with an analogous situation as the mate tries to persuade Keeney to sail back home for the sake of his wife. Moreover, O'Neill introduces, unlike Melville, a scene in which husband and wife are confronted directly. Mr. Slocum pleads to his captain: "I warn't thinkin' of myself, sir—'bout turnin' home, I mean. (Desperately). But Mrs Keeney, sir—seems like she ain't jest satisfied up here, ailin' like [...]. KEENEY: [...] That's my business; Mr. Slocum." (p. 121) In a conversation with his wife, Keeney, like Ahab, stands on the verge of renouncing his quest:

MRS. KEENEY: [...] Take me home, David, if you love me as you say. I'm afraid. For the love of God, take me home! ([...] He holds her out at arm's length, his expression softening. For a moment his shoulders sag, he becomes old, his iron spirit weakens as he looks at her tear stained face)

KEENEY: [...] I'll do it, Annie—for you sake—if you say it's needful for you. (p. 131)

KEENEY: (Sternly). Woman, you ain't adoin' right when you meddle in men's business and weaken 'em. You can't know my feelin's [...]. I got to git the ile, I tell ye. (p. 132)

Both Keeney and Ahab experience for a moment softer feelings but eventually continue in their obsessional pursuit.

The significance of the two writers' critique of their heroes' self-involvement is invested with comparable resonances in *Moby Dick* and in *Ile*. Critics have interpreted Melville's presentation of Ahab's madness as a caricature of Emersonian idealism.[17] Ahab, as a true follower of Emerson, is unable to accept that the world is void, that it does not in all points constitute an emanation from the spirit of God. Implicitly, Melville shows that the transcendentalist willingness to see in nature a spirituality which it does not possess leads to self-destruction. That nihilistic drive is coupled with a lack of compassion towards fellow human beings that betrays the selfish underpinnings of the moral principles of Transcendentalism. Ahab acts like an *isolato* because of his forced belief in Emersonian ideals. It is possible to detect in *Ile* O'Neill's embryonic satire of the same philosophical school, a satire he would develop in his cycle plays. Indeed, as I already hinted at, in *Touch*, *Mansions*, and *Capricorn*, O'Neill obliquely portrays Emerson and Thoreau in the character of Simon Harford.[18] These depictions oscillate between admiration and criticism: Simon starts as a pure idealist who wants to devote his life to writing and ends up as a ruthless and inhuman businessman. O'Neill's vision of New England Transcendentalism as corrupted arises, as in the case of Melville, from the intuition that such a philosophy does not offer an adequate view of the universe. Like Ahab who fails to understand that his mad quest is purposeless, Keeney fails to see that his wife and his crew's well-being is more important than the pride that can be derived from a successful commercial trip. Like Ahab, he exhibits the main defect of Transcendentalism, i.e., isolationism. Through their common satire of that fierce individualism, O'Neill and Melville reveal their humanitarian viewpoints.

It is in its setting that *Ile* departs the most from *Moby Dick*. The action of Melville's novel takes place essentially in the South Seas. On the contrary, the icy Northern Seas form the background against which the plot of *Ile* is developed. As the steward complains: "Ice, ice, ice! Damn him damn the Artic seas, and damn this stinkin' whalin' ship of his [...]." (p. 113) Melville's beautiful seas only exist in Mrs. Keeney's mind: "I used to dream of sailing on the great, wide, glorious ocean. I wanted to be by your side in the danger and vigorous life of it all [...]. I used to love the sea then [...]. But now—I don't ever want to see the sea again." (pp. 126–129) Not only is O'Neill's vision of the ocean darker than in *Moby Dick*, his description of the ship equally lacks the romantic overtones with which Melville's novel is suffused. If the action of *Ile* takes place on a modern ship, the "steam whaler Atlantic Queen," (p. 110), Melville focuses on an ancient sail ship: "She was a ship of the old shool, rather small if anything; with an old fashioned claw-footed look about her—her venerable bows looked bearded. Her masts [...] stood stiffly up like the spines of the three old kings of Cologne [...]." (p. 164) O'Neill's reference to unpleasant features of his setting, such as the cold, soulless Northern Seas and the modern, unpoetic ship, contributes to intensifying the departures from Melville. The dramatist envisages an America essentially different from that of Melville, one in which the environment has become dehumanized.

In *Ile*, then, O'Neill offers, perhaps unconsciously, a modified version of *Moby Dick*, by emphasizing the agnostic philosophy of the novelist—and therefore envisioning a world deprived of Godly whale. He also subtly mixes these novelistic elements into a framework derived from the melodramatic tendencies of his father's theatre, epitomized by *The Count of Monte Cristo*. But *Ile* transcends the narrow limits of melodrama, since, like *Electra*, it adopts the modernist technique of quotations and collage-like composition. Needless to say, if *Ile* is patterned on *Moby Dick*, it does not constitute the masterpiece that Melville's novel represents. But it certainly reveals more depth at second reading than at first. In that task of re-evaluation, Melville's work offers precious indications.

In *Cross*, O'Neill intersperses muted reminders of *Moby Dick*. Captain Bartlett, the hero of this early one-act, is, like Ahab, "a whaling captain." (p. 142)[19] Like Melville's protagonist, Bartlett wages war "against the sky," (p. 149) with the intent to accuse God of having left him impotent ashore. Bartlett's son, Nat, has been mutilated during a voyage. He resembles Ahab who has lost his leg at sea: "NAT: [...] the damned sea he forced me on as a boy—the sea that robbed me of my arm and made me the broken thing I am!" (p. 150) In *Cross*, as in *Ile*, however, no final confrontation with the divinity or the albino whale occurs. Here again, the playwright seems to suggest that the nobility of Melville's protagonist cannot be recaptured by modern characters. Certainly, by the time he composed this one-act play, O'Neill had read *Moby Dick*, if one believes Agnes Boulton's conversation with Louis Sheaffer.[20] If Melville's impact undoubtedly affects O'Neill's work, it takes the shape of an ironic modification meant to convey an increasingly agnostic philosophy.

In 1921, commenting on his play *Diff'rent* (1920), O'Neill explicitly acknowledged being inspired by *Moby Dick*, as I mentioned in Chapter I. From this quotation, it can be inferred that O'Neill patterned the characterization of his play upon that of Melville's *Moby Dick*. Both Ahab and Caleb are passionate questers who feel ready to sacrifice everything in order to achieve their goal. But whereas Ahab's pursuit can be depicted as metaphysical, Caleb's brand of idealism is rooted in human love. Emma, his fiancee, refuses to marry him upon learning that he is not sexually pure. Caleb then decides to roam the oceans for thirty years. After all that time has elapsed, he again proposes to Emma. Forced to admit that he has lost all hopes of becoming her husband, Caleb feels desperate: "I kin only see one course out for me and I'm goin' to take it. 'A dead whale or a stove boat.' We says in whalin'—and my boat is stove! [...]." (p. 247)[21] The parallel existing between Caleb and Ahab resides in their authenticity. Once he has discovered that Emma is in love with a much younger man than himself, Caleb decides to commit suicide, as the ideal to which he adhered can no longer be attained. O'Neill ostensibly tends to belittle the merits of his protagonist, stressing the purely psychological nature of his dreams. The heroic proportions of Ahab's quest can no longer assume validity in contemporary America.

A subtle reminder of *Moby Dick* can also be traced in *Electra*. In the chapter entitled "Knights and Squires," Melville states the insular origin of the members of the crew of the "Pequod." He implies that these men can be readily associated with their continent. By becoming *isolatoes*, they symbolize their islands of origin: " [...] each isolato living on a separate continent of his own [...]." (p. 216) In *Electra*, the Mannons not only have an island of which they constantly dream but they also become synonymous with it. Orin says to Christine, in a passage quoted above, that in his dream she became equated with an idyllic island. This motif serves, in both *Moby Dick* and *Electra*, to heighten the solitude of the protagonists. Simultaneously, both writers criticize the self-enclosed personalities of their heroes.

Journey possibly constitutes a fifth example of O'Neill's indebtedness to Melville. It is reasonable to suggest influence, for at this stage of his career, O'Neill had known *Moby Dick* for two decades. If the plays I have examined so far do not evoke an actual fight with the albino whale, *Journey* briefly alludes to Melville's whale and cryptic reminders of *Moby Dick* emerge early in the drama in a conversation between Mary and Tyrone:

MARY: [...] I wasn't able to get much sleep with that awful foghorn going all night long.

TYRONE: Yes, it's like having a sick whale in the back yard. It kept me awake, too. (pp. 14–15)

Further, in the stage directions of Act III, O'Neill signals: "From a lighthouse beyond the harbour's mouth, a foghorn is heard at regular intervals, moaning like a moonful whale in labour." (p. 83) It could be argued, of course, that O'Neill drew from his personal sea experience or even from popular sayings in order to develop this type of marine imagery. His motif, however, gains significance by comparison with Melville's *Moby Dick*. As in *Ile*, *Cross*, and *Diff'rent*, O'Neill modifies some elements derived from his source although his purpose is not as ironic as in the other plays I have reviewed: his vision rather consists in a pessimistic indictment of the drastic limitations of modern American life. That the whale should be sick, "mournful," suggests that the romantic world of Melville, in O'Neill's opinion, is slowly agonizing.

Thus, my study of Melville's direct impact on O'Neill reveals profound divergences between the two authors. O'Neill altered his models in various ways, which can categorized as follows: multiple angles of vision—in *Electra*—; ironic, i.e., unexpected, contrast—in *Ile*, *Cross*, and *Diff'rent*—; and reduction to imagery—in *Journey*.

B. The Sea Mystique

O'Neill's and Melville's view of the sea as source of mysticism forms the clearest instance of the confluence linking them.[22] It is a motif already hinted at in my first section, in my analysis of *Moby Dick*, *Ile*, and *Electra*. In its complex manifestations, it helps us measure the extent of O'Neill's and Melville's fascination with the sea, hence the profundity of their "imagination matérielle." That profundity is the more evident as the two writers' mysticism is marked by ambivalence, a characteristic which Gaston Bachelard regards as a quality.

In *Omoo* (1847), Melville develops for the first time the motif of the sea as an object of mystical elevation:

[...] The Trades were blowing with a mild, steady strain upon the canvas, and the ship heading right out into the immense blank of the Western Pacific [...]. On such a night, and all alone, revery was inevitable. I leaned over the side, and could not help thinking of the strange objects we might be sailing over [...]. (p. 35)[23]

In *Redburn* (1849), the novelist amplifies such motif but underlines the dangers of his dreamers' attitude. Redburn at first experiences a mystical communion with the ocean:

Never did I realize till now what the ocean was: how grand and majestic, how solitary, and boundless, and beautiful and blue [...]. Then was I first conscious of a wonderful thing in me, that responded to all the wild commotion of the outer world; and went reeling on and on with the planets in their orbits, and was lost in one delirious throb at the center of the All [...]. (pp. 115–119)·

Redburn's insights take on a cosmic, indeed pantheistic shape, which prefigures Edmund Tyrone's identification with the essence of life in O'Neill's *Journey*. By opposition, when threatening to fall from the lofty place, where he has been dreaming, into the absysmal ocean, Redburn experiences utter fright: "For a few moments I stood awe-stricken and mute, I could not see far out upon the ocean, owing to the darkness of the night [...].I [...] expected to find myself falling— falling, as I have felt when the nightmare has been on me." (p. 133) Thus in *Redburn*, Melville presents us with a Janus-faced concept of the sea as a catalyst of revery, one which announces *Moby Dick*.

In *White-Jacket*, the novelist again concentrates on the figure of the solitary sea dreamer, albeit in a more unambiguous way. The narrator of *White-Jacket* suddenly feels unified with the universe when admiring the stars on the deck of his ship:

Then, to study the stars upon the wide, boundless sea, is divine as it was to the Chaldean Magi, who observed their revolutions from the plains [...]. And it is a very fine feeling, and one that fuses us into the universe of things, and makes us a part of the All, to think that,

wherever we ocean-wanderers rove, we have still the same glorious old
stars to keep us company; that they still shine onward and on, forever
beautiful and bright, and luring us, by every day, to die and be
glorified with them. (p. 75)

Clearly, Melville views the sea as a place where mystical union with Nature can
enrich human life. Simultaneously, his pantheism prompts him to find divine
features in both the sky and the ocean.

In *Moby Dick*, the same motif reaches a culminating point. In the Chapter
entitled "The Mast Head," Melville acquaints us at once with the marvels of sea
revery and with its dangers:

[...] The mast-head; nay, to a dreamy meditative man it is
delightful [...]. There you stand, lost in the infinite series of the sea,
with nothing ruffled but the waves. The tranced ship indolently rolls;
the drowsy trade winds blow; everything resolves you into
languor [...]. (pp. 252–253)

[...] at last he (the dreamer) loses his identity; takes the mystic ocean at
his feet for the visible image of that deep, blue, bottomless soul [...]. In
this enchanted mood, thy spirit ebbs away to whence it came; becomes
diffused through time and space; like Crammer's sprinkled Pantheistic
ashes, forming at last a part of every shore the round globe over. There
is no life in thee, now, except that rocking life imparted by a gently
rolling ship; by her; borrowed from the sea; by the sea, from the
inscrutable tides of God. But while this sleep, this dream is on ye, move
your foot or hand an inch; slip your hold at all; and your identity
comes back in horror. Over Descartian vortices you hover. And
perhaps, at mid-day, in the fairest weather, with one half-throttled
shriek you drop through that transparent air into the summer sea, no
more to rise for ever. Heed it well, ye Pantheists! (pp. 256–257)

Melville's ambivalent presentation of the ocean as generator of mystical insight
corresponds, critics have asserted, to his critique of Emerson.[24] With his
reference to pantheism, the novelist voices a veiled attack against Emerson's

idealistic philosophy while his depiction of the dreamer's admiration for his own soul in the ocean hints at Emerson's solipsism. In his mention of the "Descartian vortices," Melville points to the threat of mystical oblivion, detectable in Emerson's self-reliance. The same ambiguity, compounded with an almost verbatim transposition of Melville's description will be found in O'Neill's *Journey*.

However, prior to that drama, the playwright had already introduced in his work lyrical celebrations of the mystical ocean. In *Horizon* (1918), Robert Mayo tells his fiancee Ruth of the fascination that the sea holds for him:

> ROBERT: (musingly). So I used to stare over the fields to the hills, out there—(He points to horizon) and somehow after a time I'd forget any pain I was in, and start dreaming. There was all the mystery in the world to me then about that-far-off sea—and there still is! (p. 12)[25]

As Robert recalls his childhood attraction to the sea, one is inevitably reminded of Melville's lyrical outbursts.

In *Chris* and *Anna*, O'Neill prolongs the same theme. He offers us a view of the sea as synonymous of beauty and transcendence in Andersen's and Anna's reveries. In *Chris* (1919), the heroine confesses having undergone a psychological change since her arrival upon her father's barge: "It seemed to come over me suddenly—while we were drifting in that fog with that queer silence all about [...]." (p. 95)[26] Anna's lyrical celebration parallels the mystical insights of Melville's heroes and indicates that, in her opinion, the ocean symbolizes the total poetry of human existence:

> ANNA: [...] The sea has made me discover so many feelings I never knew I had before [...] the way I feel now I'd be happy—oh, so happy!—just forever sailing here and there, watching the sun rise and sink into the sea again day after day—and never do anything but love the sea. (p. 132)

A comparable romantic fascination for the beauty of the sea can be detected in

Andersen's enthusiastic recollections: "Freedom, that's life! No ties, no responsibilities—no guilty feelings. Like the sea—always moving, never staying, never held by anything [...] citizen of the sea which belongs to no one [...]." (p. 101) After revealing his love for Anna, Andersen again voices his admiration for the deep: "We'll not leave the sea, you and I. We'll keep it in spite of everything. And we'll go to all the ports of the world and see them all-together! And the sea shall be our mother, and the mother of our children." (p. 140) Through the relationship between Anna and Andersen, then, O'Neill sings of the oceanic marvels in a fashion recalling Melville's sea mystique, and prefiguring Edmund's memories in *Journey*. It is interesting to note that, in *Redburn* as in *Chris*, the beauty of the sea is filtered through the consciousness of innocent characters, who are, in Anderson's words, "children of the sea."

In *Anna* (1920), a revised version of *Chris*, O'Neill provides us with a comparable concept of the mystical sea. He shows us the benevolent effects of the fog, through which the heroine achieves purification: "ANNA: [...] And now— this fog—Gee [...] I love it! I don't give a rap if it never lifts! [...]. It makes me feel clean—out here—'s if I'd taken a bath." (pp. 41–42)[27] Anna's longing for the mysteries of the sea is akin to the Melvillean sailor's reveries through its lyrical and quasi-religious quality.

That motif recurs in *Ape* (1921), but this time, O'Neill emphasizes, like Melville in *Redburn* and *Moby Dick*, the negative facets of mysticism. In scene one, the playwright introduces us to Paddy, who regrets the days of the sailing vessels. Through the latter's physical descriptions, O'Neill praises the sea in a style closely related to that of *Moby Dick*:

Full sail on her! Nights and days! Nights when the foam of the wake would be flaming wid fire, when the sky'd be blazing and winking wid stars. Or the full of the moon maybe. Then you'd see her driving through the gray night, her sails stretching aloft all silver and white, not a sound on the deck, the lot of us dreaming dreams [...]. 'Twas them days men belonged to ships, not now. 'Twas them days a ship was part of the sea, and a man was part of a ship, and the sea joined all together and made it one [...]. (p. 46)[28]

To Paddy, the sea creates dreams and offers a source of spiritual illumination. As in *Redburn* and *White-Jacket*, the night atmosphere awakens the poetic faculties of the hero and the protagonist experiences a mystical union with the All, i.e., Nature. In *Ape* as in Melville's novels, the author indicates that his characters' daydreaming is far removed from reality. While in *Redburn* and in *Moby Dick*, Melville shows that the danger of these mystical insights actually resides in a threat of death, O'Neill's ambiguous stance consists only in emphasizing the fact that Paddy's reveries definitely belong to the past and do not reproduce faithfully the contours of the present day experience.

It is of course in *Journey* that O'Neill's double-sided vision of the solitary dreaming sailor duplicates the most faithfully Melville's ambivalent stance. In a celebrated scene with his father James Tyrone, Edmund indulges in lyrical descriptions strongly reminiscent of analogous episodes in *Redburn* and *Moby Dick*:

> I lay on the bowsprit, facing astern with the water foaming into spume under me, the masts with every sail white in the moonlight, towering high above me. I became drunk with the beauty and singing rhythm of it, and for a amoment I lost myself—actually lost my life. I was set free! I dissolved in the sea, became white sails and flying spray, became beauty and rhythm, became moonlight and the ship and the high dim-starred sky! I belonged, without past or future, within peace and unity and a wild joy, within something greater than my own life, or the life of Man, to Life itself! To God, if you want to put it that way [...]. (p. 134)

The parallels reside in the presentation of the sea as harbinger of God, the view of the universe as a mirror of the soul, i.e., a sort of pantheism, and, as in *White-Jacket*, the beauty of the stars. Edmund's reverie takes the shape of a triptych. And the second instance he gives his father of his mystical communion with the sea also bears similarities to Melville's description. As in *Moby Dick*, it describes the mystical moment as a product of the sensuousness of the sea, its calm-like appearance, and its drowsiness. In this second image, Edmund, like Melville's character in "The Mast Head," stands aloft, on the "lookout" and watches things from above:

Then another time, on the American Line, when I was lookout on the crow's nest in the dawn watch. A calm sea, that time. Only a lazy ground swell and a slow drowsy roll of the ship [...] dreaming, not keeping lookout, feeling alone, and above, and apart, watching the dawn creep like a painted dream over the sky and sea which slept together. Then the moment of ecstatic freedom came [...]. (p. 134)

Like Melville, O'Neill praises the feeling of transcendence offered by such reveries. They are "like a saint's vision of beatitude. Like the veil of things as they seem drawn back by an unseen hand." (p. 135) Like Melville, then, O'Neill links positive connotations to these experiences and implies that they fuse the dreamer with the world, thus giving him a temporary knowledge of the significance of that universe: "For a second you see—and seeing the secret are the secret. For a second there is meaning." (p. 135). Thus singing of the joys of pantheism, both O'Neill and Melville betray their affinities with a phenomenon which has been identified by Alexis de Tocqueville as typical of American culture at large. In his *Democracy in America*, John Raleigh remarks, Alexis de Tocqueville affirms that Americans are pantheists at heart.[29] O'Neill's rendering of these sea visions in *Journey*, then, possesses a typically American nature which is better understood by reference to Melville.

But while O'Neill, following in the wake of Melville, celebrates the benefits of revery at sea, he also indicates—however dimly—that these lyrical outbursts present negative facets. If Melville criticizes the exaggeratedly individualistic character of New England Transcendentalism, it may not be entirely preposterous to affirm that O'Neill eventually condemns Edmund's solitary reveries for a similar reason. First, his visions present unmistakable points of confluence, focusing as they do on the self and on the All, with Emerson's concept of the private soul and of the Over-Soul. Critics have not failed to recognize this underlying motif in Edmund's daydreaming recollections.[30] In addition, as I noted earlier, O'Neill voiced an ambiguous statement about New England Transcendentalism in *Touch* (1942) and *Mansions* (1941). He expresses alternatively admiration for Simon's/Emerson's idealism and contempt for his subsequent corruption, for the unpractical nature of his lofty ideals. Considering that *Journey* was written at the same period as these works, it is possible that O'Neill would have intended Edmund as a parody of the excesses of Emerson.

Indeed, he demonstrates that Edmund's insights cannot be recaptured in modern life: "Then the hand lets the veil fall and you are alone, lost in the fog again, and you stumble on toward nowhere, for no good reason." (p. 135) Moreover, O'Neill points out how Edmund's exaggerated individualism, symbolized by his private remembrances, distances him from the members of his family. Sometimes failing to provide moral support for his parents, he becomes partly responsible for the dislocation of the Tyrone family. Thus O'Neill indicates that mystical revelations may prove dangerous in daily life. Like the novelist of the American Renaissance, the playwright exhibits a Janus-faced judgement of pantheism testifying to the richness of his craft.

C. Forms of "Imagination Matérielle."

The study of O'Neill's and Melville's mariners and mystics sheds light on the American characteristics of their works. In glorifying the freedom conferred by the sea, away from the constraints of civilization, they express a romantic theme, dear to the New World imagination. They point, through the fate of their outcast mariners, to the American absence of connection with any definite setting while through their pantheism, they reflect yet another classical American concern: the loss of faith in an institutionalized religious code.[31] Finally, through the figures of their idealistic captains, both authors reject the self-enclosed individualism which they detected in their American contemporaries.

Their sea motif can be described as romantic owing to its multiple facets and emotional connotations. In this fashion, it shows correspondences to Gaston Bachelard's definition of "imagination matérielle/ material imagination" in l'Eau et les Rêves. Both writers' sea symbol, through their characterization of mariners and mystics, elicits from the reader an infinite variety of responses, which testifies to the richness of its texture. Thus, the two artists' material imagination, based on the water element, strikes us profoundly because it reflects the perspective of sea people. Both O'Neill and Melville experience difficulty in belonging to the land, to the defiled civilization of their day. Edmund's formulation in Journey aptly summarizes this plight: "It was a great mistake, my being born a man, I would have been much more successful as a seagull or a fish.

As it is, I will always be a stranger who never feels at home, who does not really want and is not really wanted, who can never belong, who must always be a little in love with death." (p. 135) Like Edmund, the two writers voice, through highly crafted portraits of mariners and mystics, the pain of living and the desire to identify with the ocean in a pantheistic union.

CHAPTER IV. TRAGIC TENSIONS OF LAND AND SEA

Melville and O'Neill demonstrate an ambiguity of feelings towards both the land and the sea, emotions often wavering within the same work between love and hate. Such ambivalence testifies, in Bachelard's critical system described in Chapter III, to a richness of "imagination matérielle." Further, it introduces in some of their novels and plays forms of tragic tension, originating precisely from the irreconcilable character of these two poles of the human universe. I shall examine a series of polarities appearing in O'Neill's and Melville's works while showing the profound emotional division these dichotomies generate in the writers' mind. In other words, as in the preceding chapter, I shall document the various facets of the writers' romantic "material imagination." Unlike Chapter III, this part of my study will look at their material imagination from the perspective offered by the two writers' mosaic-like patterns of sea imagery.

A. The Land/Sea Polarity

The land/sea polarity is perhaps the basic tension of the works of both O'Neill and Melville. While commentators have correctly identified this feature of O'Neill's craftsmanship, they have not analyzed in detail its relationship to Melville's artistry.[1]

In one of Melville's early novels, *Redburn*, it is through a young protagonist's consciousness that the contrasts between the land and the sea are established. For Wellingborough Redburn, the crossing of the Atlantic ocean coincides with his coming of age and his emotional attitude towards both the land and the sea shifts in the course of the novel. As he leaves his home town, the hero starts dreaming of Europe:

Indeed, during my early life, most of my thoughts of the sea were connected with the land; but with fine old lands, full of mossy cathedrals and churches, and long, narrow, crooked streets without side-walks, and lined with strange houses [...]. (p. 45)

In the early pages of the novel, Melville thus endows the land with endearing characteristics. Upon leaving New York harbor, however, Redburn's enthusiasm starts abating: his love for the land is now coupled with a feeling of awe for the ocean:

> [...] Who could tell what might happen to me; for when I looked up at the high, giddy masts, and thought how often I must be going up and down them, I thought sure that some luckless day or other, I would certainly fall overboard and be drowned [...]. I thought how much better it must be, to be buried under the pleasant hedge that bounded the sunny south side of our village graveyard, where every Sunday I had used to walk after church in the afternoon; and I almost wished I was there now; yes, dead and buried in that churchyard. (p. 79)

Progressively, however, Redburn becomes aware of the challenge of the deep: "[...] after casting a last look at some boys who were standing on the parapet, gazing off to sea, I turned away heavily, and resolved not to look at the land any more." (p. 83) During the voyage, the young hero is able to record the sailor's contempt for landsmen: "[...] merchant sailors have a great idea of their dignity and superiority to greenhorns and landsmen, who know nothing about a ship; and they seem to think that an able seaman is a great man." (p. 113) This quotation, in contrast to other passages, endows the land with negative overtones. Likewise, the sea represents a place of toil: "Miserable dog's life is this of the sea! Commanded like a slave, and set to work like an ass! Vulgar and brutal men lording it over me, as if I were an African in Alabama. Yes, yes, blow on, ye breezes, and make a speedy end to this abominable voyage!" (p. 119) In the lines I have quoted, Melville expresses a theme adumbrating O'Neill's vision of a cruel sea in *Cardiff*. In a phrase also announcing O'Neill's *Cardiff*, Redburn aptly encapsulates his predicament as follows: "sailors only go round the world, without going into it." (p. 197). If the sea is terrible, the land offers little solace to the victim of the hardships of the ocean. Upon landing in Liverpool, Redburn records the corruption of the town: "But though on shore, at Liverpool, poor

Jack finds more sharks than at sea, he himself is by no means exempt from practices, that do not savor of a rigid morality." (p. 270). While the hero cherished fond memories of the land at the beginning of the story, the land now becomes suffused with evil overtones. In *Redburn* as in O'Neill's *Long Voyage*, sailors are kidnapped once they have reached the land: "staggering along that bowsprit, now came a one-eyed crimp, leading a drunken tar by the collar [...]. When the crimp had got this man and another safely lodged in a bunk below, he returned on shore [...]." (p. 321) Despite his confrontation with the cruel sea and the defiled land, Redburn confesses towards the end of the novel that his experience has been meaningful, a feeling expressed through his love for the ship on which he has been sailing: "And now the ship that we had loathed, grew lovely in our eyes, which lingered over every familiar old timber; for the scene of suffering is a scene of joy when the suffering is past; and the silent reminiscence of hardships departed, is sweeter than the presence of delight." (p. 392) The ocean allows man to measure himself against his fate: sufferings thus acquire tragic depth, a theme which runs through O'Neill's *Capricorn*. *Redburn* offers an excellent vantage point to study the nature of Melville's land/sea dichotomy. When serving as a challenge to man's ambitions, the ocean yields positive connotations, but it is described in a negative fashion in those passages focusing on the sailor plight. Likewise, the land is suggestive both of happiness, as Redburn's youthful memories indicate, and of depravity, as Melville's depiction of Liverpool demonstrates. Owing to these characteristics, *Redburn* will open an important avenue to the interpretation of O'Neill's sea plays.[2]

It is especially in *Cardiff* and *Long Voyage* that one finds equivalents to Melville's dichotomous vision of both the land and the sea. In 1914 O'Neill completed *Cardiff*, a play in which he suffused his land/sea contrast with brooding overtones, strongly evocative of Melville's *Redburn*. Through dying Yank's stream of consciousness, he describes the predicament of the sailor in a realistic form: "YANK: [...] That sailor life ain't much to cry about leavin' [...] travellin' all over the world and never seein' none of it; without no one to care whether you're alive or dead [...]." (p. 46) Redburn tells of the plight of a ship crew in almost identical terms: "sailors only go round the world, without going into it." (p. 197) Both writers, then, regard the sea as a factor of alienation. Whether O'Neill had read *Redburn* by the time he composed *Cardiff* is uncertain but owing to the precise similarity in wording, it is possible to suggest influence, an hypothesis reinforced by the pessimistic atmosphere that characterizes both works. Moreover, as in *Redburn*, O'Neill's sea is not only endowed with negative connotations, it also evokes happy memories connected with Yank's past life, a fact ostensibly demonstrating that the deep allows man to experience self-fulfillment. Indeed, in *Redburn*, the hero feels transfigured through the hardships of his sea travels and by his acceptance of the challenge of the ocean. Likewise, O'Neill indicates that in spite of its unsavory features, sailor life has provided Yank with at least a fleeting sense of happiness:

> YANK: [...] D'yuh remember the time we've had in Buenos Aires? The moving pictures in Barracas? Some class to them, d'yuh remember? [...] And the days we used to sit on the park benches along the Paseo Colon with the vigilantes lookin' hard at us? And the songs at the Sailor's Opera where the guy played ragtime—d'yuh remember them? (p. 47)

Yank thus sentimentally reflects on his sea adventures, in which his death-bed companion, Driscoll, also participated. While the ocean simultaneously suggests love and hate in *Cardiff*, the land symbolizes lost happiness, as in the initial chapters of *Redburn*, in which the young hero regrets having abandoned his family to discover the world: "YANK: (musingly). It must be great to stay on dry land all your life [...] 'way in the middle of the land where yuh'd never smell the sea or see a ship. It must be great to have a wife, and kids [...]." (p. 46) Contrary to the sea, the land is associated with the family unit and a sense of belonging, i.e., positive qualities, which, however, remain purely imaginary, for Driscoll declares: "[...] What's the use av thinkin' av ut? Such things are not for the loikes av us." (p. 46) Yank himself acknowledges the impossibility of his dream when he says: "It's too late." (p. 47) As in *Redburn*, the emotional responses triggered off by the land are two-fold: if it signifies harmony, it nonetheless serves to underscore the tragic implications of the sailor predicament, Yank's inability to lead a happy life on dry land.[3]

In the third one-act play of the "S.S. Glencairn" cycle, *Long Voyage* (1917), O'Neill offers the reader a grim depiction of London, akin to that found in *Redburn*, where Liverpool typifies corruption: "The bar of a low dive on the

London water front—a squalid, dingy room dimly lighted by kerosene lamps placed in brackets on the walls." (p. 55)[4] The analogy in setting with *Redburn* was even more evident in the first draft of *Long Voyage*, in which the playwright intended to locate the action in Liverpool.[5] The unsettling atmosphere suggested by the stage directions is heightened when Olson is about to be shanghaied by the proprietors of the bar. Talking with Freda, he comments on his past experience in terms related both to *Cardiff* and Melville's *Redburn*: "[...] I don't never ship on sea no more. I got all sea want for my life—too much hard work for little money. Yust work, work, work on ship. I don't want more." (p. 68) Olson further emphasizes the tragic quality of his fate as alcohol begins to blur his senses:

> OLSON: [...] I mean all time to go back home at end of voyage. But I come ashore, I take one drink, I take many drinks, I get drunk, I spend all money, I have to ship away for other voyage. So dis time I say to myself: Don't drink, Ollie, or sure, you don't get home. And I want to go home dis time [...]. Yust like a little boy, I feel homesick [...] (pp. 72–73)

The similarity between O'Neill's one-act play and Melville's *Redburn* is made all the more convincing through both writers' description of their characters as children. Although he has apparently reached full maturity, Olson is homesick "Yust like a little boy." This implies that in *Long Voyage* the farm possesses the idyllic qualities which it had in *Cardiff*:

> OLSON: We live [...] on farm youst a little way from Stockholm [...]. I can go back with two years' pay and buy more land yet; work on farm. (grinning) No more sea, no more bum grub, no more storms—yust nice work. (pp. 68–69)

Unfortunately, the sailor's romantic depiction of his family farm exists only in his psyche and the reader realizes that Olson will never return to his native village. In the final scene, one can detect a parallel with a passage from *Redburn*, in which the novelist introduced us to a crimp:

JOE: [...] Tike 'im to the "Amindra"—yer knows that, don't yer?—two docks above. Nick'll show yer. An' you, Nick, don't yer leave the bleedin' ship till the capt'n guvs yer this bloke's advance—full month's pay—five quid, d'yer 'ear?

NICK: I knows me bizness, ole bird. (They support Olson to the door) (pp. 75–76)

The resemblances between *Long Voyage* and *Redburn* are so obvious that one is tempted to speak in terms of influence. With Melville, O'Neill shares a dichotomous view of the land: as in *Redburn*, the land symbolizes primarily corruption; when signifying happiness, however, it acquires unreal characteristics, and, as in Melville's novel, proceeds from the imagination. In *Long Voyage*, the connotations with which the sea is invested are less ambiguous than in *Redburn*: O'Neill evokes the terrible aspects of sea life only, whereas Melville concentrates on both the servitude of the sea and its mystical appeal. One of the essential links between the two works resides in the subjective response emanating from the land/sea opposition and in the perspective from which these contrasts are considered, i.e., that of the central character. In each case, this protagonist possesses child-like features, an innocence eventually destroyed by the treacherousness of the land and the sea. But while Melville's hero attains maturity through the process of initiation, O'Neill character is totally destroyed.

It is perhaps in his masterpiece *Moby Dick* that Melville offers his most comprehensive treatment of the sea motif. Riveting his attention to the ocean, he nonetheless voices oblique statements about the nature of the land. At the beginning of the story, he identifies the deep with God and equates the earth with a materialistic sense of security: "But as in landlessness alone resides the highest truth, shoreless, indefinite as God—so, better is it to perish in that howling infinite, than be ingloriously dashed upon the lee, even if that were safety!" (p. 203) Man, Melville implies, must face the dangers of the sea in order to acquire nobility. While the land is constantly connected, in *Moby Dick*, with negative qualities, the sea is suggestive of love and hate. In describing a tempest, Melville betrays both fascination and terror:

It was a sight full of quick wonder and awe! The vast swells of the omnipotent sea; the surging, hollow roar they made, as they rolled along the eight gunwales, like gigantic bowls in a boundless bowling green; the brief suspended agony of the boat, as it would tip for an instant on the knife-like edge of the sharper waves, that almost seemed threatening to cut it in two. (p. 326)

Melville's *Moby Dick* thus includes inflated descriptions of the ocean. Further, the author explores the cruelty of the deep in stressing the primitive roots of the fear that it inspires to mankind, a fright which often develops into cosmic proportions: "[...] man has lost that sense of the full awfulness of the sea which aboriginally belongs to it." (pp. 379–380) Melville's sea is a masculine and murderous presence, as the opening lines of "The Symphony" suggest: "[...] to and fro in the deeps, far down in the bottomless blue, rushed mighty leviathans, sword fish, and sharks, and these were the strong, troubled, murderous thinkings of the masculine sea." (p. 649) Such a dark vision of the deep equally recurs in O'Neill's *Capricorn*, a drama in which, as in *Moby Dick*, the protagonists must fight with the sea in order to acquire tragic status.

In *Thirst* (1913), O'Neill depicts a cruel sea, analogous to the one celebrated by Melville in *Moby Dick*. As in the novelist's masterpiece, murderous sharks threaten the protagonists: "[...] the fins of sharks may be seen slowly cutting the surface of the water in lazy circles." (p. 3)[6] One of the characters tells us how their ship sank in a monologue that reveals the terrifying aspects of the ocean:

And then the gurgling, choking cries of the drowning! Something huge rushed by me in the water, leaving a gleaming trail of phosphorescence. A woman near me with a life belt around her gave a cry of agony and disappeared—then I realized—sharks! [...] I swam and swam with but one idea—to put all that horror behind me. (p. 14)

In this one-act, the sea engenders feelings of horror not unlike those suggested by Melville's opening description of "The Symphony," a sensation further enhanced through the heroes' subsequent declarations: "But the sky will not answer your appeals or mine. Nor will the cruel sea grow merciful for any prayers of ours." (p. 18) Unlike the sea, the land, which only exists in memory, is associated with peace and safety. The woman laments: "Must this be the end of all? I was coming home, home after years of struggling, home to success, fame and money." (p. 18) For the man, the land signifies the hope of being rescued: "With us it is only a question of whether we can hold until we sight land." (pp. 18–19) O'Neill shows, however, that his protagonists will never be able to go back ashore: they die in the last moments of the drama. The land represents in *Thirst* the image of a lost happiness that is detectable in Melville's *Redburn*, where the young hero regrets having left the security of his home town and feels appalled at the dangers of the sea. At the end of his short play, O'Neill asserts the triumph of the terrible ocean, in a mood again suggestive, albeit in a much less successful technique, of *Moby Dick*, when the three characters, the woman dancer, the gentleman, and the mulatto sailor start fighting:

> With a swift movement (the gentleman) grasps the Dancer's body with both hands and, making a tremendous effort, pushes it into the water. There is a swift rush of waiting fins [...].The sailor [...], knife in hand, springs on the gentleman and drives the knife in his breast. The gentleman rises to his feet with a shriek of agony. As he falls backward into the sea, one of his clutching hands fastens itself in the neck of the sailor's jersey. The sailor tries to force the hand away, stumbles, loses his balance, and plunges headlong after him. There is a great splash. The waiting fins rush in. The water is lashed into foam. The sailor's black head appears for a moment, his features distorted with terror, his lips torn with a howl of despair. Then he is drawn under. The sun glares down like a great angry eye of God [...]. (pp. 31–32)

In O'Neill's first nautical drama, the sea, offering only death and desolation, functions as a universe governed by the "angry eye of God," an image related to Melville's avenging deity in *Moby Dick*.

The playwright further displays a treatment of the land/sea dichotomy akin to that of Melville's *Redburn* and *Moby Dick* in *Horizon*. It was with the latter, a play deriving its impact partly from its subtle sea symbolism, that O'Neill earned his first Pulitzer Prize. In the first act of this work, the emotional qualities of the land/sea opposition are manifest in a dialogue between the two brothers Andrew and Robert Mayo. Robert, a dreamer who hates land values, compares his tastes to those of his brother:

> ROBERT: [...] You're a Mayo through and through. You're wedded to
> the soil. Father [...] (is) happy in knowing that another Mayo, inspired
> by the same love, will take up the work where he leaves off. I can
> understand your attitude, and Pa's; and I think it's wonderful and
> sincere. But I—well, I'm not made that way [...]. It's just Beauty that's
> calling me, the beauty of the far off and unknown [...] in quest of the
> secret which is hidden over there, beyond the horizon [...]. (pp. 8–9)

Robert's idyllic vision of both water and earth offers similarities with Melville's
view in *Redburn*. In equating the land with the joys of family life, O'Neill
recaptures the essence of Melville's image of a harmonious home; on the other
hand, like Redburn, Robert Mayo feels that he must go to sea in order to measure
himself with his fate. As he confesses to Ruth, his fiancee: "And I'd promise
myself that when I grew up and was strong, I'd follow that road, and it and I
would find the sea together [...]." (p. 12) As in *Moby Dick*, Robert regards the
sea as the fate, the necessary initiation that man must undergo in order to enter
adulthood. Unlike Redburn and the crew of the "Pequod," Robert eventually
refuses to assume that destiny and decides to stay on the land in order to marry
Ruth. His brother Andrew goes to sea in his stead, out of contempt for the land:
"I'm sick and tired of the whole damned business. I hate the farm and every inch
of ground in it. I'm sick of digging in the dirt and sweating in the sun like a slave
without getting a word of thanks for it [...]." (p. 28) Andrew's sudden hate for
the land contrasts sharply with Robert's initial description of his brother's passion
for the soil. In addition, O'Neill suggests that Andrew decides to go to sea
because of his former love for Ruth. By leaving the land, however, Andrew
neglects to follow the true path of his destiny, in much the same way as by
abandoning his dreams of travelling round the earth, Robert avoids being
introduced to the wonders of the sea. Towards the end of the play, O'Neill
indicates that Andrew had to suffer from the predicament of the sailor and sought
in vain happiness during his voyages. The latter explains to Robert how merciless
the sea could become, in descriptions akin to *Moby Dick* in their lyrical quality:

> ROBERT: (with eager interest). Then you were through a typhoon?

ANDREW: Yes—in the China Sea. Had to run before it under bare poles for two days. I thought we were bound down for Davy Jones, sure. Never dreamed waves could get so big and the wind blow so hard [...]. It was all-wool-and-a-yard-wide-Hell, I'll tell you. You ought to have been there. I remember thinking about you at the worst of it, and saying to myself: "This'd cure Rob of them ideas of his about the beautiful sea, if he could see it." And it would have too, you bet! (pp. 48–49)

In the final moments of *Horizon*, the playwright inserts into the fabric of his drama a dismal picture of the sea, opposed to Robert's mystical reveries. If Andrew was plagued with hardships after his departure, Robert was punished for his decision to remain on the "lee-shore," where he first proved unable to run the farm efficiently, and then slowly died of consumption. In this melodramatic work, O'Neill unconsciously duplicates a Melvillean tension between the land and the sea: as in *Moby Dick*, the ocean stands for the test that man must submit himself to in order to acquire tragic grandeur; the earth, on the contrary, is devoid of any nobility. While Melville shows in *Moby Dick* man's courageous acceptance of the challenge of the sea, O'Neill in *Horizon* dramatizes the effects of his protagonist's refusal to struggle with the fate symbolized by the ocean.

In *Capricorn* (1935), O'Neill displays a vision of the land/sea opposition which is also reminiscent of Melville's *Moby Dick*. Ethan Harford wishes to conquer the sea and, as is the case in *Moby Dick*, regards the deep as the symbol of the fate to which he must obey. He expresses his feelings of love and hate for the sea in powerful terms:

ETHAN: [...] No, I can't explain the feeling I have—it must be this ship and no other. It is because of my fate. It is the test, the particular challenge of the sea to me [...]. To me the sea meant freedom from all land values, but I find myself still enslaved by them, always obeying orders. And I feel a love for the sea and hate it for that very reason [...]. I want this chance to accept the sea's challenge, that's all. If I win, I possess her and she cringes and I kick her away from me [...]. If I lose, I give myself to her as her conquest and she swallows and spews me out in death [...]. (pp. 14–15)[7]

As in *Redburn*, *Moby Dick* or *Horizon*, the ocean represents in *Capricorn* a source of positive connotations, symbolizing as it does man's transcending destiny.

In the universe of the two writers, then, man is constantly torn apart between the beauties and horrors of the two basic poles of life. This constitutes an essential ingredient of the type of tragedy the two artists eventually develop.

B. The North/South Polarity

O'Neill's and Melville's mixture of love and hate towards the land/sea dichotomy finds echoes in their treatment of a subsidiary motif, i.e., the opposition between the South and the North Seas.

Melville's lyrical vision of the South Seas emerges clearly in *Moby Dick*, which contains some flamboyant descriptions of that part of the oceanic universe:

> Some days elapsed, and ice and icebergs all astern, the Pequod now
> went rolling through the bright Quito spring, which, at sea, almost
> perpetually reigns on the threshold of the eternal August of the Tropic.
> The warmly cool, clear, ringing, perfumed, overflowing, redundant
> days, were as crystal goblets of Persian sherbet, heaped up—flaked up,
> with rose-water snow. (p. 221)

In this quotation, it is evident that the opposition between southern and northern hemispheres resides essentially in a contrast between two types of weather: whereas the north suggests ice, the south confers a "perfumed" quality upon reality.

In *Redburn*, the northern Atlantic Ocean, on the contrary, symbolizes desolation and is therefore endowed with negative connotations:

> [...] When you go out of these Narrows on a long voyage like this of
> mine, it seems like going out into the broad highway, where not a soul
> is to be seen. For far away and away, stretches the great Atlantic

Ocean; and all you can see beyond is where the sky comes down to the water. It looks lonely and desolate enough [...]. (p. 80)

These bleak features are reinforced by Redburn's awareness of the ominous nature of the voyage: "I thought it an ill-omened voyage, and railed at the folly which had sent me to sea, sore against the advice of my best friends [...]." (p. 100)

The lyrical quality of O'Neill's delineation of the South Seas can be observed in *Ape*, when Paddy evokes his voyages on the South Seas in terms suggesting their peacefulness: "PADDY: [...] Oh, to be scudding south again [...] A warm sun on the clean decks. Sun warming the blood of you, and wind over the miles of shiny green ocean like strong drink to your lungs [...]."(p. 46) In *Ape*, O'Neill gives the reader his clearest articulation of the mood of harmony that reigns over the South Seas and like Melville, locates the source of their charm in the atmospheric qualities of their latitudes. Not only does O'Neill's lyrical presentation of the features of the South Seas parallel that of Melville, his vision of the North Seas can equally be compared to that of he novelist.

In *Cardiff*, the bleakness of the Atlantic Ocean is heavily emphasized, as Yank dies miserably on "[...] a foggy night midway on the voyage between New York and Cardiff." (p. 33) Likewise, *Zone* (1917) presents the reader with an ominous northern sea on which the "S.S. Glencairn" runs the risk of being torpedoed. In *Fog* (1914), O'Neill again associates the North Seas with a sense of threat: "The lifeboat of a passenger steamer is drifting helplessly off the Grand Banks of Newfoundland [...]. A menacing silence [...] broods over everything." (p. 85)[8] In this short play, the dramatist shows how the characters live under the constant danger of being destroyed by an iceberg. In two other works of the early years, he further explores the dark connotations suggested by the same seas. In *Anna*, the action takes place for the most part in Chris Christophersen's barge anchored in Boston's harbor. Here, the Atlantic possesses devilish characteristics as Chris exclaims: "Ay thank it's better Anna live on farm, den she don't know dat ole davil, sea, she don't know fader like me." (p. 15) The quality of the North Seas in *Ape* reveals equally dismal overtones. Indeed, it is in crossing the Atlantic Ocean that Yank loses his primitive sense of belonging, after encountering Mildred Douglas. In short, O'Neill's plays converge with Melville's novels in their treatment of the North/South Seas dichotomy, to an extent that bespeaks the two writers' kindred artistic vision.

C. The Sea as Death Symbol

A third aspect of the two writers' sea imagery resides in their common equation of the symbol of the ocean with death. In some of their works, the sea leads the character from a symbolic death to rebirth and regeneration through a ritual of initiation. Thus, in *Moby Dick*, Ishmaël undergoes an initiation into the madness of mankind, epitomized by Ahab's frenzy, and is eventually reborn as he "escape(s) alone to tell thee." Similarly, in O'Neill's plays, the protagonists often undergo a "sea change," bringing them from an ignorant life to a higher degree of consciousness through a pattern of death and rebirth. In *Journey*, Edmund has lost his old conventional self by going to the far-off confines of the earth and, as he himself poignantly confesses, he has thus discovered the true meaning of the universe. In addition to that alternation of death and rebirth, Melville and O'Neill focus on comparable images connecting the ocean with the death motif. These images can simultaneously evoke horror and peacefulness.

In *Omoo* and *White-Jacket*, Melville focuses on the demise of the sailor in terms prefiguring O'Neill's *Cardiff*. For both writers, the ocean constitutes the passage to an afterworld, as in Greek mythology. In Chapter XII of *Omoo*, entitled "Death and Burial of Two of the Crew," Melville provides a realistic and compassionate depiction of the death of two helpless sailors in a mode foreshadowing the moving evocation of Yank's last moments. The narrator of *Omoo* tells of the delirious state of his dying companion: "[...] he was often delirious, starring up and glaring around him, and sometimes wildly tossing his arms." (p. 47) This sort of frenzy can be compared with Yank's stream of consciousness in *Cardiff*. As in O'Neill's one-act, the sailors of Melville's *Omoo* die because of their isolation on the ocean: "[...] had either of them been ashore under proper treatment, he would, in all human probability, have recovered." (p. 49) Melville stresses the tragic nature of the sailors' death in indicating that they will have to be buried at sea: "As the plank tipped, the body slid off slowly, and fell with a splash into the sea." (p. 48) This notation is analogous to Yank's sad realization that he will die before reaching Cardiff and will be deprived of a grave on the land.

In *White-Jacket*, the theme of the dying sailor is presented in terms as authentic as in *Omoo* and *Cardiff* and again, the figure of the agonizing sailor shows correspondences to O'Neill's Yank:

> Shenly was lying on his back. His eyes were closed, forming two dark-blue pits in his face; his breath was coming and going with a slow, long-drawn, mechanical precision. It was the mere foundering hull of a man that was before me [...]. Pierre, who had been a "chummy" of Shenley's, spent much time in tying the neckerchief in a elaborate bow, and affectionately adjusting the white frock and trousers [...]. (pp. 315–316)

The resemblance with *Cardiff* is all the more striking through the presence of Shenly's death-bed companion, whose sense of caring forms a counterpart to Driscoll's compassionate attitude in O'Neill's play. If the image of the dying sailor in *White-Jacket* elicits saddened emotions, another episode from the same novel reflects a more ambivalent acceptance of death at sea when the narrator records the impressions he experienced upon falling accidentally overboard. He tells both of the horror and of the feeling of peace that the idea of his oncoming demise aroused in his soul:

> [...] I thought to myself, Great God! This is death! Yet these thoughts were unmixed with alarm [...]. As I gushed into the sea, a thunder boom sounded in my ear; my soul seemed flying from my mouth, the feeling of death flooded over me with the billows [...] in a trance I yielded, and sank deeper down with a glide [...] the horrible nausea was gone; the bloody, blind film turned a pale green; I wondered whether I was yet dead, or still dying [...]. For one instant an agonizing revulsion came over me as I found myself utterly sinking [...]. The life-and-death poise soon passed; and then I found myself slowly ascending, and caught a dim glimmering of light. (p. 368)

The symbol of the sea as messenger of death, evident in the passages I have quoted, has an equivalent in O'Neill's *Cardiff*. If the ambivalence of the excerpt just cited is not found as such in *Cardiff*, it nonetheless deserves being mentioned in this part of my study. It indicates that if, in general terms, both O'Neill and Melville displayed ambivalent feelings towards the deep, their attitude towards a particular motif could at times vary significantly.

In *Cardiff*, the dramatist stages the death of the sailor through techniques bearing a strong resemblance to Melville's *Omoo* and *White-Jacket*. Like the protagonists of *Omoo*, Yank feels frightened by the prospect of being buried at sea: "We won't reach Cardiff for a week at least [...]. I'll be buried at sea [...]. I always wanted to be buried on dry land." (p. 49) His sad awareness echoes Melville's description of a sea burial in *Omoo*: like Yank, the novelist's sailors are deprived of a grave on the land. Another characteristic that both *Cardiff* and *Omoo* share resides in their presentation of the dying sailor as delirious. While in *Omoo* the protagonist is "wildly tossing his arm," in *Cardiff*, Yank's feverish state prompts him to remember his entire past life and the whole play can be regarded as his "stream of consciousness." Further, both in *Omoo* and *Cardiff*, the heroes perish because of their isolation on the sea. Melville suggests that ashore the dying sailors would have been able to recover. Likewise, O'Neill indicates that Yank will die because the ship will not reach Cardiff in time: "THE CAPTAIN: [...] I can't do anything else for him. It's too serious for me. If this had only happened a week later we'd be in Cardiff in time to [...]." (p. 44) On the whole, *Cardiff* can be compared to *Omoo* through its realistic and elegiac mood but can also be interpreted by reference to Melville's *White-Jacket*. Similarities exist in the physical delineation of the dying sailor, whom the novelist depicts as "the foundering hull of a man." O'Neill also stresses the characteristics of agony on Yank's body: "[...] One of his arms is stretched limply over the side of the bunk. His face is very pale, and drops of clammy perspiration glisten on his forehead." (p. 34) A second feature shared by both *White-Jacket* and *Cardiff* consists in the presence of a death-bed companion. While Melville's Pierre feels deeply moved by the departure of his friend, O'Neill's Driscoll equally experiences sadness upon the demise of his fellow sailor: "DRISCOLL: (With a great sob). Yank! (he sinks down on his knees beside the bunk, his head on his hands [...])." (p. 50) The two artists thus regard the sea as the symbolic passage to death, a vision analogous to the Greek myth of the crossing to the Inferno and the Elysian fields. In view of these elements, it is correct to say that *Omoo* and *White-Jacket* have influenced *Cardiff*, the more so as Jean Chotia indicates that O'Neill had read some of Melville's stories by the time he started working on *Cardiff*.[9]

In his masterpiece *Moby Dick*, Melville prolonged the theme of physical annihilation at sea in a slightly different fashion by stressing the criminal nature of the ocean: "Consider, once more, the universal cannibalism of the sea; all those creatures prey upon each other, carrying on eternal war since the world began." (p. 381) The disquieting atmosphere is reinforced at the end of the novel through the poignant tableau of the sinking Pequod. The final image of *Moby Dick* is one of nearly total destruction caused by a creature of the sea, the albino whale.

Similarly, O'Neill's obsession with the "universal cannibalism" of the sea can be found in *Thirst*, in which one of the characters, the gentleman, refers to the surrounding deep with words evocative of its mournful quality:

[...] Today everything is red. The very sea itself seems changed to blood (He licks his swollen, cracked lips—then laughs—the shrill cackle of madness). Perhaps it is the blood of those who were drowned that night rising to the surface. (p. 5)

As in *Moby Dick*, the sea of *Thirst* possesses murderous characteristics. Indeed, at the end of the play, the protagonists are devoured by sharks. Thus, unlike the image of the sailor's demise, primarily associated with elegiac connotations, the figure of the sea as murderer suggests essentially fright.

D. Death in the Dark Interiors of the Sea

The two writers can also be compared through their kindred treatment of a recurrent image evocative of death at sea: the "bottom of the ocean" or "death by immersion" motif, suggesting peace and harmony throughout their canons. If it does not generate emotional division by itself, it nonetheless contributes to reinforcing the pattern of oppositions already existing in the author's novels and plays. Melville develops such an image for the first time in *Mardi* (1849) in focusing on a sunken ship:

> Pray heaven, the spirit of that lost vessel [...] may never haunt my future path upon the waves. Peacefully may she rest at the bottom of the sea; and sweetly sleep my shipmates in the lowest watery zone, where prowling sharks come not, nor billows roll. (p. 22)[10]

If in *Mardi*, Melville equates the bottom of the sea with a sleep-like death, in *Redburn*, the unreality of death, experienced at the bottom of the ocean, is even more heavily emphasized. Redburn only imagines that he is walking beneath the waters, an image conjuring up the sense of drowning:

> I felt as if in a dream all the time; and when I could shut the ship out, almost thought I was in some new, fairy world, and expected to hear myself called to, out of the clear blue air, or from *the depths of the deep blue sea* [...]. I [...] did not exactly know where, or what I was; everything was so strange and new. (pp. 116–117, my italics)

The hero's reverie indicates that he progressively loses his knowledge of being, a feeling close to death, in a setting, which, although ill-defined, may very well correspond to the bottom of the sea.

In *White-Jacket*, on the contrary, in the drowning scene I have already quoted, the sense of death appears more real. White-Jacket's fascination for the peaceful demise that awaits mankind there, or in any case beneath the surface of the water, is reflected in his harmonious description of the environment. As in *Redburn* and *Journey*, the atmosphere appears unreal and the overall impression is one of quietness: "Purple and pathless was the deep calm now around me, flecked by summer lightnings in an azure afar [...]. I wondered whether I was yet dead, or still dying." (p. 368)

In his late career, in *Billy Budd*, Melville would again revert to a similar motif by concluding his novel with a sailor song entitled "Billy in the Darbies." In this poem, sinking to the bottom of the sea does not evoke terror but elicits a certain sense of humor:

> But me they'll lash in hammock, drop me deep. Fathoms down, fathoms
> down, how I'll dream fast asleep. I feel it stealing now. Sentry, are you
> there? Just ease these darbies at the wrist, And roll me over fair! I'm
> sleepy, and the oozy weeds about me twist. (p. 132)

As in *Redburn* and *White-Jacket*, the bottom of the sea, or at least the
immersion underneath water level, suggests some degree of unreality, manifested
in the equation of death with a tranquil sleep.

In *Cross*, O'Neill introduces a comparable image of death when ghost
sailors emerge from the depths of the ocean in order to bring back Captain
Bartlett's alleged treasure: "Their hair is matted, entertwined with shiny strands
of seaweed [...]. Their flesh in the green light has the suggestion of
decomposition. Their bodies sway limply, nervelessly, rhythmically as if to the
pulse of long swells of the deep sea [...]." (pp. 159–160) Although the mention of
"decomposition" hints at a terrible, rather than mild death, the general mood is
one of resignation to physical destruction, of identification with the rhythm of the
ocean. As in *Billy Budd*, the characters are surrounded with weed and become a
part of the sea.

In *Marco* (1925), the image of the bottom of the ocean is again associated
with sweetness, as a chorus of sailors laments: "There is peace deep in the
sea [...]. When I sank drowning, I loved death [...]. Death lives in a silent sea."
(p. 274).[11] This allusion to the quiet death with which man meets when
submerged under water is reminiscent of Melville's *Mardi, Redburn,* and
White-Jacket and reappears in *Capricorn*, where Ethan confesses: "I want to let
go, go down, drown, forget [...]." (p. 79) It also recurs in *Iceman* when Hickey
requests his friends to get rid of their illusions in terms of sea imagery: "Let
yourself sink down to the bottom of the sea. Rest in peace. There's no farther you
have to go. Not a single damned hope or dream left to nag you." (p. 86) In both
Capricorn and *Iceman*, death by immersion is endowed with highly positive
connotations.

In *Journey*, O'Neill resorts to sea imagery in a more explicit mode. In one
of Edmund's reveries, he envisages a death-like situation connected with the

bottom of the sea. As in *Redburn* and *Mardi*, the image evokes an illusionary and quiet universe:

> Out beyond the harbour, where the road runs along the beach, I even lost the feeling of being on land. The fog and the sea seemed part of each other. It was like walking on the bottom of the sea. As if I had been drowned long ago. As if I was a ghost of the sea. It felt damned peaceful to be nothing more than a ghost within a ghost [...]. (p. 113)

Edmund's intuition indicates that the hero, like Redburn, loses the sense of his own identity—he becomes a ghost—as well as his sense of a stable setting, since spatial oppositions—the sea and the land—are blurred.

In summation, the symbols of the sea as harbinger of death and of death at the bottom of the ocean, although sources of conflicting emotions, definitely contribute, in their various guises, to intensifying the mood of tragic nostalgia characterizing the works of Melville and O'Neill.

E. The Ship, Sovereign of the Seas

The two writers' questing protagonists explore the seas in nearly identical vessels. In that respect, it is significant to note that both authors regret the disappearance of sailing frigates and express contempt for steamships. In *Billy Budd*, Melville casts a romantic glance upon the bygone days of sail, when sailors were noble and handsome:

> In the time before steamships, or then more frequently than now [...] a group of bronzed mariners [...] would flank [...] some superior figure [...] the "Handsome sailor." With no perceptible trace of the vainglorious about him, rather with the offhand unaffectedness of natural regality, he seemed to accept the spontaneous homage of his shipmates [...] . (p. 43)

In *Anna*, O'Neill seems to recapture a sense of nostalgia similar to that which emerges in *Billy Budd*. Like the novelist, he links the era of the sail with the authenticity of the mariners: "CHRIS: [...] Ay was on windjammer [...] Ships vas ships den—and men dat sail on dem vas real men. And now what you gat on steamers? You gat fallars on deck don't know ships from mudscow." (p. 76) In *Ape*, Paddy voices the identical yearning to retrieve the epoch of sail during which men were handsome and courageous:

> Oh, there was fine beautiful ships them days—clippers wid tall masts touching the sky—fine strong men in them [...]. Oh, the clean skins of them, and the clear eyes, the straight backs and full chests of them! Brave men they was, and bold men surely! (p. 45)

Clearly, Melville and O'Neill share a regret for the passing of the clipper ship era. They describe the interior and the crew of their vessels in related modes. They attribute analogous characteristics to the forecastle of the ships in which their mariners are cruising: a cramped and dark setting serves, in their novels and plays, as the home of an international crew, symbolic of the American "melting pot."

In *White-Jacket*, the writer develops this image in some detail: "And thus, with our counterlikes and dislikes, most of us men-of-war's men harmoniously dove-tail into each other, and by our very points of opposition, unite in a clever whole [...]." (p. 156) As in the plays of O'Neill, Melville's ship becomes a microcosm of the universe, a metaphor further amplified in the depiction of the crew of the "Pequod:" "They were nearly all Islanders in the Pequod [...]. An Anarcharsis Clootz deputation from all the isles of the sea, and all the ends of the earth [...]." (pp. 216–217) In "Midnight, Forecastle," the artist lists the different nationalities of the sailors living in the cramped forecastle; "First Nantucket Sailors," "Dutch Sailor," "French Sailor," "Iceland Sailor," "Maltese Sailor," "Sicilian Sailor," "China Sailor." (pp. 269–276) By gathering sailors from various parts of the world, Melville's forecastle is associated with positive overtones. In prolonging Melville's theme of the "melting pot," O'Neill reveals a deeper interest than his predecessor for the cramped space of the forecastle.

In the opening stage directions of *Cardiff*, O'Neill emphasizes the cramped characteristics of such a setting:

> An irregular shaped compartment, the sides of which almost meet at the
> far end to form a triangle. Sleeping bunks about six feet long, ranged
> three deep in a space of three feet separating the upper from the lower,
> are built against the sides [...]. Four of the men are pulling on pipe and
> the air is heavy with rancid tobacco smoke. (pp. 33–34)

The space in which the sailors live stifles its occupants with a horrid smell. In this
repulsive environment, O'Neill portrays an international crew reminiscent of
Melville's *Moby Dick*. Throughout his "S.S. Glencairn" cycle, the playwright
carefully details the various nationalities of the members of the crew: "A
Norwegian, Paul, is soflty playing some folk song on a battered accordion."
(*Cardiff*, p. 34); Olson is "a Swede with a drooping blood mustache." (*Cardiff*,
p. 35); Driscoll is a "brawny Irishman with the battered features of a
prizefighter" (*Cardiff*, p.35); Ivan is a "Rooshan swab." (*Long Voyage*, p. 65);
Jack is a "Young American with a though, good-natured face." (*Zone*, p. 85). As
in *Moby Dick*, O'Neill attempts to present his ship as a microcosm of the
universe.

In *Ape*, the dramatist again combines the description of the crew's
traditional abode with the "melting pot" metaphor:

> The firemen's forecastle of a transatlantic liner an hour after sailing
> from New York for the voyage across. Tiers of narrow, steel bunks,
> three deep, on all sides [...] the room is crowded with men, shouting,
> cursing, laughing, singing—confused, inchoate uproar swelling into a
> sort of unity [...] All the civilized white races are represented [...]. (p.
> 39)

After having established the narrow aspects of the forecastle, O'Neill continues to
evoke the various nationalities of the sailors in attempting to reproduce their
opposite languages: "Salute [...] gesundheit [...] La Touraine [...] Bloody
Dutchman! [...]." (p. 40) From this quotation, it is evident that *Ape* bears strong
resemblances to Melville's "Midnight, Forecastle."

Both men regard the forecastle as a place of exile, as a refuge from the conflicts occuring on land. In *Redburn*, the novelist compares sailors to outcasts who "only go round the world, without going into it [...]. They but touch the perimeter of the circle; hover about the edges of terra firma [...] They would dream as little of traveling inland to see Kenilworth [...] as they would of sending a card overland to the Pope, when they touched at Naples." (p. 197)

In *White-Jacket*, Melville refines this motif in a manner that prefigures O'Neill's *Zone* and presents us with a poet isolated in the midst of his fellow sailors:

> Lemsford was a poet; so thoroughly inspired with the divine afflatus, that not even all the tar and tumult of a man-of-war could drive it out of him [...]. Now Lemford's great care, anxiety, and endless source of tribulation was the preservation of his manuscripts [...]. He had a little box [...] in which he kept his papers and stationery [...]. Added to this was the deadly hostility of the whole tribe of ship-underlings [...] both to the poet and his casket [...]. They hunted out his hiding-places like pointers, and gave him no peace night or day. (pp. 42–43)

In *Moby Dick*, Ishmaël confesses from the start that voyaging allows him to resolve psychological tensions experienced on land:

> Call me Ishmaël. Some years ago—never mind how long precisely— having little or no money in my purse, and having nothing particular to interest me on shore, I thought I would sail about a little and see the watery part of the world. It is a way I have of driving off the spleen, and regulating the circulation. Whenever I find myself growing grim about the mouth; whenever it is a damp, drizzly November in my soul [...] then I account it high time to get to sea as soon as I can. (p. 93)

But whereas *Moby Dick* offers an optimistic view of sea life, *White-Jacket* contains bitter comments on the social implications of coexistence in the forecastle.

In *Zone*, O'Neill articulates a compelling statement about the fate of the outcast. To him, as to Melville, the forecastle constitutes a space of alienation, a motif which he endows with exclusively negative and pessimistic overtones. In this short drama, he provides the reader with an unconscious transposition of the motif of the poet figure Melville inserted into the fabric of *White-Jacket*. Smitty, the protagonist of *Zone*, is estranged from the rest of the crew and appears, like Lemsford, constantly worried about the preservation of love-letters hidden in a little box: "Smitty opens the suit-case and takes out a small black tin box, carefully places this under his mattress, shoves the suit-case back under the bunk, climbs into his bunk again, closes his eyes and begins to snore loudly." (p. 82)[12] Although Smitty, unlike Lemsford, does not write full-length manuscripts, his letters suggest that he shares with Melville's hero the qualities of a dreamer. Like Lemsford, his intellectual superiority earns him only contempt on the crew's part: "COCKY: Be the airs 'e puts on you'd think 'e was the Prince of Wales." (p. 87) While the sailors of Melville's *White-Jacket* hunted out Lemsford's hiding places, the crew of the "S.S. Glencairn" tie Smitty down in order to read his love letters. Driscoll's reading intimates that Smitty, like Ishmaël, has run away from the land because he no longer could resolve the psychological conflicts that had besieged him on the continent: "[...] You have run away to sea loike the coward you are." (p. 106) The similarity between *Zone* and *White-Jacket* is further reinforced by the identical settings in which the crisis takes place. *White-Jacket* focuses on a man-of-war and *Zone* presents us with a ship used for a military transport of ammunition in a war situation. In depicting the hostility between sailors having abandoned the land, O'Neill adopts a more pessimistic viewpoint than Melville, for, unlike the novelist, he fails to detect in sea life a way of "regulating the circulation."

F. Marine Imagery

Melville's and O'Neill's sailors, while cruising on their ships, were fascinated by natural phenomena connected with the ocean such as the fog, calms, and the merging of sky and water. In addition, O'Neill and Melville demonstrated interest in the "Quest pattern," and the "Blessed Islands" motifs, which also contributed to the development of their marine imagery. Both writers treated these attributes and motifs of the sea as constrasting literary images and leitmotifs, reinforcing the tragic tensions already inherent in their works.

The Quest Pattern

O'Neill and Melville regard their characters' voyages as physical symbols of a spiritual quest which fails to provide an eventual sense of enlightenment. In *White-Jacket*, Melville universalizes the quest pattern and considers it as an essential feature of the human predicament at large:

> As a man-of-war that sails through the sea, so this earth that sails through the air. We mortals are all on board a fast-sailing, never sinking world frigate, of which God was the shipwright [...] the port we sail from is for ever astern [...] our last destination remains a secret to ourselves and our officers [...]. Life is a voyage that's homeward bound [...]. (pp. 372–374)

The metaphysical implications of the motif are clearly articulated through the equation of human life with a pointless sea journey. The existence of an afterlife, Melville implies, appears extremely dubious. In *Moby Dick*, he further develops his ironic and pessimistic concept of our fate and underscores heavily the elusiveness of man's pursuit of ideals:

> Were this world an endless plain, and by sailing eastward we could for ever reach new distances, and discover sights more sweet and strange than any Cyclades or Islands of King Solomon, then there were promise in the voyage. But in pursuit of those far mysteries we dream of, or in tormented chase of that demon phantom that, some time or other, swims before all human hearts; while chasing such over this round globe, they either lead us on in barren mazes or midway leave us whelmed. (p. 340)

A similar pessimistic outlook on the purpose of man's life, expressed in terms of nautical imagery, recurs in the works of O'Neill.

In O'Neill's early sea plays, Melville's quest pattern re-emerges in *Thirst*. Before sinking, the ship in which the protagonists of that playlet were cruising, ventured in little known waters. Says the gentleman: "We are far out of the beaten track of steamers. I know little of navigation, yet I heard those on board say that we were following a course but little used." (p. 10) If the destination of the voyage in *Thirst* is left uncertain, in the one-act plays of the "S.S. Glencairn" cycle, the sailors also appear to be roaming purposelessly through the seas. In *Cardiff*, Yank's various voyages around the globe have failed to offer him permanent happiness, an impression which his death-bed reminisicences contribute to establish:

> YANK: [...] I always like Argentine [...]. All except that booze, cana. How drunk we used to get on that, remember? Remember the night I went crazy with the heat in Singapore? And the time you was pinched by the cops in Port Said? And the time we was both locked up in Sidney for fightin'? (p. 48)

As the narrator of *Moby Dick* suggests, Yank's quest has led him in "barren mazes" and has left him midway "whelmed," a fate also experienced by Olson in *Long Voyage*. O'Neill's Scandinavian sailor has constantly been sailing the seas without any clearly defined objective. In *Horizon*, one can observe a universalizing technique analogous to that which Melville displayed in *White-Jacket*. Indeed, the goal of the character's cosmic voyage appears ill-defined and the nature of death is unidentified: "And this time I'm going! It isn't the end. It's a free beginning—the start of my voyage!" (p. 79) Although Robert asserts that death constitutes a new start, the dramatist stresses the fact that the hero's vision is highly subjective. In his late career, O'Neill reverted to the quest motif with equally universal and pessimistic overtones in *Iceman*, where, as in *Horizon* and *White-Jacket*, human life is implicitly compared with a voyage: "LARRY: [...] It's the No Chance Saloon. It's Bedrock Bar, the End of the Line Café, the Bottom of the Sea Rathskeller! Don't you notice the beautiful calm in the atmosphere? That's because it's the last harbor!" (p. 25) Harry Hope's bar epitomizes the last refuge of characters who have been disappointed in their search for happiness. O'Neill's allusion to the last "harbor" implies movement and evokes the image of a voyage endowed with cosmic and allegorical characteristics: it is the ultimate haven in human existence to which O'Neill refers. In this sense, the nautical imagery recalls that of *White-Jacket*, where the quest motif acquires equally universal and bleak overtones. Throughout his dramatic career, then, O'Neill portrayed sailors and "land" characters embarked upon a quest for the absolutes of life. His protagonists, however, like those of Melville, are doomed never to possess the ideal for which they are yearning.

The "Blessed Islands" Motif

The "Blessed Islands" perform an archetypal role that confers upon O'Neill's and Melville's sea works a mythic dimension. Indeed the "Fortunate or Blessed Isles" were already sung of by the Ancient Greeks, who compared them to earthly paradises. In the case of O'Neill, the influence of Nietzsche may also have been important in the development of such image.[13] In O'Neill and Melville, they can either signify temporary relief for the weary sea traveller, or, in a few rare instances, they can evoke feelings of awe and terror. Again, this "double consciousness," to speak with Emerson, characterizes O'Neill's and Melville's richly endowed "imagination matérielle." The "Blessed Islands" motif is to be found in *Typee* and *Electra*, in which it assumes the shape of a leitmotif. As I have dealt with these two works in the preceding chapter, I shall now concentrate on other novels and plays from the two writers' canons.

In Melville's *Omoo*, the narrator lyrically praises the wonders of the Motoo-Otoo island:

It is of coral formation; and all around, for many rods out, the bay is so shallow, that you might wade anywhere. Down in these waters, as transparent as air, you see coral plants of every hue and shape imaginable:—[...] tufts of azure, waving reeds like stalks of grain, and pale green buds and mosses [...] and around Motoo-Otoo have I often paddled of a white moonlight night, pausing now and then to admire the marine gardens beneath. (p. 184)

These lyrical evocations foreshadow the splendor of the lagoon in *Mardi*: "But how tranquil, the wide lagoon, which mirrored the burning spots in heaven! Deep down into its innermost heart penetrated the slanting rays of Hesperus like a shaft of light, sunk far into mysterious Golcondas, where myriad gnomes seemed toiling [...]." (p. 157) In his later years, Melville modified his presentation of the Blessed Island motif, in the tales entitled "The Encantadas" (1856). These islands share with those of *Omoo* and *Mardi* an enchanted quality, although they symbolize, in the end, desolation and death:

> In many places the coast is rock-bound, or, more properly, clinker-bound; tumbled masses of blackish or greenish stuff like the dross of an iron-furnace, forming dark clefts and caves here and there, into which a ceaseless sea pours a fury of foam [...] the dark, vitrified masses [...] present a most Plutonian sight. In no world but a fallen one could such lands exist. (p. 133)[14]

Melvile's dichotomous vision of the "Blessed Isles" foreshadow O'Neill's seascapes.

In *Cross*, it is in one of those "Blessed Islands" that Captain Bartlett finds a shelter after the sinking of his frigate. There, he buries a treasure before returning to America: "Their second day in the island [...] they discovered in a sheltered inlet the rotten, waterlogged hulk of a Malay prau [...]. The Kanakas went over the prau [...] and they found in two chests...treasure, of course." (pp. 143–144) In *Diff'rent*, the connotations attached to the same islands equally suggest peace and harmony and tend to conjure up an atmosphere of Edenic innocence. Caleb Williams, the mariner of *Diff'rent*, tells his fiancé he has experienced in these isles a sexual freedom, from which the inhabitants of New England could never benefit:

> And them native women—they're different [...]. That night when she swum out and got aboard when I was alone, she caught me by s'prise. I wasn't expectin' nothin' o' that sort. I tried to make her git back to land at fust—but she wouldn't go. She couldn't understand enough English for me to allow to tell her how I felt—and I reckon she wouldn't have seed my p'int anyhow—her bein' a native. (A pause). And when I was afeered she'd catch cold goin' round all naked and wet in the moonlight—though it was warm—and I wanted to wrap a blanket round her [...]. (p. 219)

Although in his first years of composition, O'Neill expresses his fascination for the beauty of the "Blessed Isles" in a style which recalls Melville's, in his later years he endows the same motif with negative overtones close to those found in "The Encantadas."

In *Misbegotten*, he refers to the motif of the "Blessed Islands" in an oblique manner by suggesting that the sense of happiness and relief derived from a stay in these islands could at best constitute a pipe-dream:

> TYRONE: [...] We can kid the world but we can't fool ourselves, like most people, no matter what we do—nor escape ourselves no matter where we run away.Whether it's the bottom of a bottle, or *a South Sea island*, we'd find our own ghosts there waiting to greet us [...]. (p. 87, I italicize)

The bitter overtones of O'Neill's and Melville's marine imagery comes clearly to the fore in this facet of the "Blessed Islands" motif.

The Fog

Melville resorts to such an image in *Redburn*, in a passage foreshadowing, through its blurred presentation of the outside world, O'Neill's *Fog*: "It was on a Sunday we made the Banks of Newfoundland; a drizzling, foggy, clammy Sunday [...]. The decks were dripping with wet, so that in the dense fog, it seemed as if we were standing on the roof of a house in a shower." (p. 136) The narrator further emphasizes the weird atmosphere in which this part of the voyage took place as everything was "flat and calm." (p. 136) In *Fog*, O'Neill offers the reader an analogous image of the dense fog, of quietness and unreality:

> The lifeboat of a passenger steamer is drifting helplessly off the Grand Banks of Newfoundland. A dense fog lies heavily upon the still sea. There is no wind and the long swells of the ocean are barely perceptible. The surface of the water is shadowy and unreal in its perfect calmness. (p. 85)

The similarity between Melville's *Redburn* and O'Neill's *Fog* is further emphasized through the identical setting of both works, i.e., the Banks of

Newfoundland. While Melville seems to have introduced this image in *Redburn* only, O'Neill resorted to it in various plays, particularly in *Cardiff* when telling of Yank's passage from life to death. The fog there serves to prepare the audience for the symbolic, the unreal nature of the action, which occurs on "a foggy night midway on the voyage between New York and Cardiff." (p. 3) In *Anna*, the strange power of the fog dominates the stage: "ANNA: [...] I love this fog! Honest! It's so [...] funny and still. I feel as if I was—out of things altogether." (p. 41) In *Anna* as in *Redburn*, the fog obliterates the distinction between reality and illusion. In *Journey*, the dramatist utilizes the fog image in order to underline Mary's psychotic behavior. The ominous atmosphere of the fog, pointing to Melville's *Redburn*, corresponds to the emotional turmoil assailing the heroine:

> There is a pause of dead quiet. Then from the world outside comes the melancholy moan of the foghorn, followed by a chorus of bells, muffled by the fog, from the anchored craft in the harbour. Mary's face gives no sign she has heard, but her hands jerk and the fingers automatically play for a moment on the air [...]. (p. 92)

In Edmund's lyrical outbursts, it is the illusionary quality of the fog that acquires a symbolic value, duplicating the one it received in *Redburn*:

> The fog was where I wanted to be. Halfway down the path you can't see this house. You'd never know it was here. Or any of the other places down the avenue. I couldn't see but a few feet ahead. I didn't meet a soul. Everything looked and sounded unreal. Nothing was what it is. That's what I wanted—to be alone with myself in another world [...]. (p. 113)

The fog motif, in O'Neill's and Melville's works, symbolizes a quasi-supernatural universe, which as it constantly bespeaks fear, constitutes an instance of the two artists' convergent nautical imagery.

Calms

Both writers utilized the image of the calms in order to stress the fierceness of the physical, psychological, or metaphysical crises, to which these doldrums form a prelude. In *Mardi*, Melville weaves this particular image into the texture of his work in a manner that prefigures O'Neill's *Capricorn*. Indeed, calms affect the characters' psyche to the point of near madness:

> To a landsman a calm is no joke. It not only revolutionizes his abdomen, but unsettles his mind; tempts him to recant his belief in the eternal fitness of things; in short, almost makes an infidel of him [...] he grows madly skeptical [...]. He begins to feel anxious concerning his soul. (pp.7–8)

In *Moby Dick*, calms foreshadow the terrible storm which will destroy the "Pequod" and qualify as signs of bad omen:

> [...] the profound calm which only apparently precedes and prophesies of the storm, is perhaps more awful than the storm itself; for, indeed, the calm is but the wrapper and envelope of the storm; and it contains it in itself, as the seemingly harmless rifle holds the fatal powder [...]. (p. 387)

This terrifying aspect of the calms corresponds closely to the imagery of O'Neill's *Capricorn*. In "Benito Cereno" (1856), Melville again insists on the dangerous effects of that natural phenomenon, which represents a brooding introduction to Captain Delano's strange adventures:

> The morning was one peculiar to that coast. Everything gray. The sea, though undulated into long roods of swells, seemed fixed, and was sleeked at the surface like waved lead that has cooled and set in the smelter's mould. The sky seemed a gray surtout. Flights of troubled gray fowl, kith and kin with flights of troubled gray vapors among which they were mixed, skimmed low and fitfully over the waters, as swallows over meadows before storms. Shadows present,

foreshadowing deeper shadows to come. (p. 217)[15]

In "Benito Cereno" as in *Moby Dick*, the calms prefigure a storm, "deeper shadows to come." In O'Neill's *Capricorn*, the calms function as a literary device pointing to the fatal outcome of the action. Here, O'Neill, like Melville in *Mardi*, depicts a group of landsmen, the Harfords of Massachusetts, who feel driven to madness by the awfulness of the calm: "ELIZABETH: [...] My God, it's all so mad, this calm!" (p. 83) Like Melville, O'Neill expresses the metaphysical doubts of which the passengers become the victims through Reverend Dickey's formulation: "[...] in this calm one doubts. Perhaps God cares nothing about justice for man." (p. 85) The resemblance in situation between Melville's *Mardi* and O'Neill's *Capricorn* is strengthened through the fact that in both works, the protagonists blame the Captain for the weather conditions. The narrator of *Mardi* comments: "At length, horrible doubts overtake him as to the Captain's competency to navigate his ship." (p. 8) Conversely, in *Capricorn*, Warren, the owner of the ship, accuses the Captain of incompetence:

> It's the cursed luck of this calm, this calm. The trouble with you, Captain, is your mind is not on the voyage. You're worrying about other things, your personal affairs, not your duty to the ship, its owner, its freight, its passengers—[...]. (p. 69)

In *Capricorn* as in *Moby Dick* and "Benito Cereno," the calms announce the psychological storm which eventually crushes the characters: Ethan and Nancy feel desperate after killing the Captain of the ship. To Melville as to O'Neill, the calms image intensifies contrasts with subsequent accelerations in the rhythmical pattern of the work. It also allows the writers to explore the innermost recesses of the characters' souls, thereby shedding light on metaphysical issues.

The Sky/Sea Tension

The two writers were interested in the fundamental opposition between the sky and the sea, a dichotomy which they often viewed in sexual terms. In *Moby Dick*, the novelist considers both the dissimilarity between sky and sea and their fusion:

It was a clear steel-blue day. The firmaments of air and sea were hardly separable in that all-pervading azure; only, the pensive air was transparently pure and soft, with a woman's look, and the robust and man-like sea heaved with long, strong, lingering swells, as Samson's chest in his sleep. Hither, and thither, on high, glided the snow-white wings of small, unspeckled birds; these were the gentle thoughts of the feminine air ; but to and fro in the deeps, far down in the bottomless blue, rushed mighty leviathans, sword-fish, and sharks; and these were the strong, troubled, murderous thinkings of the masculine sea. (p. 649)

In O'Neill's works, one can detect a similar image, for the playwright opposes the two elements in sexual terms while eventually stressing their intimate connection. In his early poems, he offers a precise equivalent of Melville's imagery in *Moby Dick*:

> Whimsical dreams of wind
> Stirring the sea's face
> to a tender smiling;
> And the peace of a twilight
> When the sea and sky
> become one. (p. 71, poem 47)

As in *Moby Dick*, the air represents a feminine element, which succeeds in pacifying the bold, masculine sea. Their juxtaposition recalls *Moby Dick*, where "the firmaments of air and sea were hardly separable." In *Journey*, Edmund evokes a related image while dreaming of former mystical revelations: "(I was) watching the dawn creep in like a painted dream over the sky and sea which slept together." (p. 134) In this play, the dramatist provides us with a muted reminder of Melville's sexual fusion of the sky and the ocean: a certain degree of ambiguity can be detected in "slept together." Moreover, like Melville, O'Neill asserts the union of the two elements, which owing to the night setting, appear inseparable. It could be argued that, through the sky/sea contrast, O'Neill developed, along the lines of Melville, an image expressive of an animistic conception of the deep. In summation, the close parallels generated through the quest pattern, the "Blessed Islands," the fog, calms and sky/sea motifs I have described in O'Neill and

Melville, do raise the question of a possible direct influence between the two writers' marine imagery.

G. Back to the Lee-Shore

The myriad of motifs I have dealt with in this chapter once more evidence the multi-faceted nature of O'Neill's and Melville's romantic vision of the sea symbol. Such richness of texture naturally betrays the writers' profound reverence for the sea as a shaping force of their imagination, or rather of their "imagination matérielle." Simultaneously, the artists' ambivalence towards sea life prefigures the power of their ultimate tragic vision. To obtain a better understanding of this tragic sense, we must, at the end of this odyssey, turn back to the land, to the "lee-shore," where human conflicts, no longer benefitting from the soothing influence of the sea, take on their full tragic dimension.

CHAPTER V. TALES OF YANKEES AND PURITANS

At the core of O'Neill's and Melville's concept of tragedy lies their pessimistic—and needless to say, highly personal—vision of the double-consciousness of American society. On the one hand, they lament the failure of Puritan, Calvinistic religious and moral manifestoes, i.e., the impossibility for America to fulfill the ideals of Winthrop's sermon, "A Model of Christian Charity".[1] They were, in some senses, "New England" writers, as both had spent either their childhood or part of their adulthood in that region of the United States.[2] They consequently translated their impressions about New England in several of their works. In addition to satirizing the gradual decline of American Puritanism—or in a more generic sense Protestantism—, they also deplored the defects of the opposite American traditon, i.e., that of the more secular, rational, Yankee turn of mind, best epitomized in the works of Benjamin Franklin. To that Yankee spirit, they ascribed the birth of the so-called American materialism. Connections between the two types of thought I have just described do exist, of course, as for instance the well-known work ethic of Protestantism may at times coincide with Yankee mercantilism. This is precisely why this chapter will consider simultaneously the two writers' critique of both Puritan and Yankee ingredients in American society. Accordingly, my study will not restrict itself to a depiction of society life on New England shores, but will indeed encompass the entire American landscape. It will examine the writers' view of American society, philosophy, and religious life. More often than not, these components of American civilization have either a Yankee or Puritan origin. O'Neill and Melville regretted that instead of becoming a New Jerusalem, New England—and later America at large—became corrupted by greed, materialism as well as by religious intolerance.[3] To them, the Yankee and Puritan heritage of America is both social and religious, a double-sided view which this chapter proposes to explore in its various aspects.

A

Deploring the mercantile character of American society, a phenomenon which they considered as both a product of the early Puritan work ethic and the "Yankee philosophy" of Benjamin Franklin, Melville and O'Neill underscored the spiritual blindness of the American salesman or businessman.

In "Benito Cereno", Melville concentrates on the naivety of the merchant Captain Delano. In this masterful short story, the novelist links his critique of American materialism to that of American optimism.[4] "Benito Cereno" is concerned with Delano's inability to see beneath the surface of things. At the beginning of the story, the merchant is presented as such: "[...] Captain Amasa Delano, of Duxbury, in Massachusetts, commanding a large sealer and general trader[...]." (p. 217) Having established the New England origin and "Yankee," merchant-like nature of Captain Delano, Melville at first obliquely narrates events from the viewpoint of his protagonist. He subsequently shifts to an omniscient point of view and explains the elements of the plot that had initially remained obscure to the anti-hero. Having sighted an approaching ship in difficulty, the "San Dominick," Delano comes to its rescue and discovers that its Spanish Captain, Benito Cereno, is pale and exceedingly tired. Until the very end of the story, Delano fails to understand that Benito Cereno has been the victim of a mutiny led by a negro called Babo. Captain Delano lacks any sense of evil and is therefore incapable of objectifying it correctly in the outside world. As strange incidents occur on the "San Dominick," he cannot interpret them properly and suspects the Spanish captain :

> Why was the Spaniard so superfluously punctilious at times, now heedless of common propriety in not accompanying to the side his departing guest? [...].What imported all those day-long enigmas and contradictions, except they were intended to mystify, preliminary to some stealthy blow? (pp. 279–180)

In offering to his reader a rational account of the black slaves' revolt aboard the "San Dominick" in the second part of his short story, Melville ironically points to Delano's blindness. The nature of the incidents that took place aboard Benito

Cereno's vessel was far from innocent, as the following excerpt indicates:

> [...] on the fifth day of the calm, all on board suffering much from the heat, and want of water, and five having died in fits, and mad, the negroes became irritable, and for a chance gesture, which they deemed suspicious—though it was harmless—made by the mate, Raneds, to the deponent in the act of handing a quadrant, they killed him [...]. (p. 296)

After commiting that murder, the slaves had taken Benito Cereno prisoner and were planning a mutiny when Delano arrived on board. Interestingly, Melville uses allegorical characterization. Throughout his short story, he associates three characters with well-defined sets of values: Delano with naivety and materialism, Benito Cereno with decay and Babo with evil. "Benito Cereno" thus constitutes a clear artistic articulation of Melville's attack against American materialism and optimism.

O'Neill's most memorable portrait of the American merchant, reminiscent in some aspects of Melville's Delano,[5] is perhaps Marco Polo. In *Marco*, O'Neill analyses the conflict between Eastern idealism and American materialism by opposing the merchant Marco Polo to Princess Kukachin. This long epic work charts the psychological evolution of Marco at first in his native Venice and subsequently in his travels through Asia. Having fallen in love with a Venetian lady, Marco composes a poem which unveils to the readers his materialistic personality:

> "You are lovely as the gold in the sun,
> Your skin is like silver in the moon,
> Your eyes are black pearls I have won.
> I kiss your ruby lips and you swoon,
> Smiling your thanks as I promise you
> A large fortune if you will be true,
> While I am away earning gold
> And silver so when we are old
> I will have a million to my credit
> And in the meantime can easily afford

A big wedding that will do us credit
And start having children bless the Lord!" (pp. 224–225)

O'Neill implies tongue-in-cheek that Marco Polo is unable to conceive of spiritual love. To him, marriage is synonymous with financial security, and children—significantly in the plural—represent a further sign of wealth, the manifestation of God's grace ("Bless the Lord!"). Thus, Marco does not apprehend the deeper significance of things beneath their materialistic surface and remains unaware of the evil consequences that his attitude can entail. Assuming responsibilities in the kingdom of the Khan, he modifies Eastern morality along commercial principles:

MARCO: [...] My tax scheme, Your Majesty, that got such wonderful results is simplicity itself. I simply reversed the old system. For one thing I found they had a tax on excess profits. Imagine a profit being excess! [...]. I wrote on the statute books a law that taxes every necessity in life, a law that hits everyman's pocket equally, be he beggar or banker! (p. 256)

O'Neill further illustrates this Melvillean theme in a scene between Marco and Princess Kukachin. The merchant fails to notice the Princess' love for him, except for one moment when "their lips seem about to meet in a kiss. She murmurs [...] Marco!/Marco (his voice thrilling for this second with oblivious passion) Kukachin!/Maffeo: [...] One Million [...]/Marco: [...] What, Uncle? Did you call?" (pp. 279–180) Marco's lack of intelligence, his naivety, and his optimistic nature are fateful to others: the poor inhabitants of Jang-Frau are overburdened with taxes and Princess Kukachin dies of grief while Marco leads a self-contented life in Venice. At the end of the play, O'Neill explicitly equates the Venetian merchant with the modern American businessman:

The play is over [...] a man rises [...] he is dressed as a Venetian merchant of the later thirteenth-century. In fact, it is none other than Marco Polo himself [...]. Arrived in the lobby his face begins to clear of all disturbing memories of what had happened on the stage [...]. His car [...] draws up at the church [...]. Marco Polo, with a satisfied sigh at the sheer comfort of it all, resumes his life. (p. 304)

O'Neill once more critizes, this time straightforwardly, the businessman's unawareness of unspoken truths and reliance on the superficial pleasures of existence.

In his masterpiece *Iceman*, the artist offers an extremely skillful and synthetic treatment of the same issue. In this late play, he exposes the metaphysical roots of American materialism through the character of Theodore Hickmann. From the start, his sense of confidence, comparable to that of a salesman, and his immaturity, his "boyish" nature are emphasized: "His face is round and smooth and big-boyish with bright blue eyes, a button nose, a small, pursed mouth [...]. His expression is fixed in a salesman's smile of self-confident affability and hearty good fellowship." (p. 76) However Yankee-like Hickey may appear, O'Neill carefully introduces information concerning the Protestant heritage of his character, as Hickey himself voices criticism towards his own background: "[...] You've heard the old saying, 'Ministers' sons are sons of guns.' Well, that was me, and then some. Home was like a jail. I didn't fall for the religious bunk." (pp. 231–232) In the course of action, Hickey optimistically suggests that, in order to achieve happiness, the bums of Harry Hope's bar should abandon their illusions. O'Neill condemns Hickey's philosophy: towards the end of the play, the protagonist proves unable to live without the illusion that he killed his wife out of love. Hickey seeks refuge in madness while the *habitués* of the bar return to their normal activities. In *Iceman*, O'Neill formulates, with the help of Hickey's character, a compelling statement about his vision of the adolescent aspect of American society. A better understanding of that satire is arrived at when O'Neill's drama is compared whith Melville's critique of Yankee/Puritan optimism and materialism in "Benito Cereno."

B

Second, Melville and O'Neill challenge what they regard as the American view of the negro based on racial prejudice.[6] Originating in Puritanism, that racial bias also affects the more Yankee-minded part of America. Refusing to associate the black character with evil, O'Neill and Melville endow him with an aura of innocence that white protagonists rarely possess in their works. In other words, the two writers are linked through their innovative emphasis on humanitarian issues.

In *Moby Dick*, Melville offers a subtle treatment of that theme when uttering his compassion for the black boy Pip, who goes mad in the pursuit of the whale: "Black Little Pip! [...]. Poor Alabama boy! On the grim Pequod forecastle, ye shall ere long see him, beating his tambourine, prelusive of the eternal time, when, sent for the great quarter-deck on high, he was bid strike in with angels and beat his tambourine in glory [...]." (pp. 216–217) In this early chapter, entitled "Knights and Squires," Melville confers upon Pip a spiritual quality, one that gives the boy foreknowledge of "eternal time." In a subsequent passage of the novel, "Midnight, Forecastle," the artist contrasts Pip's innocence to Ahab's ferocity:

> Pip [...] Duck lower, Pip, here comes the royal yard! It's worse than being in the whirled woods, the last day of the year! [...]. White whale, shirr! [...]. That anaconda of an old man swore 'em in to hunt him! Oh, thou big white God aloft there sowewhere in yon darkness, have mercy on this small black boy down here: preserve him from all men that have no bowels to feel fear! (p. 276)

Pip's foolish raving contains profound truths about the nature of the conflict between man and God. While Ahab possesses "no bowels to feel fear," Pip exhibits no such pride towards the divinity. Melville emphasizes the boy's goodness in the episode recording his death at sea: neither Ahab, nor the "big white God" could protect him against such a fate. By comparison to innocent Pip, Melville intimates, both the Captain and God qualify as sinful creatures. Clearly, the novelist modifies the traditional connotations associated with the black and white colors in an attempt to question the validity of the negative vision of the negro that some of their contemporaries harbored. In subsequent chapters, the writer continues to show the effects of Pip's purity on Ahab. Immediately before the final chase, the mad Captain is involved in a conversation with the black boy and confesses being moved by his fundamental goodness: "Thou touchest my inmost centre, boy: thou art tied to me by cords woven of my heart-strings [...]. See [...] man [...] full of the sweet things of love and gratitude." (p. 631) Throughout the novel, then, Pip is associated with the force that generates human compassion and understanding.[7]

In *Chillun* (1923), O'Neill dramatizes a similar racial intolerance in primarily psychological terms. To that end, he illustrates the negative effects of miscegenation on Ella Downey's spiritual balance. Although from Irish Catholic stock, Ella seems to be endowed with the prejudices of the Puritan/Yankee society in which she lives.[8] After marrying a negro named Jim Harris, Ella becomes progressively obsessed with the color of her husband. She wishes that Jim would fail in his university examinations and in Act II, scene ii, she even attempts to kill him. At the end of the play, however, both protagonists finally succeed in reaching a compromise. In this melodramatic work, O'Neill indicts the association of the black character with evil, a concept rooted in insanity, as Ella Downey's psychotic behavior would seem to intimate. As Jim poignantly confesses his love for Ella, his essential goodness is vividly contrasted to his wife's wickedness:

> JIM: [...] I don't ask you to love me—don't dare to hope nothing like that! I don't want nothing—only to wait [...]—to serve you—to lie at your feet like a dog that loves you [...] to become your slave!—yes, your slave—your black slave that adores you as sacred. (p. 108)[9]

Although she feels moved by Jim's authenticity and self-abnegation, Ella Downey cannot always repress her Puritan-like feelings of hate towards the negro. In Act II, scene iii, the heroine addresses an African mask, which functions as a symbol of her husband's identity, in frankly revengeful terms: "ELLA: [...] (threatening the Congo mask). It's you who're to blame for this! [...] Black! Black! Black is dirt! You've poisoned me! I can't wash myself clean! Oh, I hate you ! Why don't you let Jim and I be happy?" (p. 129) O'Neill later indicates that Jim is the innocent victim of both Ella Downey, who attempts to murder him, and God, who fails to protect him against the evil nature of the white race. In the very last scene of the work, Jim voices his anger against such an insensitive deity: "ELLA: [...] will God forgive me, Jim? JIM: Maybe He can forgive what you have done to me [...] but I don't see how He's going to forgive [...] Himself." (p. 132) In *Chillun*, O'Neill offers a sympathetic vision of the negro, comparable in some aspects to Melville's *Moby Dick*, particularly in the dramatist's denunciation of God's cruelty towards the black character.

C

O'Neill and Melville did not only exhibit a bleak outlook towards the realities of the New England and America of their day, they also voiced identical opinions of American history. Like Whitman, they were obsessed with the past, that "dark, unfathomed retrospect."[10] Disappointed with the negative aspects of American democracy with which they were continually confronted, they sought to interpret the historical patterns that had provoked such corruption of New England ideals. Living in two different centuries, they of course riveted their attention on divergent historical events. While O'Neill was fascinated by the Civil War and the America of the early nineteenth century, Melville wrote about the American Revolution. Nonetheless, it should be remarked that both writers chose periods of crises, resulting in radical changes in the history of the United States. Moreover, both located the source of historical process in the individual consciousness.

Melville's concept of American history can be found in *Israël*, a neglected novel published in 1855. In this work, the writer describes the gradual decline of American democracy through the fate of one of its most ardent defenders, Israël Potter. The career of Melville's hero again offers satiric comments on the Puritan idea of New England as a New Jerusalem. Having fought in Bunker Hill during the Revolutionary War, Israël is made a prisoner by the British and is sent to Europe. With the help of a few friends, he manages to escape to Paris, where he meets Dr. Franklin. In the scenes between these two protagonists, Melville adopts a mildly ironical tone towards the wisdom of Dr. Franklin: "the incredible seniority of an antediluvian seemed his [...] the years of sapience [...]. He seemed to be seven score years old; that is, three score and ten of prescience added to three score and ten of remembrance, makes just seven score years in all." (pp.65–66)[11] The novelist further debunks Franklin's Quaker-like behavior in recording the conversation between the two characters at dinner time:

(Franklin)—How many glasses of port do you suppose a man may drink at a meal?

(Israël)—The gentleman at White Waltham drank a bottle at a dinner.

—A bottle contains just thirteen glasses—that's thirty-nine pence, supposing it poor wine. If something of the best, which is the only sort any sane man should drink, as being the least poisonous, it would be quadruple that sum, which is one hundred and fifty-six pence, which is seventy-eight two-penny loaves. Now, do you not think that for one man to swallow down seventy-two two-penny rolls at one meal is rather extravagant business? [...]. My honest friend , if you are poor, avoid wine as a costly luxury; if you are rich, shun it as a fatal indulgence. Stick to plain water [...]. Pastry is poisoned bread. Never eat pastry. Be a plain man, and stick to plain things [...]. You must not be idle. Here is poor Richard's Almanac, which, in view of our late conversation, I commend to your earnest perusal [...]. (p. 75–76)

Not only does Melville debunk the stature of Benjamin Franklin by showing the emptiness of his logic, he also puts in serious doubt the validity of a masterpiece of Puritan/Yankee literature: *Poor Richard's Almanac*. Indeed, the code of moral conduct contained in that book seems to be of little help to Israël Potter for, after attempting to live according to Dr. Franklin's ideals, Israël dies a miserable man. After his interview with Franklin, Israël is doomed to a fifty-year exile in London. At that point, the hero's name acquires symbolic overtones, as suggested by the very title of the last chapters: "Israël in Egypt." Melville thus establishes a Biblical parallel between his hero, the representative of the elect nation, the new Jerusalem, and the ancient people of Israël. When he is finally allowed to return to America, Israël, unlike his namesake, fails to find the Promised Land. He is confronted with the indifference of a country for which he idealistically sacrificed everything. Returning to his native town, he discovers that the vestiges of his childhood have vanished:

Here [...] my father would sit, and here, my mother, and here I, little infant, would totter between, even as now, once again, on the very same spot, but in the unroofed air, I do. The ends meet [...]. He was repulsed in efforts after a pension by certain caprices of law. His scars proved his only medals. He dictated a little book, the record of his fortunes. But long ago it faded out of print—himself out of being—his name out of memory. He died the same day that the oldest oak on his native hills was blown down. (p. 3O1)

Although the Revolutionary War was fought in a humanitarian spirit, Melville suggests, American society quickly degenerated and rendered the citizen's individual fulfillment impossible.

In *Electra*, O'Neill develops the main theme of Melville's *Israël*, i.e., the failure of the pursuit of happiness within the context of American democracy. In his Civil War trilogy, the Mannons of New England epitomize the perversion of American democratic values for, in the universe of the play, murder and incest reign supreme. It could be argued that in this play, O'Neill's vision of New England culminates in a satiric counterpoint to the Puritan concept of the New Jerusalem and to the moral precepts of Benjamin Franklin. From the start, the two representatives of the townspeople, Louisa and Ames, intimate the psychological depravity of the Mannons:

AMES: [...] They don't want folks to guess their secrets.

LOUISA: The Mannons got skeletons in their closets same as others! Worse ones (lowering her voice almost to a whisper—to her husband). Tell Minnie about old Abe Mannon's brother David marryin' that French Canuck nurse girl he'd got into trouble. (p. 691)

Further, O'Neill's vision in *Electra* resembles that of Melville in *Israël* for, while Israël suffers from the indifference of a dehumanized world, Lavinia Mannon eventually buries herself alive.

In *Touch*, O'Neill dramatizes episodes in the life of Major Melody, who, having emigrated to the United States, discovers that the American dream is mere illusion. Major Melody hoped to find better opportunities in New England than in his native Ireland. He is bitterly disappointed when failing to marry his daughter to a rich Yankee. Through his predicament, it is the corruption of American democracy that O'Neill indicts. A family friend tells us how Melody came to be a victim of social injustice:

CREGAN: [...] Con spoke wid the airs ow a lord. "Kindly inform your master," he says, "that Major Cornelius Melody, late of his Majesty's Seventh Dragoons, respectfully requests a word with him." Well, the flunky put an insolent sneer on him."Mr. Harford won't see you," he says. And then, glory be, there was a fight! (pp. 154–157)[12]

Eventually, O'Neill shows, Melody is forced to abandon all illusions. His confession is suffused with moments of a poignant emotional intensity:

Begorra, if that wasn't the mad Major's ghost speakin'! But be damned to him, he won't haunt me long, if I know it! I intend to live at my ease from now on and not let the dead bother me, but enjoy life in my proper station as auld Nick Melody's son. I'll bury his Major damned red livery ov bloody England deep in the ground so he can haunt its grave if he likes, and boast to the lonely night ov Talavera and the ladies of Spain and fightin' the French. (p. 169)

O'Neill prolongs this Melvillean theme in *Mansions*, the second play of his cycle. There, he examines the tragic effects of what he typifies as the decay of American civilization on the character of Sara Melody, the major's daughter. The action takes place between 1832 and 1841 and again represents a dramatization of essential episodes of American history. The playwright illustrates how, because of the harsh business ethics surrounding her, Sara is unable to find happiness in marriage. In short, the greed of the society in which she lives prevents Sara from achieving a satisfactory sense of psychological balance. Like Israël in Melville's novel, the course of American history deprives O'Neill's heroine from her quest for personal happiness.

D

Not Only did O'Neill and Melville record the malevolent effects of a culture inherited in part from New England Puritanism and American materialism upon the private consciousness. They also enhanced their critique of American society through a pointed attack of Transcendentalism, which constituted a major intellectual movement of nineteenth century New England.

Through Transcendentalism, it is American philosophy at large that the two writers are satiziring. Although considered in many ways as the exact counterpart of Puritanism, American transcendentalism, Perry Miller has demonstrated in *Errand into the Wilderness,* can be viewed as a romantic version of the Puritan ethic and shows correspondences to the literature of the early seventeenth century.[13]

Further, the critic F.O. Matthiessen mentions in *American Renaissance* that Melville both admired and rejected Emersonian principles. Upon hearing the sermons of Emerson, the novelist had felt enormously impressed although he eventually came to regard the philosopher's optimistic mood as inadequate in an American context. Commenting on Emerson's poetic delight in nature, Melville clearly expressed this emotional ambivalence: "Mr.E. is horribly narrow here. He has his Dardanelles for every Marmora—but he keeps nobly on, for all that!"[14] In his burlesque work *Confidence,* written in 1857, Melville discussed in artistic forms the overly enthusiastic nature of American Transcendentalism.

In Chapter XXXVI, entitled "A Mystic," he offers a portrait of an idealistic person, whom critics have compared to Emerson:[15]

> [...] A blue-eyed man, sandy-haired, and Saxon-looking; perhaps five-and-forty; tall, and, but for a certain angularity, well made; little touch of the drawing-room about him, but a look of plain propriety of a Puritan sort, with a kind of farmer dignity. His age seemed betokened more by his brow placidly thoughtful, than by his general aspect which had that look of youthfulness in maturity [...] he seemed a kind of cross between a Yankee peddler and a Tartar Priest, though it seemed as if, at a pinch, the first would not in all probability play second fiddle to the last. (p. 224)[16]

This mystic, significantly named Mark Winsome, possesses an engaging personality, evident in his dignity and youthfulness. And yet, Melville subtly introduces ironic overtones in his delineation of this Emerson surrogate by comparing him to a Yankee peddler and a Tartar priest.

Moreover, the confidence-man subtly demonstrates the exaggeratedly optimistic conclusions that might be arrived at, should one follow Emerson's concept of the goodness of all objects of nature. Feigning to adopt an Emersonian viewpoint, he confesses to believe in "the latent benignity of that beautiful creature, the rattle-snake." (p. 225) Melville's satirical vision of Emerson is compounded in *Confidence* by his description of the philosopher's disciple, Henry David Thoreau.

In Chapter XXXVII, the novelist introduces Egbert, the mystic's student, in the practical nature of whom critics have indeed detected characteristics reminiscent of Thoreau.[17] Egbert, like Thoreau, applies the principles of Emerson/Mark Winsome in his daily life. The mystic presents his pupil to the confidence-man in a most enthusiastic fashion:

> I wish you to know Egbert. Egbert was the first among mankind to reduce to practice the principles of Mark Winsome—principles previously accounted as less adapted to life than the closet [...] it is by you that I myself best understand myself. For to every philosophy are certain rear parts, very important parts, and these, like the rear of one's head, are best seen by reflection. Now, as in glass, you, Egbert, in your life, reflect to me the more important part of my system. He, who approves you, approves the philosophy of Mark Winsome. (pp. 233–234)

Melville subsequently indicts the nature of Egbert's practical vision of Transcendentalism when his confidence-man comments: "[...] if mysticism, as a lesson, ever came in his way, he might, with the characteristic knack of a true New-Englander, turn even so profitless a thing to some profitable account." (p. 236) Instead of developing into a democratic morality, Egbert's theories degenerate into sheer greed. Indeed, Egbert refuses to lend money to the confidence-man, thereby proving selfish, under the pretext that friendship cannot be corrupted by such proposals. At this point, Melville voices the criticism that the idealism of Transcendentalism can become synonymous with lack of generosity. Thus in *Confidence*, Melville shows that Transcendentalism, a product of New England civilization, presents marked flaws.

As I have already pointed out in Chapters I and III, O'Neill's notes for *Touch*, preserved at the Beinecke, reveal that he patterned his character Simon Harford upon both Ralph Waldo Emerson and Henry David Thoreau.[18] Although he manifests sympathy for his Transcendentalist protagonist in *Touch*, O'Neill adopts a more pessimistic viewpoint towards the disintegration of Simon's idealistic theories in *Mansions*. It is precisely in that respect that he shows deep affinities with Melville. Like the novelist, he implies that the Transcendentalist refusal to face the evil underpinnings of the universe can lead to disastrous consequences. Although at the beginning of the drama, Simon still believes "with Rousseau, as firmly as ever, that at bottom human nature is good and unselfish," (p. 9)[19] he cynically describes the deceptive aspects of Rousseau-like Transcendentalism after taking over his father's business:

> What is evil is the stupid theory that man is naturally what we call virtuous and good—instead of being what he is, a hog. It is that idealistic fallacy which is responsible for all the confusion in our minds, the conflicts within the self, and for all the confusion in our relationships with one another [...]. (p. 172)

In their examination of the possibilities of life on the land, the two writers analyze what they view as the drawbacks of American materialism, American racial intolerance, American history and Emersonian Transcendentalism. Beyond Melville's and O'Neill's critique, one perceives a romantic mood of nostalgia for an Edenic America. In the background of their pessimistic works, looms the pale reflection of a Paradise Lost. As O'Neill himself declared: "The United States [...] is the greatest failure [...]. We are the greatest example of 'What shall it profit a man if he shall gain the whole world and lose his own soul?' We had so much and could have gone either way."[20] It is the painful realization that America itself is responsible for its woes that confers upon both writers' works their dark and bitter overtones.

E

O'Neill and Melville, far from restricting their considerations to American society, also probe the nature of the religious legacy of New England, a legacy that extends beyond the narrow confines of New England valleys. At times, their critique even comprises any American religious cult worshipping a harsh deity, be it Protestant or Catholic. They bemoan the fact that faith can no longer offer any sense of comfort to the victim of American philistinism. They criticize

Calvinism, which, they affirm, glorifies, along the lines of seventeenth century American Puritanism, a cruel divinity and thus fails to provide for the spiritual needs of man. Melville transcribes this issue in *Moby Dick*, thereby reflecting the prevalent tendencies in the religious thinking of the first half of the nineteenth century.[21] Likewise, throughout his career, O'Neill was intrigued with the nature of the link between man and God. He once confessed to Joseph Wood Krutch: "Most modern plays are concerned with the relation between man and man and man, but that does not interest me at all. I am interested only in the relation between man and God."[22] Although some of O'Neill's works, e.g. *Ape*, are dealing with sociological issues, it is nonetheless true that most of his plays explore the conflict between man and a harsh, often Calvinistic, deity. Being of Irish-Catholic extraction, he adopts, unlike Melville, the viewpoint of an outsider towards the pressure of Puritanism. His plays dramatize a double process, i.e., the decay of Calvinism and the influence of Catholicism due to the Irish immigration to the United States. Like Melville, however, O'Neill satirizes what he considers as the cruelty of a religion based on predestination in some of his plays. While the former concentrates on the chasm between Calvinism and Unitarianism, the latter focuses on the dichotomy between Puritan orthodoxy and Catholic liberalism.[23] Moreover, it should be remarked that to O'Neill, this contrast is not always well-defined: his brand of Catholicism, derived from his Irish forebears, had acquired austere features owing to centuries of Protestant domination.[24] And as I shall demonstrate in this section, in America, even Catholics or Yankees seem haunted by a revengeful, Puritan-like divinity. If both Melville and O'Neill reject Calvinism, their attitude is perhaps motivated by a belief in democratic values, none of which lend credence to a doctrine affirming the "Innate Depravity" of mankind and presenting divine election as the only way to salvation. Both artists certainly cast a highly critical glance at the religious legacy of New England.

They did not, however, limit their investigations to the decay of American Protestantism and the failure of Christianity, they suggested solutions in order to alleviate the sufferings of the individual in a godless universe. In the end, they came to regard stoic acceptance as the only possibility left to mankind and, prefiguring Camus's existential philosophy, they encouraged man to assume the limitations of an esssentially absurd world.[25] Even if, at that late stage, their language was still suffused with nostalgia for a lost religion.

Needless to mention, I shall not deal, in the course of this analysis with the various historical and theological divergences between Protestant cults. Neither O'Neill nor Melville did confine their vision of Protestantism to one single denomination, as Melville depicts Quakers in *Moby Dick* and as O'Neill attacks in turn the First Congregational Church of New England, Protestant Fundamentalism, and the pietist methodism of frontier missions respectively in *Electra, Mansions*, and *Iceman*. Both were more concerned, however, with a subjective rendition of Protestantism.[26]

In *Moby Dick*, Melville seeks to interpret aspects of the opposition between man and the ruthless deity of Puritanism. Viewed from Ahab's perspective, that deity, having deprived man of free-will, may well be responsible for sin. In the white whale, it is possible to see a reflection of Ahab's own madness. The Captain, however, regards it as God's symbol on earth. Moby Dick represents a modern equivalent of the Old Testament Leviathan, which God sent to Jonah in order to submit his rebellious character. The novelist suggests that, considered from Ahab's viewpoint, the godly whale possesses a potential for evil. Moby Dick exhibits "such an infernal aforethought of ferocity, that every dismembering or death that he caused, was not wholly regarded as having been inflicted by an unintelligent agent." (p. 282) In his search for the Albino whale, Ahab ironically pledges his allegiance to the Puritan God of hatred: "I leap with thee; I burn with thee; would fain be welded with thee; defyingly I worship thee." (p. 617) Earlier, Melville had already indicated that Ahab was predestined to be a rebel, and ultimately to be lost: "The path to my fixed purpose is laid with iron rails, whereon my soul is grooved to ruin." (p. 296) But the novelist highlights the tragic plight of Ahab when in "The Symphony," he stresses his humanity :

That glad, happy air, that winsome sky, did at last stroke and caress him; the step-mother world, so long cruel—forbidding—now threw affectionate arms round his stubborn neck, and did seem to joyously sob over him, as if over one, that forever willful and erring, she could yet find it in her heart to save and to bless. From beneath his slouched hat Ahab dropped a tear into the sea; nor did all the Pacific contain such wealth as that one wee drop. (p. 650)

Although Ahab, in spite of his pride, is still able to feel moved by the beauty of nature, the Calvinist God passes a death sentence upon him. The Captain realizes the impossibility of any salvation and accuses God of forcing him to commit evil:

> What is it, what nameless, inscrutable, unearthly thing is it; what cozzening, hidden lord and master, and cruel, remorseless emperor commands me; that against all natural lovings and longings, I so keep pushing, and crowding, and jamming myself on all the time; [...] making me ready to do what in my own proper natural heart, I durst not so much as dare? (pp. 652–653)

Instead of acknowledging his own pride, Ahab arraigns God himself: "Where do murderers go, man! Who's to doom, when the judge himself is dragged to the bar?" (p. 653) This desperate philosophy is further evinced in the final chase, in which Ishmaël alone escapes from the sinking of the "Pequod."

In *Moby Dick*, however, Melville opposes Ishmaël's viewpoint towards that of the Captain. Ishmaël does not respond with hate to God's cruelty: on the contrary, he develops the principles of an existential philosophy, seeking refuge in human companionship. My concepts of the "absurd" and "existentialism," are derived from Albert Camus's works and have been set forth in detail in Chapter II. Melville clearly regards human fellowship as the only means of achieving personal happiness in an uncongenial universe. In "A Squeeze of the Hand," he expresses this idea in referring to Ishmaël's desire for companionship:

> Squeeze! Squeeze! Squeeze! All the morning long; I squeezed that sperm till I myself melted into it [...] and I found myself unwittingly squeezing my co-laborer's hand in it [...]. Come; let us squeeze hands all round; nay, let us all squeeze ourselves into each other; let us squeeze ourselves universally into the very milk and sperm of kindness. (p. 527)

In "The Hyena," Melville summarizes that absurdist philosophy concretely illustrated by Ahab's fate: "[...] prospects of sudden disaster, peril of life and limb [...] and death itself, seem [...] jolly punches in the side bestowed by the unseen and unaccountable old joker." (p. 329) But if God is an old joker, Melville is still able at this point in his career, to envision a somewhat optimistic solution to man's helplessness, consisting in the sense of brotherhood evident in the above quotation from "A Squeeze of the Hand." His atttitude wavers on the border-line between religious criticism and atheism.

The existential vision of *Moby Dick* is prolonged and eventually modified in Melville's late epic poem, *Clarel*. In this work, he deals with themes developed in his earlier novel in a more didactic fashion. Throughout most of this epic poem, he articulates an even bleaker view of Calvinism in following the religious quest of Clarel, who in the hope of finding new ways to renew the vigor of his faith undertakes a pilgrimage to the old Jerusalem. He only discovers ashes and desolation in the Holy Land. Melville weaves this plot into the study of the failure of Christianity to provide for the spiritual need of modern man through several characters, representing various religious beliefs. The first of these to come under scrutiny is American Puritanism. In his travels, Clarel meets Nehemiah, whom Melville associates with the pathetic offshoot of Puritanism, i.e., of Protestant fundamentalism: "In Calvin's creed he put his trust;/Praised heaven, and said that God was good,/And his calamity but just." (p.122)[27] Nehemiah does not experience any crisis of faith. Melville shows, however, that reality belies the hero's optimistic expectations when the latter dies sleepwalking into the Dead Sea. Through this burlesque episode, the novelist derides the Puritan reliance on the goodness of the divinity. Derwent, on the contrary, seems to be aware of the contradictions inherent in the Protestant faith. He almost voices his anger against the God that allows evil to exist in the world: "Derwent bit the lip;/Altered again, had fain let slip/'Throw all this burden upon HIM;'/But hesitated." (p. 360) He still maintains, however, ameliorative views and believes that one should stick to the transcending values of the religious myth: "Have faith, which, even from the myth,/Draws something to be useful with/In any form some truths will hold;/Employ the present-sanctioned mold [...]." (p. 361) While Derwent symbolizes the opposing responses elicited by American Puritanism, Rolfe condemns the decline of the latter. The democracy that it helped to create has only offered chaos, he argues. The threat is that Catholicism and Atheism will take advantage of that state of decay: "Rome and the Atheist have gained:/These two shall fight it out—these two [...]." (p. 234) Another character subsequently implies, however, that Catholicism is as inadequate as Protestantism in satisfying the spiritual needs of modern man: "Know,/Whatever happen in the end,/Be sure 'twill yield to one and all/New Confirmation of the fall/of Adam." (p. 483) Melville seems to indict both Catholicism and Protestantism in their emphasis on the "innate depravity" of mankind. Starting with a critique of American Protestantism, he enlarges his scope of investigation and concludes with the decay of Christianity at large. O'Neill similarly rejects all religious systems in *Iceman*. At the end of *Clarel*, sometimes described as a religious conversion to life, the novelist hesitates between agnosticism and a return towards a more frankly religious attitude.[28] After all the attacks he has levelled against Protestantism in the course of the poem, this ending, needless to say, seems somewhat contrived, not unlike that of O'Neill's *Days*. On the one end, Melville hopes that Clarel will live to see that "death but routs life in victory." (p. 523) However, the religious connotation of that line is superseded by the frankly humanistic mode of thinking that will allow man to arrive at such solution: "Clarel, thy heart, the issues there but mind [...]." (p. 523) Clearly, man's spiritual freedom above any religious dogma is strongly asserted. In short, biblical language and humanistic context coexist. This probing attitude foreshadows the existentialism of O'Neill's *Journey* and *Iceman*, even if it somewhat tempers *Moby Dick*'s agnosticism. The hero of the poem, Melville implies, should continue to hope for enlightenment in his solitary quest for meaning, even though God has withdrawn from the world. This double consciousness is not unlike that of O'Neill in his later plays: on the one hand, the playwright depicts in these plays a universe devoid of God but on the other, consistently resorts to imagery derived from religion, as the "confessional" motif of *Iceman* and *Journey* makes abundantly clear.[29] This, of course, betrays a profound sense of nostalgia for the lost certainty of the existence of God.

In a number of his plays, Eugene O'Neill articulated a literary attack against New England Protestantism similar to that of Melville. Like the novelist, he rejected the Calvinist angry God, who seeks vengeance upon mankind. In his so-called New England plays, as well as in some dramas less specifically situated within the confines of that region of the United States, he offered a Melvillean portrayal of God as the author of sin.[30] Accordingly, I have decided to include in this discussion of O'Neill's New England religious legacy, plays such as *Thirst*, *Brown*, *Capricorn*, and *Iceman*, which are divorced from the New England setting. They concentrate on the more specifically "Yankee" heritage of America and yet they offer a vision of a God akin to that of *Moby Dick*.

In *Thirst*, already discussed in my chapters on sea symbolism, the curtain falls on a striking scenic image, after the sharks have devoured the occupants of the raft: "The sun glares down like a *great angry eye of God*. The eerie heat waves float upward in the still air like the souls of the drowned. "(p. 32, my italics) In *Thirst*, O'Neill accuses the "great angry eye of God" of having plotted the death of his protagonists and implies that God is a murderer, a blood-thirsty deity similar to Moby Dick. The divinity that governs the universe of *Thirst* is nameless, although it possesses qualities generally associated with the harsh God of the Puritans.

Cross, another representative early play, is set on the California coast. O'Neill focuses on the character of Mrs. Bartlett, who possesses the unmistakable qualities of the playwright's New England types. Mrs. Bartlett, upon hearing that her husband once committed a murder during his voyages in the South Sea, starts hating him. O'Neill derides her obsession with sin, which prompts her to forfeit human compassion: she even refuses to christen her husband's ship in an attempt to make him confess his guilt. The dramatist resorts to caricature in order to express his contempt for his heroine's concept of the "innate depravity of the human soul:"

MRS. BARTLETT: Confess your sin [...]. Confess to God and me [...].

MR. BARTLETT: The schooner will sail at dawn [...]. Will ye christen her with your name afore she sails?

MRS. BARTLETT: (firmly). No [...] I've never refused in anything that's right—but this be wicked wrong [...] (shrinking from him in terror). No. Don't you touch me! Don't you touch me! (She hobbles quickly out of the door in the rear, looking back frightenedly over her shoulder to see if he is following [...]). (pp. 157–159)

As in the works of Melville, O'Neill's Calvinistic God is deaf to the sufferings of mankind: when sinking into madness, Captain Bartlett receives no help from his wife nor does God listen to his complaints. Thus, in the "ironic fate" that crushes his characters, O'Neill offers an equivalent of the Calvinistic sense of predestination.

In his early masterpiece *Desire*, the dramatist satirizes the same deity through one of his representatives on earth, Ephraïm Cabot:

CABOT: [...] God hain't easy [...]. God's hard not easy! God's in the stones! Build my church on a rock—out o' stones and I'll be in them! That's what he meant to Peter! [...] stones. Ye kin read the years o' my life in them walls, every day a hefted stone, climbin' over the hills up and down, fencin' in the fields that was mine, whar I'd made thin' grow out o'nothin'—like the will o' God, like the servant o' His hand. (p. 172)[31]

It is significant that O'Neill should identify the Calvinist God worshipped by Ephraïm with the hardness of stones. It is a divinity that remains indifferent to the sufferings of both Eben Cabot and Abbie Putnam and punishes these young lovers for undulging in sexual pleasure. After killing her own child, Abbie is condemned to a miserable death. This heavy penalty is administered through the hands of an avenging deity, comparable to that governing the universe of *Moby Dick*.

In *Brown*(1925), O'Neill deals especially with American materialism. However, he manages to introduce satirical comments on a Protestant-like God, albeit in more abstract terms than in *Desire*. Dion Anthony describes God as a cosmic joker: "[...] I got paint on my paws in an endeavor to see God! (He laughs widly—claps on his mask) But that Ancient Humorist had given me weak eyes [...]." (p. 334)[32] O'Neill thus creates an image reminiscent of Melville's vision of God as the "unseen and unaccountable old joker" in *Moby Dick*.

In *Interlude* (1927), the playwright explores the consequences of New England life for the psychological balance of his heroine, Nina Leeds. Finding it difficult to believe in the stern God of Puritan New England, whom she calls "God the father," Nina dreams of a benevolent "God the mother" figure. She utters her new faith during her pregnancy: " [...] I feel my child live [...] moving in my life [...] my life moving in my child [...] breathing in the tide I dream and breathe my dream back into the tide [...]. God is a mother." (p. 591)[33] At one point, Nina even affirms that the feminine God she envisions has come to govern the world, as she says: "Our account with God the Father is settled." (p. 646). At the end of the play, however, after experiencing disappointment in love, she is forced to recognize the victory of God the Father, the harsh God of New England, when she compares her life to a dark interlude in the electrical display of that ruling divinity. In *Interlude*, O'Neill again offers a bleak picture of a God treating man as a mere toy.

In *Dynamo* (1928), he concentrates on the fanatic personality of Reverend Light which is evident in his very physical description:

> He is a man in his early sixties, sligtly under medium height, ponderously built. His face is square, ribbed with wrinkles, the forehead low, the nose heavy, the eyes small and grey blue, the reddish hair grizzled and bushy, the stubborn jaw weakened by a big indecisive mouth. His voice is the bullying one of a sermonizer who is the victim of an inner uncertainty that compensates itself by being boomingly over-assertive. (p. 6)[34]

Reverend Light's stubborn and bullying nature constitutes a satiric comment on the Puritan divinity whom he worships. In a subsequent interior monologue, the priest's fanaticism reaches its culminating point:

> LIGHT: [...] But, Lord, Thou Knowest what a thorn in the flesh that atheist, Fife, has been since the devil brought him next door! [...]. How long, O Lord? [...]. Does not his foul ranting begin to try Thy patience? [...]. Is not the time ripe to smite this blasphemer [...]? [...] Lord God of Hosts, why dost Thou not strike him? [...] If thou didst, I would proclaim the awful warning of it all over America! [...] I would convert multitudes, as it was once my dream to do! [...] (p. 8)

The terrible God to whom Reverend Light has devoted his life also conditions the world of *Moby Dick*. Further, Reuben Light, the Reverend's son, becomes the victim of the divinity represented by his father. He dies of electrocution, crushed by a fate controlled by that Puritan deity.

In two plays written in the thirties, *Electra* and *Capricorn*, O'Neill once more reverts to the theological issues with which he had been concerned in

Brown and other plays of his "experimental" period. In the *Electra* trilogy, completed in 1931, he dramatizes the effects of divine wrath upon the Mannons' spiritual welfare. A strong sense of fate pervades the play, one against which the Mannons are left impotent. Christine, who has murdered her husband, accuses the Puritan God of being indifferent to the sufferings of mankind: "But God won't leave us alone. He twists and wrings and tortures our lives with others' lives until—we poison each other to death!" (p. 759) O'Neill further evidences the cruelty of the Puritan deity through a skillful use of scenic language: in Act IV of *The Haunted*, he associates God with the sun, as he had already done in *Thirst*: "On the ground floor, the upper part of the windows, raised from the bottom, reflect the sun in a smouldering stare, as of brooding revengeful eyes." (p. 857) The ensuing tragic action of *Electra* also contributes to establish the dangerous nature of the New England divinity for, as in *Moby Dick*, that deity seeks to annihilate the protagonists. Eventually, the reader realizes that Christine's initial prophecy has been fulfilled, as Lavinia buries herself alive in the family mansion. In Act I of *Homecoming*, Christine had described the Mannon estate in the following words: "Each time I come back after being away it appears more like a sepulchre! The 'whited' one of the Bible—pagan temple front stuck like a mask on Puritan gray ugliness!" (p. 699) Unmistakably, the bleak vision of *Electra* finds echoes in *Capricorn*.

In that play, during the voyage that leads them through the seas of the South Atlantic ocean, the Harfords of Massachusetts become corrupted. A mysterious fate plagues them with calms, on account of which their ship fails to move, and that fate drives them mad. The Reverend Samuel Dickey, one of the passengers, functions as the representative of the Puritan God on board. He articulates the cause of the predicament of the protagonists in religious terms: "[...] The calm is the punishment of God for the sin on this ship." (p. 75) Dickey himself seems to be punished by the God he worships and eventually comes to deny the validity of His justice. He even acknowledges having had a sexual relationship with a whore, Leda, another passenger of the ship:

DICKEY: Yes, I confess last night I talked with her and everything suddenly became innocent and clear to me. It did not matter what I did. There was no sin, no God. Life was innocent and beautiful, without guilt [...]. I have no money. The ministry is the most ill-paid calling.

Of course, if you were sure of a reward hereafter for doing without in this world—sure of the justice of God—but in this calm one doubts. (pp. 84–86)

The fate which is at work in *Capricorn* drives the main protagonist to his death: Ethan, the captain, decides to commit suicide after failing to break a record during the voyage. The Melvillean universe of this unfinished work deprives man of any hope of salvation.

Like Melville, O'Neill started with a critique of Puritanism and later adopted an agnostic viewpoint towards life. In *Iceman*, the dramatist presents his readers with a universe in which the human quest for meaning constitutes the only possibility of redemption. In this respect, O'Neill prefigures, like Melville in some chapters of *Moby Dick*, the works of artists-thinkers such as Camus. It is in courageously facing the absurdity of his fate that the hero achieves nobility. Larry Slade appears, like Ishmaël, to be reconciled with his plight and his attitude glorifies man's capacity to endure: "LARRY: [...] I'll be a weak fool looking at the two sides of everything till the day I die. May that day come soon! [...]." (p. 258) Although Larry expresses a longing for death that Ishmaël fails to utter, he nonetheless envisions, along the lines of Melville's protagonist, lonely intellectual questing as the ultimate fate of mankind. Further, in *Journey* and *Misbegotten*, O'Neill suggests that human companionship can alleviate the sufferings of the man lost in a frightening universe. In these two plays, he again aligns himself on *Moby Dick*, in which the author conceives of friendship in a similar fashion (in "A Squeeze of the Hand"). In *Journey*, having lost faith in God, the members of the Tyrone family can at least find some relief, albeit ephemeral, in one another. In *Misbegotten*, through the sense of compassion that Josie Hogan confers upon him, Jim Tyrone finds the strength to survive in a universe from which God has withdrawn. In these two dramas, written respectively in 1941 and 1943, O'Neill offers an unconscious dramatization of existential issues dealt with in Melville's *Moby Dick*. One could argue, of course, that these three plays, steeped as they are in Christian language, betray O'Neill's veiled "need of God." Indeed, the confessional pattern of *Iceman*, the pieta imagery of *Misbegotten*, and the biblical "Joseph" motif of these late plays[35] show that O'Neill could not totally outgrow a religious mode of communication. However, this nostalgia for a lost faith remains at the level of imagery, which is often subverted, as the ironic use of Christ symbolism in *Iceman* indicates. The major tonality of these late plays is humanistic rather than religious. Nonetheless, the buried religious metaphors of these works present affinities with Melville's ambiguous stance in *Clarel*. In summation, O'Neill's entire career reflects a view of Puritanism and humanism remarkably convergent with that of Melville.

F

A comparison between O'Neill's and Melville's critique of Puritanism/Protestantism sheds light on the playwright's specifically American literary sensitivity in religious matters. The dramatist expresses these concerns in a more oblique fashion than Melville. Whereas the novelist personifies the power of the Puritan God—but not necessarily his essence—through the symbol of the white whale, O'Neill's Calvinistic deity remains off-stage: his identity is revealed through the effects of his wrath on the protagonists of the play. Secondly, O'Neill may satirize, unlike Melville, the harsh divinity of Puritanism through his ministers, as in *Dynamo* and *Capricorn*. That caricatured portrait is perhaps motivated by the different medium in which O'Neill works: with such a method he hopes to present his critique in more convincing dramatic terms. In spite of these technical divergences, O'Neill's and Melville's metaphysical probings culminate in similar philosophical attitudes. Disappointed with the sterility of New England Puritanism, they posit existentialism as a valid moral principle. They finally accept, not without some regret for the benefits of a secure faith, Job's "submission to unreason." In Chapter 114 of *Moby Dick*, "The Gilder," Melville aptly summarizes the evolution of his philosophical journey in a fashion that could apply to O'Neill as well: "We do not advance through fixed gradations, and at the last one pause:—through infancy's unconscious spell, boyhood's thoughtless faith, adolescence's doubt (the common doom), then scepticism, then, disbelief, resting at last in manhood's pondering repose of if. But once gone through, we trace the round again; and are infants, boys, and men, and Ifs eternally." (p. 602) The sceptical philosophy delineated by Melville in this passage, also typical of O'Neill, can be regarded as a fundamental characteristic of American thought. In short, O'Neill's and Melville's works reflect the disintegration of American belief in the institutionalized Christian God. An essential factor linking their canons thus lies in their constant search for a code to replace degenerated New England Puritanism.[36]

CHAPTER VI. AN AMERICAN TRAGEDY

O'Neill and Melville repeatedly sought to articulate new tragic forms. Their efforts culminated in works such as *Moby Dick, Electra, Journey*, and *Iceman*, in which they tried to modify patterns inherited from Sophocles and Shakespeare in order to express what they thought to be the tragic implications of American experience.[1] In other words, they transposed in their works a tradition—established by certain European writers—, which attributed nobility to the common man. They amplified that tendency to fit the specificity of New World life. Indeed, Melville and O'Neill can be regarded as reinterpreters of the domestic tragedy genre established in the eighteenth century by Denis Diderot with *The Illegitimate Son* (1757) and *The Father of a Family* (1758). In that respect, they also follow in the wake of Gotthold Ephraim Lessing with his melodrama *Miss Sara Sampson* (1755). Among more recent instances of this phenomenon, one should not fail to mention Ibsen and Strindberg, who developed a realistic or pre-expressionistic drama staging middle-class characters in *A Doll's House* (1879), *Ghosts* (1881), and *The Dance of Death* (1901).[2] Adhering to such motif, our two American writers depict in their various works either lower or middle-class characters, the latter being often insecure about their social status. In addition, they endow their American common men with a capacity for suffering and understanding constituting the essence of tragedy.

A

Although it might at first seem exaggerated to regard *Moby Dick*, written primarily in narrative form, as a tragedy, the critic F.O. Matthiessen does not hesitate to consider that masterpiece as such.[3] Should one trust Melville's avowed aims in *Moby Dick*, one would inevitably come to the conclusion that he did capture the essence of tragic character:

So that there are instances among them of men, who, named with Scripture names [...] and in childhood naturally imbibing the stately

dramatic thee and thou of the Quaker idiom; still, from the audacious,
daring, and boundless adventure of their subsequent lives, strangely
blend with these unoutgrown peculiarities, a thousand bold dashes of
character, not unworthy a Scandinavian sea-king, or a poetical Pagan
Roman. And when these things unite in a man of greatly superior
natural force [...] receiving all nature's sweet or savage impressions
fresh from her own virgin voluntary and confiding breast, and thereby
chiefly [...] to learn a bold and nervous lofty language—that man
makes one in a whole nation's census—a mighty pageant creature,
formed for noble tragedies. (pp. 169–170)

Melville's purpose is aptly formulated in a subsequent chapter entitled "Knights
and Squires:" "[...] to meanest mariners, and renegades and castaways, I shall
hereafter ascribe high qualities, though dark; weave round them tragic graces."
(p. 212) Moreover, the tragic quality of *Moby Dick* can be measured by the
various sources that presided over its composition. F.O. Matthiessen has shown
that, in writing *Moby Dick*, Melville had been influenced by Shakespeare.
Melville's notes reveal that he was fascinated by *Anthony and Cleopatra* and
King Lear and that he also read Hawthorne's *Mosses from an Old Manse* while
at work on his epic masterpiece.[4] In *Moby Dick*, he attempted to provide
novelistic equivalents to Shakespeare's and Hawthorne's vision of the "blackness"
of the human heart.

Similarly, O'Neill repeatedly voiced his fascination for the ancient dramatic
form invented by the Greek playwrights :

[...] The one eternal tragedy of man in his glorious, self-destructive
struggle to make the Force express him instead of being, as an animal
is, an infinitesimal incident in its expression. And my proud conviction
is that this is the only subject worth writing about and that it is
possible—or can be—to develop a tragic expression in terms of
transfigured modern values and symbols in the theatre which may to
some degree bring home to members of a modern audience their
ennobling identity with the tragic figures on the stage [...].[5]

Like Melville, O'Neill experimented with the old form of tragedy in an effort to reflect the quality of contemporary American life and, as the above quotation would seem to indicate, to dramatize man's nobility in accepting his fate. To him, the theatre "[...] should give us what the church no longer gives us—a meaning. In brief, it should return to the spirit of Greek grandeur. And if we have no Gods, or heroes to portray, we have the subconscious, the mother of all gods and heroes."6

Although European models such as Shakespeare, Nietzsche and Schopenhauer undoubtedly contributed to the development of O'Neill's and Melville's tragic vision, the two writers unconsciously translated the ideals of two American artists-thinkers, i.e., Ralph Waldo Emerson and Arthur Miller. Often lending grandeur to the American common man, O'Neill and Melville offered literary equivalents of the theories contained in Emerson's essay entitled "Tragedy." There, the poet envisions the failure of the individual pursuit of happiness as the source of human tragedy and stresses in that respect the role performed by man's personal wishes as well as by his ability to resist vice:

[...] The first and highest conceivable element of tragedy in life is the belief in Fate or in Destiny, that the order of nature and events is constrained by a law not adapted to man nor man to that, but which holds on its way to the end, blessing him if his wishes chance to lie in the same course, [...] crushing him if his wishes lie contrary to it, [...] and careless whether it cheers or crushes him [...]. That is the terrible idea that lies at the foundation of the old Greek tragedy and makes the poor Oedipus and Antigone and Orestes the objects of such hopeless commiseration.

The next tragic element in life is the hindrance of private felicity by vice. The senses would make things of all persons for our behoof. Our enjoyments are cruel [...]. Only that good which we taste with all doors open: not separate, but in the chain of beings, so that the spark freely passes, makes all happy as well as us, [...] only that is godlike. Other enjoyments [...] are false, and degrade all the partakers and ministers [...]. In the base hour, we become slave holders. We use persons as things and we think of persons as things. (pp. 1O9).7

Most importantly, it is in the human consciousness that these conflicts take place: "tragedy seems to have its origin not so much in external events as in consciousness; that is, in 'temperament'" (p. 11O). Both O'Neill and Melville, like Emerson, assign a major role to "Temperament" in their tragic works by tracing the frustration of man's private desires.

The twentieth-century American playwright Arthur Miller has attempted in his theater essays to codify the specificity of American tragedy. In an essay entitled "Tragedy and the Common Man," he explains his personal concept in some detail:

> I believe that the common man is as apt a subject for tragedy in its highest sense as kings were. On the face of it this ought to be obvious in the light of modern psychiatry, which bases its analysis upon classic formulations, such as the Oedipus and Orestes complexes, for instance, which were enacted by royal beings, but which apply to everyone in similar emotional situations.(p. 3)[8]

Miller suggests that tragedy arises when common man lays down his life to insure his sense of dignity and makes sincere attempts to evaluate himself justly. In this process of tearing apart the cosmos, he discovers moral laws and acquires the tragic grandeur with which Sophocles endowed his aristocratic characters. Tragedy, then, is optimistic because it demonstrates our will to achieve humanity. In another essay, "The nature of Tragedy," Miller argues that tragedy brings knowledge and enlightenment to mankind and that it indicates who and what we are, what we must be. In other words, tragedy shows man in his struggle for happiness. As the ensuing analyses will show, O'Neill and Melville, intent as they are on depicting the plight of the American common man, can be described as retracing Emerson's footsteps and foreshowing those of Miller.

In some of their works, our two writers concentrate on the psychological turmoil of characters crushed by the dichotomy between good and evil. Their vision of such a polarized universe, often found in the early works, bears marked affinities to Puritan theology. Focusing upon their characters' gradual initiation into evil and upon their subsequent corruption, they illustrate a theme which R.W.B. Lewis had described as typical of all New World literature, i.e., the fall from innocence of the American Adam.[9] In the following pages, I shall examine in detail the two artists' treatment of such tragic motif. I shall also analyze its concomitants, i.e., the failure of the individual pursuit of happiness and the crisis of identity. Instead of charting the effects of their heroes' apprehension of the good and evil tension in purely external terms, O'Neill and Melville examine this opposition in offering us a glimpse of these protagonists' psyche, a feature preventing their works from degenerating into mere melodrama.

Far from consistently achieving the degree of coherence found in the works of Sophocles or Shakespeare, however, Melville and O'Neill frequently compose "incomplete" tragedies. With the possible exceptions of *Moby Dick*, *Desire*, *Iceman*, and *Journey*, works on which I shall focus, the two writers tend to evolve tragic forms which do not completely recapture the grandeur of Sophocles's plays. Experimenting with the limits of tragedy, Melville and O'Neill affirm the tragic potential of the common man while simultaneously indicating that true tragedy is impossible in contemporary America. Such tragedies could be termed "ironic" for they undercut the nobility of the protagonist, of whom they had initially suggested the dignity.

B

In the early romances, Melville studies the impact of the inescapability of the initiation into evil upon the individual consciousness, thereby indicting a cruel God who permits man's total corruption. Indeed, the world Melville envisions in the early romances up to *Redburn* is governed by a cruel deity akin to that of New England Puritanism. That God determines the fate of the novelist's characters. In other words, the presence of a ruling divinity is not yet questioned in these early novels, as it would be in *Moby Dick* and the later works.

In *Typee*, the main character's discovery of evil occurs when he understands that the natives of the Typee valley are not as innocent as he had hitherto imagined. Trying to escape that island, he is forced to kill one of its inhabitants. Melville records Tom's emotional turmoil upon committing murder and thus traces the consequences of his first contact with evil. Although *Typee* is not a truly tragic work, it constitutes, focusing on the psychological balance of an ordinary person, a step in the evolution that would lead Melville to create *Moby Dick*.

In his first period, O'Neill, like Melville, often considers that the universe is orchestrated by a cruel, Puritan-like God. For instance, the "angry eye of God" ordains much of the characters' tragic destinies in *Thirst*. O'Neill develops in his early short dramas a vision of tragedy related to that of Melville in *Typee*. Indeed, the common sailors of the "S.S. Glencairn" are confronted with the evil world surrounding them. The tragic loss of innocence constitutes the linking theme of O'Neill's early cycle. In *Cardiff*, the dramatist shows how dying Yank, a poor and harmless sailor, was once led to commit murder:

YANK: And that fight on the dock at Cape Town (His voice betrays great inward perturbation).

DRISCOLL: (hastily) Don't be thinkin' av that now.' Tis past and gone.

YANK: D'yuh think he'll hold it up against me?

DRISCOLL: (mystified) Who's that?

YANK: God. They say He sees everything. He must know it was done in fair fight, in self-defense, don't yuh think?

DRISCOLL: Av course. Ye stabbed him, and be damned to him for the skulkin' swine he was, after him tryin' to stick you in the back, and you not suspectin'. Let your conscience be aisy. I wisht I had nothin' blacker than that on my soul. I'd not be afraid av the angel Gabriel himself. (p. 48)

In *Cardiff*, O'Neill seems to regret that Yank's soul had to come into contact with evil and his sense of nostalgia finds a poignant expression in Driscoll's soothing comments.

In the opening chapters of *Redburn*, Melville describes the optimistic expectations of Wellingborough Redburn who embarks on his first sea voyage as a simple sailor:

[...] Far away and away stretches the Atlantic ocean [...]. It seemed too strange, and wonderful, and altogether incredible, that there could really be cities and towns and villages and green fields and hedges and farm-yards and orchards, away over that wide blank of sea, and away beyond the place where the sky came down to the water. (pp. 80–81)

If at the beginning of the action, Redburn is associated with innocence, he is initiated into evil upon his arrival in England. The novelist offers a vision of an uncongenial Liverpool adumbrating O'Neill's *Long Voyage*:

The pestilent lanes and alleys, which [...] go by the names of Rotten-row, Gibraltar place, and Booble alley, are petrid with vice and crime; to which perhaps, the round globe does not furnish a parallel. The sooty and begrimed bricks of the very houses have a reeking, Sodom-like, and murderous look. (p. 265)

Through the plight of young Redburn, Melville implies that an essential part of maturation consists in the acceptance of the human potential for evil.

Comparable themes emerge in O'Neill's *Long Voyage*. That playlet tells of the tragic predicament of a Scandinavan sailor named Olson, who, after being shanghaied, can no longer return to his native country. In this early work, O'Neill dramatizes Olson's initiation into sin in terms that are reminiscent of Melville's *Redburn*. Like the novelist's hero, Olson possesses the innocence of childhood: he is "a stocky, middle-aged Swede with round, childish blue eyes." (p. 59) Like Redburn, he is confronted with the malignant nature of a setting comparable to that of Melville's Liverpool, i.e., the corruption of a London low dive. O'Neill conjures up the morbid atmosphere of the environment through characterization:

FAT JOE, the proprietor, a gross bulk of a man with an enormous stomach [...]. At one of the tables, front, a round-shouldered young fellow is sitting, smoking a cigarette. His face is pasty, his mouth weak, his eyes *shifting and cruel*. He is dressed in a shabby suit, which must have once been cheaply flashy, and wears a muffler and a cap. (pp.

55–56, I italicize.)

Through his "cruel" eyes, Joe's companion qualifies as a representative of evil. On the contrary, Olson symbolizes goodness and naivety, as his spontaneous confession indicates: "You know, Miss Freda, my mother get very old, and I want to see her. She might die and I would never—."(p. 73) Olson will never see home again: instead, Fat Joe and his partner will imprison him on another ship, the "Amindra." O'Neill illustrates the conflict between good and evil in psychological terms in showing how Olson's innocent soul is eventually shattered by a threatening universe. Like Melville in *Redburn*, he depicts the clash between a sincere person and a frightening environment. The fate of the two writers' common men is rendered even more tragic through the dark overtones of the setting, either Liverpool or London.[10]

In a play which represents the culmination of his early career, *Desire*, O'Neill again develops the tragic conflict between good and evil with an elegiac regret for a lost innocence. The universe of *Desire,* dominated by the angry God of Puritanism, opposes the authenticity of Eben Cabot to the scheming nature of Abbie Putnam. O'Neill subsequently dramatizes the corruption of his young male figure. He describes Eben, a farmer, in terms befitting his animality: "His defiant, dark eyes remind one of a wild animal's in captivity [...]. There is a fierce repressed vitality about him." (p. 137) When Abbie seduces him, Eben can no longer escape initiation into evil. The playwright hints at Abbie's potential for mischief from the start: "Abie is thirty-five, buxom, full of vitality. Her round face is pretty but marred by its rather gross sensuality. There is strength and obstinacy in her eyes [...]." (p. 155) The heroine's evil nature is reflected in the "hard determination" through which she plans to eventually possess the Cabot farm. O'Neill masterfully dramatizes Eben's attraction to Abbie in Act II, scene ii. In this powerful scenic image, to use Tiusanen's phrase, the future lovers feel each other's presence through the walls of their respective rooms: "Abbie hears him. Her eyes fasten on the intervening wall with concentrated attention. Eben stops and stares. Their hot glances seem to meet through the wall." (p. 171) Once Eben's initiation is completed, the tragic rhythms accelerate and Abbie and Eben are both destroyed. As Eben feels jealous towards his father, to whom Abbie is married, the heroine kills her baby son in order to prove her superior love for Eben. The two younger protagonists finally expiate their guilt and fully understand the implications of their tragic predicament. Eben accepts to stand by Abbie till the end in spite of the murder she has committed. In *Desire*, O'Neill manages to create a truly tragic work in which man can achieve nobility in assuming the desperate nature of his fate. *Desire*, which has often been regarded as O'Neill's first tragedy,[11] acquires that status through its mythical framework, i.e., its reliance on the Phaedra legend, and through its characters' capacity to understand and suffer. Thus, although *Desire* shows us protagonists besieged by Oedipal fixations, the ending of the play transcends these limitations into genuine tragic qualities.

C

Whereas the works of O'Neill's and Melville's early careers show characters trapped in a fallen Eden and therefore could be regarded as examples of a religious tragedy, the novels and plays of later years possess a radically different quality.

In *Moby Dick*, Melville demonstrates how the universe can be interpreted in two widely opposed modes, i.e., Ahab's and Ishmaël's. The two protagonists react in divergent fashions towards the riddle of the world, towards the existence of the good and evil dichotomy. In that novel, one senses Melville's first attempts at creating a code of ethics that would subsequently develop in *Pierre* and *Billy Budd* into an outspoken existential life attitude. Ishmaël and Ahab, the central figures of *Moby Dick*, are both unaristocratic persons, about whom critics have often remarked that they constituted two facets of a single protagonist.[12] It is appropriate, then, to study their psychological evolution in parallel fashion. Ahab discovers what he takes to be the evil nature of God while madly pursuing the white whale. In the chapter entitled "The Symphony," Melville indicates that Ahab fully understands the nature of his plight. About to be destroyed by the whale, the captain sentimentally remembers the family life he enjoyed in the past:

> I have seen them (his wife and child)—some summer days in the morning. About this time—yes, it is his noon nap now—the boy vivaciously wakes; sits up in bed; and his mother tells him of me, of cannibal old me; how I am abroad upon the deep, but will yet come

back to dance him again [...]. By heaven, man, we are turned round and round in this world, like yonder windlass, and Fate is the handspike [...]. (pp. 652–653)

Melville endows his ordinary hero with a capacity for understanding, which the protagonists of his earlier works lacked. As Captain Peleg had already put it in the chapter entitled "The Ship," "stricken, blasted, if he be, Ahab has his humanities!" (p. 177) Because he possesses a profound ability to express human love, Ahab's final destruction by the forces of evil is all the more tragic.

Ahab's eventual madness prevents him, however, from achieving total tragic stature. Ishmaël, on the contrary, succeeds in transcending the tragic tension between good and evil within his consciousness. Throughout the novel, Ishmaël takes part in the captain's murderous quest and consequently comes in touch with evil. Melville aptly symbolizes Ishmaël's temporary involvement in Ahab's pursuit by reference to the myth of Ixion. At the climax of the "fiery hunt," Ishmaël is called upon to take the post of Ahab's bowsman. When the whale destroys the "Pequod," Ishmaël for a moment appears to follow Ahab in his final doom, but is eventually rescued:

I was he whom the Fates ordained to take the place of Ahab's bowsman [...]. So, floating on the margin of the ensuing scene, and in full sight of it, when the half-spent suction of the sunk ship reached me, I was then, but slowly, drawn towards the closing vortex [...]. Like another Ixion I did revolve. Till, gaining that vital centre, the black bubble upward burst; and now, liberated by reason of its cunning spring, and owing to its great buoyancy rising with great force, the coffin life-buoy shot lengthwise from the sea, fell over, and floated by my side. Buoyed up by that coffin, for almost one whole day and night, I floated on a soft and dirgelike main. (p. 687)

Saved by a "coffin life-buoy," Ishmaël learns the fundamental and necessary duality of human existence: life and death are linked as are good and evil. If Ishmaël participates in Ahab's evil quest, he eventually ceases to revolve down the vortex that swallows the captain and manages to escape destruction: "And I only am escaped alone to tell thee." (p. 687) The message the hero will offer the world consists in the affirmation of the fundamental coexistence of good and evil. Indeed, at the beginning of the novel, he had placed his trust in friendship, as his relationship with Queequeg indicated. Having spent a night in the same crowded inn, the two men shared a single bed and formed a loving pair. Said Ishmaël: "You had almost thought I had been his wife." (p. 118) During the voyage, the outcast hero had also been sensitive, unlike Ahab, to the goodness of the whale, particularly of baby whales:

> [...] as human infants while suckling will calmly and fixedly gaze away from the breast, as if leading two different lives at the time; and while yet drawing mortal nourishment, be still spiritually feeding on some unearthly reminiscence; even so did the young of these whales seem looking up towards us, as if we were but a bit of Gulf-weed in their new-born sight. Floating on their sides, the mothers also seemed quietly eyeing us. One of these little infants that from certain queer tokens seemed hardly a day old, might have measured some fourteen feet in length and some six feet in girth. (p. 497)

Ishmaël, as a spiritual voyager, discerns the innocence of the whale, while Ahab is obsessed with the evil character of Moby Dick. By the end of the novel, then, the reader realizes that Ishmaël has learned to integrate through the filtering process of his private soul the opposed facets of existence. Remaining constantly aware of the simultaneous existence of good (the infant whales) and evil (Captain Ahab), he refuses, unlike his commander, to adhere solely to the values of evil. Moreover, able to courageously face the horror of life, Ishmaël qualifies as a precursor to Larry Slade's existential philosophy. For the text of *Moby Dick* is interspersed with references to the existential dilemma with which man, trapped in a contingent universe, is faced. Thus, in "The Quarter-Deck," Ahab exclaims: "All visible objects, man, are but pasteboard masks [...]. If man will strike, strike through the mask! How can the prisoner reach outside except by thrusting through the wall?" (p. 262) In "The Hyena," Ishmaël realizes: "There are certain queer times and occasions in this strange mixed affair we call life when a man takes this whole universe for a vast practical joke [...] and [...] the joke is at nobody's expense but his own." (p. 329) Further, in "The Line," the novelist reflects: "All men are enveloped in whale-lines. All are born with halters round their necks." (p. 387) Thus in *Moby Dick*, the tragic tension between good and evil resolves itself in a near-existential stance.

In *Iceman*, O'Neill identifies the good/evil dichotomy as the source of tragic action, but, like Melville in *Moby Dick*, suggests that a psychological balance between the two forces may be struck. As in *Moby Dick*, the loss of innocence affects two characters, Hickey and Larry Slade. While Hickey, like Ahab, becomes mad, Larry Slade succeeds in integrating the principles of good and evil within the boundaries of his consciousness. In doing so, he qualifies as a spiritual voyager, belonging to Ishmaël's progeny.[13] Like the Melvillean protagonist, Slade is eventually able to face the absurdity of existence and to tell the world of his experience, after escaping Hickey's doom.

At the beginning of the action, Theodore Hickmann is described in terms implicating his innocence: "[...] His expression is fixed in a salesman's winning smile of self-confident affability and hearty good fellowship [...]. He exudes a friendly, generous personality that makes everyone like him on sight [...]." (p. 76) O'Neill intimates, however, that Hickey's goodness cannot resist the test of evil, when, in the last act, he confesses having murdered his wife. Like Ahab, Hickey achieves near-tragic grandeur by realizing the weakness of his own soul but appears unable to accept the limitations of his predicament to the full :

So I killed her [...]. I remember I heard myself speaking to her, as if it was something I'd always wanted to say: "Well, you know what you can do with your pipe dream now, you damned bitch!" [...]. No! That's a lie! I never said! Good God, I couldn't have said that! If I did, I must have gone insane [...]. Yes, Harry of course, I've been out of my mind ever since! All the time I've been here! You saw I was insane, didn't you? (pp. 241–243)

Hickey attempts to convince both himself and the bums of Harry Hope's bar that he acted out of madness. Like Melville's demented captain, he has failed to understand the interdependence existing between good and evil and as a result is destroyed by forces beyond his control. If Hickey's confession parallels Ahab's moment of awareness in "The Symphony," both characters lack the strength necessary to bear the psychological burden of their plight. Ahab continues to pursue the whale in a frantic fashion while Hickey loses his sanity. It is through another character, Larry Slade, that *Iceman* acquires the status of tragedy.

Critics have suggested that Larry Slade and Hickey represented two sides of the same coin.[14] O'Neill's characterization thus shows correspondences to Melville's *Moby Dick*, in which Ishmaël and Ahab can be viewed as complementary personalities. Like Ishmaël, Larry participates in Hickey's attempts at destroying human illusions but finally escapes total annihilation. He appears capable of striking a balance between the various poles of human existence. Throughout the play, Larry resists being converted to Hickey's optimistic philosophy. Rather, he observes the latter from a distance and comments bitterly on his attitude: "LARRY: [...] (then in his comically intense, crazy whisper). Be God, it looks like he's going to make two sales of his peace at least! But you'd better make sure first it's the real McCoy and not poison." (p. 87) Larry is aware of the dangerous aspects of Hickey's personality and yet at the end of the tragedy, it becomes apparent that he identifies with his philosophy to some extent:

> Ah, the damned pity—the wrong kind, as Hickey said! Be God, there's no hope! I'll never be a success in the grandstand—or anywhere else! Life is too much for me! I'll be a weak fool looking with pity at the two sides of everything till the day I die! [...] Be God, I'm the only real convert to death Hickey made here. (p. 258)

Like Ishmaël, who understands both the malignity and the goodness of the whale, Larry not only comprehends the nature of violence and death, he also recognizes the value of love and compassion. In spite of his cynical behavior, Larry adopts a soothing attitude towards Parritt, who feels remorseful after having betrayed his mother. As Parritt leaves the stage in order to commit suicide, Larry's sense of charity towards other human beings is clearly manifested to the reader:

> LARRY: (torturedly arguing to himself in a shaken whisper). It's the only way out for him! [...] (He half rises from his chair just as from outside the window comes the sound of something hurtling down, followed by a muffled, crunching thud. Larry gasps and drops back on his chair, shuddering, hiding his face in his hands [...]). (pp. 257–258)

Like Ishmaël, Larry still adheres to the values represented by love and acquires tragic nobility by maintaining a psychological balance between the opposed principles of morality. The heroes of *Iceman* and *Moby Dick* indicate that while evil may eventually triumph, man must retain illusions and pipe-dreams in order to preserve spiritual sanity. Ahab and Hickey become preys to madness for having failed to stick to those saving illusions.[15]

D

While *Moby Dick* still shows us the signs of the power of God, *Pierre* represents a step further in the evolution that leads Melville towards the philosophical substance of *Billy Budd*. In *Pierre*, the hero no longer manages to integrate the tension between good and evil. That opposition remains unresolved in a Godless universe. In this respect, *Pierre* possesses analogies with O'Neill's *Electra*, in which Orin also proves unable to synthesize the good and evil dichotomy in a universe increasingly alienated from its creator. Thus, *Pierre* and *Electra* point the way towards the agnostic worlds of *Billy Budd* and *Journey*. Simultaneously, both Pierre and Orin are destroyed by the evil part of the dichotomy as both commit suicide. Unlike Larry Slade and Ishmaël, they are crushed by evil and do not entirely master the ultimate enlightenment generally associated with tragic figures.

In *Pierre* as in *Electra*, initiation into evil takes the shape of the protagonists' inability to resist their incestuous longings for their sisters. The parallels between the two works are so striking that the critic Joyce D. Kennedy even conjectured that O'Neill might have been directly influenced by Melville.[16] This impression is reinforced by the fact that both works rely on the stories of Orestes and Hamlet.

Indeed, both novel and play express the brothers' love for their sisters in marked melodramatic terms. Thus in *Pierre*:

> Pierre did not seem to hear her; his arm embraced her tighter [...] "Call me brother no more! [...]. I am Pierre and thou Isabel, wide brother and sister in the common humanity [...]. The demi-gods trample on trash, and Virtue and Vice are trash!" Swiftly he caught her in his arms: "From nothing proceeds nothing. Isabel! How can one sin

in a dream?" (pp. 380–381)

O'Neill similarly dramatizes the incestuous love between sister and brother in Act III of *The Haunted*, in which Orin feels remorseful and nearly confesses the secret cause that prompted him to kill Adam Brant:

ORIN: [...] ([...] he stares at her and slowly a distorted look of desire comes over his face) [...] Perhaps I love you too much, Vinnie! [...]. There are times when you don't seem to be my sister but some stranger with the same beautiful hair—(he touches her hair caressingly [...]). (p. 853)

O'Neill's and Melville's male protagonists would wish to obliterate the reality of their family link with the heroines. It is out of thinly disguised love for their sisters that they become involved in violent actions: Pierre in inflicting a fatal psychological blow to Mrs. Glendinning, and Orin in murdering Christine's lover.

At the core of the tragic quality of both *Pierre* and *Electra* lies the heroes' desperate attempts at defining their link with the deity, a quest in which they would eventually hope to find a resolution of the good and evil dichotomy. Both Orin and Pierre come to the bitter conclusion that no God can improve the tormented relationships in which they are engaged with their sisters. The hero of *Pierre* never succeeds in understanding his relationship with the deity, a failure best expressed through his sudden discovery of Plotinus Plinlimmon's pamphlet "Chronometricals and Horologicals." This treatise, advising the reader not to seek to interpret God, tells of the impossibility of reconciling the horror of the human plight and divine goodness. In other words, Pinlimmon suggests, "in things terrestrial (horological) a man must not be governed by ideas celestial (chronometrical)." (pp. 298–299) Struck with the "profound Silence" of God's voice, Pierre nearly "runs, like a mad dog, into atheism." (pp. 290 and 299) God remains indifferent to Pierre's struggle with the opposed poles of the good and evil dichotomy. The hero qualifies as an American Enceladus, a character who, in his efforts to attain divine status, is confined to the earth:

[...]You saw Enceladus the Titan, the most potent of all the giants,

writhing from out the emprisoning earth [...] still turning his uncon-
querable front toward that majestic mount eternally in vain assailed by
him [...]. Enceladus was both the son and grandson of an incest; and
even thus, there had been born from the organic blended heavenliness
and earthliness of Pierre, another mixed, uncertain, heaven-aspiring,
but still not wholly earth-emancipated mood [...]. (pp. 480–483)

Orin Mannon, another New World Enceladus, feels estranged from heavenly God
and consequently gropes in the darkness of the earth. He dimly realizes that the
must rely on his own strength in order to survive the psychological crisis that the
forces of good and evil generate in his soul:

ORIN: And I find artificial light more appropriate for my work—
man's light, not God's—man's feeble striving to understand himself, to
exist for himself in the darkness! It's a symbol of his life—a lamp
burning out in a room of waiting shadows! (p. 387)

In *Pierre* as in *Electra*, one witnesses a tendency to leave the tragic
consequences of the good and evil dichotomy unresolved, against an agnostic
background. These two works, then, prefigure further developments in their
authors' careers, i.e.,*Billy Budd* and *Journey*.17

E

The action of *Billy Budd* is filtered through the consciousness of three
protagonists: Billy Budd, Claggart, and Captain Vere. Again, as in *Moby Dick*,
Mevlille's main character has been selected for his non-aristocratic nature. The
godless world of the novel renders the good/evil dichotomy even more
threatening. At the beginning of his narrative, the novelist stresses Billy Budd's
innocence:18 "[...] Billy came; and it was like a Catholic priest striking peace in
an Irish shindy. Not that he preached to them or said or did anything in
particular; but a virtue went out of him, sugaring the sour ones [...]."(p. 47)
Whereas Billy is the epitome of purity and goodness, Claggart, the master-at-
arms, is associated with evil. Melville contrasts the civilized personality of
Claggart with the natural authenticity of the sailors of the "Bellipotent:"

> Claggart was a man about five-and-thirty, somewhat spare and tall, yet of no ill figure upon the whole. His hand was too small and shapely to have been accustomed to hard toil [...]. This complexion singularly contrasting with the red or deeply bronzed visages of the sailors, and in the sunlight, though it was not exactly displeasing, nevertheless seemed to hint of something defective in the constitution and blood. (p. 64)

Melville feels utter contempt for Claggart: his satiric thrust is evident in his suggestion that the character suffers from "something defective in the constitution and blood." The writer later associates him more straightforwardly with evil: "Now something such an one was Claggart, in whom was the mania of an evil nature, not engendered by vicious training or corrupting books or licentious living, but born with him and innate, in short 'a depravity according to nature.'" (p. 76). While Claggart represents evil, Captain Vere recalls Ahab through his iron-will: "[...] He had seen much service, been in various engagements always acquitting himself as an officer mindful of the welfare of his men, but never tolerating an infraction of discipline [...]." (p. 60) Captain's Vere wisdom is flawed: the death sentence that he passes upon Billy, after the latter accidentally killed Claggart, is motivated by his monomaniac obsession with discipline. Captain Vere comes to symbolize, like Claggart, the forces of evil to which Billy falls a victim. In this short work, then, Melville indicates that, in a godless universe, the tension between good and evil at best remains unresolved. Indeed, unlike Ishmaël whose intellectual acumen he lacks, Billy Budd does not integrate the poles of that dichotomy and is eventually crushed by his destiny. Initially compared with the Lamb of God, Billy fails to experience Christ's resurrection. However, man's tragic grandeur, Melville implies, originates in his courageous acceptance of the inescapability of that predicament, as Billy stoically endures his punishment. This view exhibits point of confluence with Camus's philosophy of the Absurd. Naturally, the slight restriction I introduced in the preceding chapter needs to restated here. Melville's language and imagery are to some extent religious in form ("lamb of God") but the ironic undercut betrays the author's ambiguous stance.[19]

In *Journey*, O'Neill concentrates on the souls of the members of an average American family. There, as in *Billy Budd*, the tension between good and evil remains unresolved because O'Neill no longer allows his characters, like Larry

Slade, to bring about the fusion between these two moral principles. Although Edmund can be regarded as an observer and therefore as a replica of Slade, he never exhibits the latter's courage in front of the absurd. Tension manifests itself in the relationship between the two sons of the family, Edmund and Jamie Tyrone. O'Neill locates the source of Edmund's fundamental purity in his mystical nature, in his admiration for the sea. Edmund has preserved a kind of natural innocence, and has not yet fallen a victim to civilization. In the following scene, however, he witnesses the confession of his brother who is associated with the depravity of the city. Jamie tells of his life on Broadway in cynical terms:

> [...] I picked Fat violet [...]. By the time I hit Mamie's dump I felt very sad about myself and all the other poor bums in the world. Ready for a weep on any old womanly bosom [...]. Imagine me sunk to the fat girl in a hick town hooker shop! Me! Who have made some of the bestlookers on Broadway sit up and beg! (p. 139–141)

Upon hearing his brother, Edmund acquires knowledge of evil. Further, Jamie indicates that he had already initiated adolescent Edmund into sexuality : "I've had more to do with bringing you up than anyone. I wised you up about women, so you'd never be a fall guy, or make any mistakes you didn't want to make." (p. 144) Clearly, Edmund's innocence, O'Neill implies, cannot resist the test of experience. In *Journey*, the playwright asserts the tragic essence of the conflictual rhythm of the human universe. Having lost faith in the Catholicism of their youth, the heroes of *Journey* cannot transcend the limitations of the good/evil dichotomy but nonetheless exhibit a capacity for enduring and suffering, which constitutes a primary component of tragedy.[20] Like Melville in *Billy Budd* and in some passages of *Moby Dick*, O'Neill develops in *Journey* a vision of tragedy related to existential philosophy, according to which man, entrapped in an absurd situation, is condemned to an "exile without remedy."[21]

The three stages that mark O'Neill's and Melville's treatment of the American Adam theme, i.e., the good and evil opposition, are remarkably parallel: religious nostalgia, balance between the dual forces of nature, and finally unresolved tension coupled with an existential philosophical stance. These represent the various modes in which O'Neill and Melville experiment with the concept of tragedy in an essentially American context. They do not always, as my analysis of *Electra* following that of *Iceman* indicates, move from one stage to the other in a purely chronological order, but the pattern is consistently present.

F

Both O'Neill and Melville saw tragedy as a consequence of their characters' failed attempts at interpreting the essence of human nature and of God. As a result, the failure of the individual pursuit of happiness forms a concomitant tragic theme in the two writers' works. Indeed, while Jefferson's "Declaration of Independence" seemed to guarantee the rights of the individual to be free and happy within the confines of American society, O'Neill and Melville invariably show, in their tragic works, that these ideals have been progressively thwarted by circumstances.Thomas Jefferson affirmed: "We hold these truths to be self-evident, that all men are created equal; that they are endowed by their creator with certain unalienable rights; that among these are life, liberty, and the pursuit of happiness [...]."[22] Ironically, they assert that their characters are themselves responsible for their lack of happiness. It is in the excessive self-reliance of their heroes that the two writers locate this tragic motif. Although I have already dealt with this motif in connection with the two writers' sea motif and attack of Transcendentalism, my perspective here is more purely pyschological. This theme is manifested in such works as *Moby Dick*, *Iceman*, or *Journey*, in which the central characters are fully self-enveloped. They qualify as mono-maniacs incapable of sharing their emotions with the outside world and their fellow human beings. F.O. Matthiessen defined that characteristic of Melville's tragic thought as such: "tragedy (is) a fearful symbol of the self-enclosed individualism that, carried to its furthest extreme, brings disaster both upon itself and upon the group of which it is part."[23] Accordingly, these protagonists remain unable to assume the full consequences of their tragic mistakes. They prefer to confine themselves in a quasi-psychotic isolation, as is the case for Ahab, Pierre, Hickey and the heroes of *Electra*.

In the early pages of *Moby Dick*, Melville suggests the self-enclosed character of his protagonist: "Captain Ahab remained invisibly enshrined within his cabin." (p. 197) Ahab's isolation becomes even clearer in the chapter entitled "The Doubloon," in which the protagonist confesses being egotistical:

(on the doubloon) [...] You saw the likeness of the three Andes'
summits; from one a flame; a tower on another; on the third a crowing
cock; while arching over all was a segment of the partitioned zodiac,
the signs all marked with their usual cabalistics, and the keystone sun
entering the equinoctial point at Libra. Before this equatorial coin,
Ahab, not unobserved by others, was now pausing.
"There is something very egotistical in mountain-tops and towers, and
all oher grand and lofty things; look here,—three peaks as proud as
Lucifer. The firm tower, that is Ahab; the volcano, that is Ahab; the
courageous, the undaunted, and victorious fowl, that, too, is Ahab; all
are Ahab; and this round gold is but the image of the round globe,
which, like a magician's glass, to each and every man in turn but
mirrors back his own self [...]." (p.541)

Ahab's individualism causes his doom: it prompts him to devote all his energy to
his quest, which ends in total destruction. Ahab's narcissistic personality thus
provokes the tragic outcome of the voyage. Likewise, his monomaniac chase
prevents him from understanding fully the desperate nature of his predicament.
Similarly, in *Iceman* and *Journey*, O'Neill locates the tragic flaw of some of his
characters in their inability to relate to their surrounding universe.

Like Ahab, Hickey in *Iceman* becomes demented in the pursuit of quixotic
ideals. In his endeavors to demonstrate that man can live without pipe-dreams,
Hickey forfeits human love and kills his wife. His exaggerated individualism
results in death and insanity. Failure to relate to the outside world is satirized as
strongly by O'Neill in *Iceman* as by Melville in *Moby Dick*. In *Journey*, Mary
Tyrone's drug-addiction forces her to retire into isolation. Her self-enclosed
personality resembles that of Captain Ahab since her individualism provokes the
disintegration of her family unit. In the last scene of the play, her behavior
verges on madness:

Mary appears in the doorway [...]. Her face is paler than ever. Her eyes
look enormous. They glisten like polished black jewels [...]. She seems
aware of other objects in the room, the furniture, the windows,
familiar things she accepts automatically as naturally belonging there

but which she is too preoccupied to notice.

JAMIE: [...] The Mad Scene. Enter Ophelia! [...]

Then Mary speaks, and they freeze into silence again, staring at her. She has paid no attention whatever to the incident. It is simply a part of the familiar atmosphere of the room, a background which does not touch her preoccupation; and she speaks aloud to herself, not to them. (pp. 150–151)

In this scene, Mary Tyrone identifies herself completely with her past and even dresses as a young girl. Her quest to recreate the past results in alienation. Because of her withdrawal, the heroine fails to grasp and assume the deep implications of her predicament and instead of achieving tragic grandeur, finds shelter in a quasi-psychotic attitude. It is precisely through a depiction of these self-reliant protagonists that O'Neill and Melville succeed in making us feel the ironic, indeed tragic consequences of the failure of the pursuit of individual happiness in the New World.

Ultimately, this theme merges with that of the crisis of identity, another source of tragic tension within the boundaries of American society. Both O'Neill and Melville envision this absence of a firm, clearly established sense of self as typical of the American experience. Indeed, in *Confidence*, Melville has a mystic declare "What are you? What am I? Nobody knows who anybody is." (p. 228). Comparably, in *Brown*, Dion Anthony expresses a fundamental anxiety about the nature of his identity:

Why am I afraid to dance, I who love music and rhythm and grace and song and laughter? Why am I afraid to live, I who love life and the beauty of flesh and the living colors of earth and sky and sea? Why am I afraid of love, I who love love? Why am I afraid, I who am not afraid? [...] Why was I born without a skin, O God, that I must wear armor in order to touch or to be touched? [...] Why the devil was I ever born at all? (p. 315)

Thus, these two motifs complement the tragic poignancy of O'Neill's and

Melville's vision of the American Adam theme.

G

As described in this chapter, the two writers' concept of tragedy, relying mostly on the good and evil duality, could be adequately typified, in Doris V. Falk's words, as a "tragedy of tensions."[24] Moreover, O'Neill and Melville develop near-tragedies based on fragmented themes—such as the good/evil dichotomy, the failure of the pursuit of happiness, the quest for identity—, which would not, taken in isolation, lend a tragic stature to their works. It is most notably, therefore, to their ability to establish an ironic mode of tragedy that O'Neill and Melville owe their merits as tragic writers. This notion of irony differs from that displayed by classical tragedy-writers. Indeed, the irony in this case does not reside in the spectator's knowledge of facts to which the protagonist has no access, as in Sophocles's plays. In implying, however, that some of their protagonists—including Orin, Pierre, Hickey and Ahab—are too weak to accept the bleakness of their predicament, Melville and O'Neill depict "ungodly, godlike" men, towards whom they exhibit an ambiguous atttitude of both rejection and admiration. [25] Possible exceptions to such patterns exist: Eben and Abbie, Ishmaël, and Larry, characters whose tragic qualities are unquestionable.

But most often, the two writers' use of irony signifies an unexpected reversal of viewpoint, an alternation of love and contempt towards their creatures. The complex stance that the two writers adopt towards their tragic protagonists allows them, in Michael Manheim's words, to "transcend melodrama."[26] If O'Neill's writings do not achieve the status of full tragedies, then, their modernity prevents them from being considered side by side with such melodramas as *The Count of Monte Cristo*.

Both writers' characters only possess the potential for tragic enlightenment, a potential which they cannot fully develop owing to their exaggeratedly self-reliant nature and their inability of being concerned with issues transcending their private psychological universes. Reversing Whitman's optimistic view of life in America, O'Neill and Melville thus offered searingly tragic songs of American experience, constituting significant variants upon classic tragic concepts.

CHAPTER VII. IN SEARCH OF POETIC REALISM

In their tragic works, O'Neill and Melville were in search of a form of realism which could adequately reflect their thematic concerns. Although they were separated by almost a century of literary innovations, their vision of such realism often coincided. Indeed, if Melville composed in a period antedating the advent of naturalism, and wrote in a style which some critics have regarded as purely romantic, he nonetheless paralleled O'Neill, whose drama was undoubtedly influenced by Zola's theories, in his ability to envision realistic passages prefiguring the playwright's own brand of realism. In other words, it is possible to regard the two writers' experiments with form, which prompted them to explore such opposed genres as romanticism, naturalism, and expressionism, as variations on a basic realistic model. Should one wish to define that style, one might turn to Elia Kazan's notion of "poetic realism," i.e., a rendering of reality subtly blended with moments of subjective insights and lyrical outbursts.[1] That formal characteristic corresponds to Richard Chase's definition of the American romance genre in his study *The American Novel and Its Tradition*. To Chase, the term "romance" signifies:

> an assumed freedom from the ordinary [...] requirements of verisimili-
> tude [...] a tendency toward melodrama and idyl; a more or less formal
> abstractedness and, on the other hand, a tendency to plunge into the
> underside of consciousness; a willingness to abandon moral questions or
> to ignore the spectacle of man in society, or to consider these things
> only indirectly or abstractly [...]. Being less committed to the
> immediate rendition of reality than the novel, the romance will more
> freely veer toward the mythic, allegorical, and symbolistic forms.[2]

And indeed, O'Neill's and Melville's realism possesses a subjective, poetic nature, which can be detected in a marked use of symbolism and myth in their rendering of reality. Their craftsmanship prompts them to create forms comparable to Chase's romance through their metaphysical and cosmological preoccupations. In the course of this analysis, it will often be necessary to focus on tiny points of confluence between the two authors. These elements would not by themselves justify a comparison between O'Neill and Melville. Viewed in conjunction with the thematic characteristics I have delineated in previous chapters, however, they contribute to enhance the patterns of similarity linking both artists.

A. The Symbolic Method

To both O'Neill and Melville, symbolism proceeds mainly from the writer's consciousness and reveals highly subjective features. The most striking instance of their use of romantic symbolism is located in their sea imagery, which has been examined in Chapters III and IV. But their romantic symbolism manifests itself in other domains, especially in their use of the color white as well as in their fire and electricity imagery.[3]

A comparative study of the values that the two artists attach to white provides interesting insights into the specific characteristics of their related symbolic techniques. In *Moby Dick*, Melville inverts the traditional connotations associated with white in linking it to evil in his chapter entitled "The Whiteness of the Whale." In a brilliant novelistic passage, the author seeks to explain why the color white should provoke such fright in the heart of mankind. In order to equate white with atheism, he resorts to a form of virtuoso style:

Is it that by indefiniteness it (the color white) shadows forth the heartless voids and immensities of the universe [...]. Or is it, that in essence whiteness is not so much colour as the visible absence of colour, and at the same time the concrete of all colours; is it for these reasons that there is such a dumb blankness, full of meaning, in a wide landscape of snows—a colourless, all-colour of atheism from which shrink? [...]. Like wilful travellers in Lapland, who refuse to wear colouring glasses upon their eyes, so the wretched infidel gazes himself blind at the monumental white shroud that wraps all the prospect around him. And of all these things the Albino whale was the symbol.

Wonder ye then at the fiery hunt? (pp. 295–296)

In "The Whiteness of the Whale," Melville utilizes the color white in order to convey a fear of annihilation, as evidenced in his reference to a "monumental white shroud." Further, white evokes the albino whale itself. As the latter symbolizes evil throughout the novel, it can be argued that the writer endows white with negative overtones.

In *Ape*, O'Neill also resorts to the technique of inverted color symbolism and suffuses white with emotions of terror, harshness, loss of identity and evil. In that work, the writer shows us how Yank, the stoker, loses his sense of being through his fatal encounter with Mildred Douglas, who, during her confrontation with Yank, is associated with the color white:

> While the other men have turned full around and stopped dumb-founded by the spectacle of Mildred standing there in her white dress, Yank does not turn far enough to see her [...]. He sees Mildred, like a white apparition in the full light from the open furnace doors [...]. As she looks at this gorilla face, as his eyes bore into hers, she utters a low, choking cry, and shrinks away from him, putting both hands up before her eyes to shut out the sight of his face, to protect her own. This startles Yank to a reaction. His mouth falls open, his eyes grow bewildered [...].
>
> MILDRED:...Take me away! Oh, the filthy beast! (pp. 57–58)

It is the color white, represented by Mildred, that shocks Yank into the recognition of his predicament, for in the following scene, Yank starts brooding about the significance of her apparition and ceases to enjoy working in the forecastle. He clearly has lost his sense of belonging to the steamship and hence feels deprived of selfhood:

> [...] She was all white. I thought she was a ghost [...]. I was scared, get me? I thought she was a ghost, see? She was all in white like dey wrap around stiffs [...]. She didn't belong, dat's what. But Christ, she was

funny lookin'! Did yuh pipe her hands? White and skinny. Yuh could
see de bones through 'em. And her mush, dat was dead white, too [...].
(pp. 62–64)

In *Ape* as in *Moby Dick*, the color white triggers unconventional emotions. In
O'Neill's play as in Melville's novel, it signifies nothingness, loss of being, as
manifested through the indefinite nature of Mildred's whiteness; it symbolizes
death: the heroine is equated to a ghost; and it elicits terror, as Yank confesses: "I
was scared." The subsequent action of *Ape* also signals that the color white
epitomizes the forces of evil. In attempting to retrieve his sense of personal unity,
Yank meets with his death in the New York Zoo, a tragic ending finding its
source in his initial confrontation with Mildred's mysterious whiteness. Both
O'Neill and Melville thus modify the usual connotations of the white color
symbolism to offer a plastic equivalent of the spiritual crises through which their
protagonists are evolving.[4]

The two artists explored the possibilities of fire imagery with an equally
innovative imagination. In the chapter entitled "Try-Works" of *Moby Dick*,
Melville develops this type of symbolism effectively in a passage where fire
confers a grotesque and hellish aspect upon the "Pequod:"

The hatch, removed from the tops of the works, now afforded a wide
hearth in front of them. Standing on this were the Tartarean shapes of
the pagan harpooners, always the whale ship's stokers. With huge
pronged poles they pitched hissing masses of blubber into the scalding
pots, or stirred up the fires beneath, till the snaky flames darted,
curling, out of the doors to catch them by the feet [...]. Here lounged
the watch [...]. Their tawny features, now all begrimed with smoke and
sweat, their matted beards, and the contrasting barbaric brilliancy of
their teeth, all these were strangely revealed in the capricious
emblazonings of the works. As they narrated to each other their unholy
adventures, their tales of terror told in words of mirth; as their
uncivilized laughter forked upwards out of them, like the flames from
the furnace; [...] then the rushing Pequod, freighted with savages, and
laden with fire, and burning a corpse, and plunging into the blackness

of darkness, seemed the material counterpart of her monomaniac commander's soul. (pp. 533–534)

In "The Try-Works," Melville employs fire imagery in order to create grotesque effects. He compares the "Pequod" to a hellish furnace, and stresses the link existing between the burning ship and the mad captain.

A similar atmosphere pervades scenes of O'Neill's *Ape* where a sort of frenzy prompts Yank to willingly identify with the fire of the stokehole. O'Neill alludes to a hellish universe in a scenic image reminiscent of Melville's "Try-Works:"

Dat's fresh air for me! Dat's food for me! I'm new get me? Hell in the stokehole? Sure! It takes a man to work in hell. Hell, sure, dat's my fav'rite climate. I eat it up! I git fat on it! It's me makes it hot! It's me makes it roar! It's me makes it move! (p. 48)

Both the "Pequod" and the liner of *Ape* possess infernal characteristics. Moreover, the fire and the ship are "the material counterpart(s)" of both Yank's and Ahab's souls. In *Moby Dick* and *Ape*, fire symbolism is used in kindred fashions in order to stress the psychological turmoil of the central characters.

Like many American writers, O'Neill and Melville admired the elemental forces of nature, of which electricity or thunder constituted a prominent symbol.[5] Electricity becomes a part of their romantic symbolism primarily in *Moby Dick*, *Pierre*, *Dynamo* and *Interlude*. In the chapter entitled "The Candles," the author of *Moby Dick* describes how the "Pequod" is assailed by a terrible storm:

All the yard-arms were tipped with a pallid fire; and touched at each tri-pointed lightning-rod-end with three tapering white flames, each of the three tall masts was silently burning in that sulphurous air, like three gigantic wax tapers before an altar. (p. 614)

In *Moby Dick*, the symbol of electricity is endowed with religious attributes, as indicated by Melville's allusion to the candles and the altar.

In *Pierre*, the novelist refers to electricity in order to underline the mysterious beauty of the heroine, Isabel, and to intimate the secret link between the physical and spiritual realms of experience:

> For ever all these things, and interfusing itself with the sparkling electricity in which she seemed to swim, was an ever-creeping and condensing haze of ambiguities. Often, in after-times with her, did he recall this first magnetic night, and would seem to see that she then had bound him to her by an extraordinary atmospheric spell—both physical and spiritual [...]. This spell seemed one with that Pantheistic master-spell, which eternally locks in mystery and in muteness the universal subject world, and the physical electricalness of Isabel seemed [...] moulded from fire and air, and vivified at some Voltaic pile of August—clouds heaped against the sunset. (p. 213)

Thus, the symbol of electricity/thunder serves to express the fundamental sense of polarity typifying our universe, acquiring simultaneously a divine and supernatural character. To some extent, *Moby Dick* and *Pierre* can throw light on the nature of O'Neill's electricity symbol in *Dynamo* and *Interlude*.

In *Dynamo*, the storm symbol sustains the flow of action throughout the play. Its impact is asserted in the opening stage directions of the play: "It is evening. In the background between the two houses the outlines of the maples are black against a sky pale with the light of quarter-moon. Now and then there is a faint flash of lightning from far-off and a low mumble of thunder." (p. 5). Here, O'Neill resorts to the electricity symbol in order to establish the dark mood of the drama. In an ensuing love scene between Ada and Reuben, the playwright reintroduces his symbol and, as in *Pierre*, fuses love and electricity:

> REUBEN: [...] We'll walk out to the top of Long Hill. That's where I was all during the storm that night after I left here. And that's the right place for us to love—on top of that hill—close to the sky—driven to love by what makes the earth go round—by what drives the stars through space! Did you ever think that all life comes down to electricity in the end, Ada? (p. 62)

In *Dynamo* as in *Pierre*, electricity constitutes the principle generating the rhythm of the universe because in both works, its divine quality allows the protagonists to experience love. In O'Neill's play, however, the symbol of electricity is full of the fragrance of death for, at the end of the play, it brings about Reuben's demise: "He (Reuben) throws his arms out over the exciter [...]. There is a flash of bluish light about him [...]. Reuben's voice rises in a moan [...]." (p. 101) Starting with a vision of the electricity symbol identical to that of Melville, O'Neill regards the dynamo, i.e., man-controlled electricity, as a destructive force, interweaving in his work bitter overtones totally absent from Melville's novels.

In *Interlude*, he also develops a comparable symbol, perhaps in a more oblique fashion. At the end of the play, Nina Leeds affirms the divine nature of electricity: "Strange Interlude! Yes our lives are merely strange dark interludes in the electrical display of God the Father!" (p. 681) In *Interlude* as in *Dynamo*, O'Neill insists, following in the wake of Melville's *Pierre* and *Moby Dick*, on the cosmic significance of electricity but posits the dynamo as a symbol of the artificiality of the modern world. A joint study of O'Neill's and Melville's electricity symbolism thus sheds light on the playwright's romantic imagery and reveals the bleakness of his philosophy.

O'Neill's and Melville's symbolism also finds its origin in Puritan typology, a characteristic particularly noticeable in their biblical allusions. Interestingly, both resorted to this type of symbolism in an inverted mode, in an attempt to unmask the false saviors of our modern universe.

Both O'Neill and Melville were avid readers of the Bible. By integrating Biblical symbolism into their novels and plays, they betrayed their affinities with the American tradition of Puritanism and idealism described by Ursula Brumm, W.H. Auden, and F.O. Matthiessen. In *American Renaissance*, Matthiessen notes the similarity between Melville and Emerson: to both "every natural fact is a symbol of some spiritual fact," which corresponds to "the tendency of American idealism to see a spiritual significance in the material universe." (pp. 242–243) W.H. Auden offers a further commentary on this tradition in *The Enchafed Flood*, as he describes *Moby Dick* in terms of an elaborate synecdoche. *Moby Dick* contains many instances of parable and typology of the following type: as X is in one field of experience, so is Y in another. Such analogical method bears points of confluence with composition techniques used by both the Church Fathers and Jonathan Edwards.[6] Ursula Brumm, in *Die Religiöse Typologie im Amerikanischen Denken* further refines this concept and firmly establishes the link existing between Puritanism and the American Renaissance.[7] That connection resides primarily in the role of Typology. In *Moby Dick*, Brumm claims, the author, under the inspiration of Puritanism, sees manifestations of God in the outside world. The universe of that epic novel is godly in all details, a concept reminiscent of Calvinism. Often endowed with an emblematic value, Melville's characters are also impregnated with Puritan features. Conversely, in some of his plays, O'Neill appears to be familiar with the Puritan method of typological symbolism. In works such as *Rope* and *Desire*, in which the protagonists represent modern equivalents of Biblical figures, O'Neill modifies the function of Puritan typology. Like Melville in *Moby Dick*, he suggests that the behavior of X twentieth-century character corresponds to the attitude of Y Biblical *persona*. In short, both O'Neill and Melville can be likened through their adherence to typological symbolism, a tendency that manifests itself in several of their works.

In *Moby Dick*, Melville implies tongue-in-cheek that Ahab does not possess the grandeur of his Biblical namesake, who achieved royal status. In the short story "Bartleby, the Scrivener," the novelist compares his protagonist to Christ in order to subsequently debunk his tragic potential. In these two instances of typology, in which a specific character is compared to a Biblical hero, Melville manipulates irony effectively. Likewise, in *Desire*, O'Neill establishes derisive parallels between his *dramatis personae* and Biblical protagonists. Ephraïm Cabot constitutes a modern equivalent of the harsh Old Testament God but does not retain his divine essence. Like Melville in "Bartleby," the playwright refers to Christ in *Iceman*. Indeed, the central figure of that drama, Hickey, can be equated to a corrupted Savior. Although, at the beginning of the drama, his mission appears holy, he is eventually unmasked as a murderer: his gospel contains only words of evil. These few examples indicate how O'Neill and Melville could ironically contrast the shabbiness of the present and the glorious nature of the past.

The most striking parallel in the two writers' typological symbolism consists undoubtedly in their kindred use of the Abraham motif. In *Billy Budd*, Melville intimates that Captain Vere's plight is analogous to Abraham's dilemma, when God ordered him to sacrifice his son. Vere realizes the harshness of a law which demands that Billy Budd be executed. In announcing the death sentence to the hero, the narrator conjectures that Vere

> in the end may have developed the passion sometimes latent under an exterior stoical or indifferent. He was old enough to have been Billy's father. The austere devotee of military duty, letting himself melt back into what remains primeval in our formalized humanity, may in the end have caught Billy to his heart, even as *Abraham* may have caught young Isaac on the brink of resolutely offering him up in obedience to the exacting behest. But there is no telling the sacrament—seldom if in any case revealed to the gadding world—wherever, under circumstances at all akin to those here attempted to be set forth, two of great Nature's nobler order embrace. (p. 115, italics mine)

In this novella, Melville resorts to typology in an attempt to stress the absence of God in our modern universe. For, if Isaac is eventually rescued by the divinity, Billy Budd is condemned without mercy. Melville adopts a pessimistic viewpoint towards the Biblical father image, one probably rooted in personal experience. He depicts a world devoid of compassion, a world in which the son is crushed by the cruelty of the father. Similarly, in *Rope* (1918), O'Neill formulates a compelling statement about the nature of our modern experience through the device of typological symbolism.

In that early play of the sea, the dramatist introduces a New England farmer symptomatically named Abraham Bentley. O'Neill's satirical goals are evident in the very physical description of the protagonist in the opening stage directions:

> Abraham Bentley appears in the doorway and stands, blinking into the shadowy barn. He is a tall, lean stoop-shouldered old man of sixty-five. His thin legs, twisted by rheumatism, totter feebly under him as he shuffles slowly along with the aid of a thick cane. His face is gaunt, chalk-white, furrowed with wrinkles, surmounted by a skinny bald scalp fringed with scanty wisps of white hair. His eyes peer weakly from beneath bushy, black brows. His mouth is a sunken line drawn in under his large, beak-like nose. A two weeks' growth of stubby patches of beard covers his jaws and chin. He has on a threadbare brown

overcoat but wears no hat. (p. 167)[8]

Bentley's caricatural physique belies the nobility that his very name confers upon his personality. Throughout the one-act, Bentley recites passages from the Bible in a fashion that betrays his insanity. Through dialogue, O'Neill further undercuts the seriousness of his character's behavior. The tragic stature of Abraham the patriarch cannot be recaptured by O'Neill's New World citizen:

> [...] He looks toward the sea and his voice quavers in a doleful chant [...] "Woe unto us! for the day goeth away, for the shadows of the evening are stretched out" (He mumbles to himself for a moment—then speaks clearly). Spyin' on me! Spawn o' the pit! (He renews his chant). "They hunt our steps that we cannot go in our streets: our end is near, our days are fulfilled: for our end is come." (p. 168)

The unfolding of the action of *Rope* offers yet a third ironic twist to the story of Abraham, one comparable to that found in *Billy Budd*. As Luke Bentley, the family son, comes back to the paternal home after years spent at sea, O'Neill juxtaposes the motif of the Prodigal son with that of the Abraham/Isaac relationship.[9] Bentley/Abraham then seems compelled by a divine order to sacrifice his offspring and accordingly lends Luke a rope in the apparent hope that he will hang himself. Unlike Isaac or Billy, Luke refuses to accept death:

> LUKE: (grabbing Bentley's shoulder and shaking him—hoarsely). Yuh wanted to see me hanging there in real earnest, didn't yuh? You'd hang me yourself if yuh could, wouldn't yuh? And yuh my own father! Yuh damned son of a gun! Yuh would, would yuh? I'd smash your brains out for a nickel! (He shakes the old man more and more furiously [...] giving his father one more shake, which sends him sprawling on the floor). Git outa here! Git outa this b'fore I kill yuh dead! [...] (pp. 192–193)

In this passage of his one-act play, O'Neill introduces a striking departure from the original biblical pattern in order to comment bitterly, like Melville, on the function of divine justice. While in *Billy Budd*, the hero is not saved by God, in

Rope, the protagonist spontaneously revolts against the father figure, whose behavior Luke decodes as a wish to administer godly justice. Like Melville, O'Neill expresses his personal anxieties and conflicts in this work: the relationship prevailing between Bentley and Luke duplicates the mixed feelings of love/hate O'Neill experienced towards his own father. Although O'Neill departs from a source identical to that of Melville in *Billy Budd*, divergences between the two writers can nonetheless be traced. Like Melville, O'Neill uses the Abraham motif to present us with an ironic portrait of contemporary realities. However, the bleakness of his vision exceeds that of the novelist. First, O'Neill dramatizes the conflict between man and God in a powerful, indeed melodramatic work, whereas Melville seeks to compose a stoic and serene novella. Secondly, his derisive stance, unlike that of Melville, verges on caricature, whether through characterization or dialogue. Vere, on the contrary, retains a certain degree of nobility. O'Neill's method, based like Melville's on Puritan typology, amplifies the novelist's already intense despair. From a structural point of view, one should note O'Neill's and Melville's double consciousness about the nature of symbol: in their literary universe, the symbol can be either romantic or Puritan, i.e., typological. This double nature, this mixture of freedom and rigidity in symbolic form, constitutes a paradox, an ambiguity of attitude that enriches rather than empoverishes the works of the two artists.

B. Myth-Making

Over the years, numerous studies on the nature and function of myth in society and literature have been published. In *Mythes, Rêves et Mystères*, Mircea Eliade submits that myth differs from the dream in its universal traits. In a related study, *Aspects du Mythe*, Eliade defines myth as a true story taking place in the era of the great beginnings and of the creation of the universe.[10] Roger Caillois, in *Le Mythe et L'Homme*, conceives of the mythical situation as a projection of human psychological conflicts for which the mythical hero finds an ideal solution.[11] On the other hand, Joseph Fontenrose in *The Ritual Theory of Myth* insists on the justifying function of myth: it provides a rationale for existing institutions and therefore possesses a socio-political role.[12] O'Neill's and

Melville's mythical allusions fulfill the functions described by those critics: in referring to Prometheus, they voice an oblique statement about the creation of the universe; they reflect the psychological conflicts experienced by the protagonists and provide explanations for existing customs. Moreover, in resorting to myth, O'Neill and Melville are both seeking to lend artistic coherence to their works. They replace their themes within a larger context and show the continuity existing between ancient and modern times. Simultaneously, the two authors also use myth in order to undercut the stature of their protagonists, who often lack the grandeur of their mythical counterparts.

O'Neill's and Melville's use of the myth of Orestes has formed the object of so many critical studies that I wish to limit my remarks on this subject to a short paragraph.[13] The dramatic patterns of *Pierre* and *Electra* unfold along lines strongly reminiscent of Orestes' story. Both Orestes and Pierre attempt to avenge the paternal honor and accordingly engage in conflictual relationships with their mothers. Isabel Banford, Pierre's half-sister, qualifies as a latter-day counterpart to Electra, for in leaving his manorial estate to live with Isabel as her husband, Pierre indirectly provokes the demise of his mother. Characteristically, the plot of *Electra*, like that of *Pierre*, owes a great deal to the myth of Orestes. Indeed, Lavinia Mannon urges her brother Orin to take the life of Adam Brant, Christine Mannon's lover. She thus hopes to punish her mother for plotting the death of the family head, Ezra Mannon. As a result of Orin's violent deed, Christine eventually commits suicide. Further, the two writers utilize the myth of Orestes in order to show both the perennial quality of their characters' behavior but also to deflate the nobility of these protagonists. Indeed, if Pierre and Orestes do bear resemblances to the Greek hero, they cannot attain his final tragic stature although their initial qualities had indicated their potential for enlightenment. As in the case of color symbolism, then, O'Neill and Melville invert the significance of their myths, hinting at the fact that they do no longer reflect adequately the American experience. Pierre and Orin remain the prisoners of purely psychoanalytical woes, and consequently fail to recapture Orestes' degree of transcendence.

A similar ironic twist emerges from the two writers' references to the myth of Prometheus. Commentators have emphasized the profound similarities existing between Melville's Ahab and the classical Prometheus.[14] Like the latter, Ahab is in revolt against the gods. In the chapter entitled "The Candles" of *Moby Dick*, the novelist describes the hero's taking hold of the lightning chains and waving of the fiery harpoon in terms evocative of Prometheus's theft of fire: "[...] dashing the rattling lightning links to the deck, and snatching the burning harpoon, Ahab waved it like a torch among them [...]." (pp. 617–618) Melville introduces an ironic ingredient in his comparison between Ahab and Prometheus. Unlike the ancient hero, Ahab does not offer fire to the crew in the hope of improving their lives but to threaten them. Moreover, by forcing them to continue in the quest, he eventually provokes their death.

As John Henry Raleigh suggested, O'Neill presents in *Dynamo* a disguised portrait of the mythical Prometheus.[15] Reuben Light is so fascinated by electric light that he wishes to bring its power to mankind at large, a desire akin to Prometheus's action. Towards the end of the play, he confesses his ambition to become a new savior for humanity:

> [...]That centre must be the Great Mother of Eternal Life, Electricity, and Dynamo is her Divine Image on earth! Her power houses are the new churches! She wants us to realize the secret dwells in her! She wants some one man to love her purely and when she finds him worthy she will love him and tell him who will bring happiness and peace to men! And I'm going to be that saviour—the miracle will happen tonight. (p. 84)

Despite references to Christ, one could interpret this passage as an adaptation of the myth of Prometheus for, like the Greek hero, Reuben brings fire/electricity to the human world and is eventually punished for his hubris. Like Melville, O'Neill introduces ironic allusions in his portrait of Reuben/Prometheus. As was the case with Ahab, Reuben's theft fails to provide any sense of comfort and well-being to the community in which he lives. On the contrary, the dynamo qualifies as a dangerous object which kills its worshippers. But O'Neill's vision seems to be even darker than that of Melville: whereas the fire Ahab brings to mankind is natural, that which Reuben extols is purely artificial as it proceeds out of the dynamo, a human creation. O'Neill thus emphasizes to a greater extent than

Melville the opposition existing between his twentieth century protagonist and nature. While using a mythical framework identical to that of Melville, the dramatist eventually formulates an intensely personal, ironic and pessimistic statement about the status of modern man. Not only do O'Neill and Melville develop kindred forms of symbolism and related mythical patterns, they also utilize techniques based on the principle of literary quotation.

C. Literary Quotation

In *Moby Dick* and *Ape*, the two artists subtly interspersed quotations from Dante's *Divine Comedy*. In this fashion, they sought to achieve essentially two goals: first, to reinforce the structural unity of their novel or play, and second, to establish a derisive parallel with modern reality. As I have shown in the case of their use of myth, the two authors regard literary quotation as the means of voicing a pessimistic viewpoint about contemporary American experience.

In "The Grand Armada," the author of *Moby Dick* transposes episodes reminiscent of Canto XXVII in "Paradiso," particularly in the image of the circling whales. The critic Marius Bewley attributes this influence to the fact that Melville had read Cary's Dante in 1848.[16] In this Canto, Dante, turning from Beatrice, admires the intense light around which spin the nine concentric circles of the angelic intelligences, while great wheels of fire shoot forth sparks. Dante's vision finds an equivalent in Melville's depiction of the whales:

> [...] we glided between two whales into the innermost heart of the shoal, as if from some mountain torrent we had slid into a serene valley lake. Here the storms in the roaring glens between the outermost whales, were heard but not felt. In this central expanse the sea presented a smooth satin-like surface [...]. Yes, we were now in the heart of every commotion. And still in the outer distance we beheld the tumults of the outer concentric circles, and saw successive pods of whales, eight or ten in each, swiftly going round and round, like multiplied spans of horses in a ring [...]. (pp. 495–496)

While in the *Divine Comedy*, the concentric circles lead to God, in *Moby Dick*, they culminate in an image of primeval innocence, which, Bewley contends, closely parallels Dante's work. Indeed, Melville compares baby whales to "human infants [...] still spiritually feeding on some unearthly reminiscence [...]."(p. 497) Melville thus quotes from Dante in order to introduce in his novel a vision of supreme and divine goodness. He modifies, however, his source and confers an ironic turn on its significance by inserting the quotation into a specific context. The image of the circling whales, evocative of purity, contrasts sharply with Ahab's evil nature. Unlike Dante, Melville suggests that the principle of goodness is crushed by the forces of corruption. In *Ape*, O'Neill offers an equally ironic treatment of a quotation lifted from the *Divine Comedy*.

In an article entitled "O'Neill's Use of Dante in *The Fountain* and *The Hairy Ape*," Robert J. Andreach claims that O'Neill draws inspiration both from Dante's "Purgatorio" and "Paradiso" in several scenes of *Ape*.[17] While in scene iii, the dramatist inverts the pattern of Cantos XXCIII and XXXII in the "Purgatorio," scenes iv and viii reflect O'Neill's ironic vision of Dante's spiritual journey in the "Paradiso." In the "Purgatorio," Beatrice, who has left footprints in hell in order to give hope to Dante, enters in a flaming procession to reproach the poet for his sins. When she commands him to look at her, he is so ashamed that he drops his eyes to the stream. After confessing his faults, he is led by Beatrice in his ascent to the stars. Andreach contends that an equivalent of the confrontation between Dante and Beatrice can be found in the scene opposing Mildred to Yank. At the precise moment when the heroine appears, the fiery furnaces are open, an image reminiscent of Beatrice's flaming procession: "(Yank) sees Mildred, like a white apparition in the full light from the open furnace doors." (p. 58). In *Ape* as in the "Purgatorio," the hero becomes painfully aware of his identity in front of the white and fiery apparition. But while in the *Divine Comedy*, the sinner is finally saved, in *Ape*, the protagonist is doomed to death after his encounter with the messenger of God. In the subsequent scenes of the play, Yank feels irretrievably estranged from society. Both O'Neill and Melville imply that Dante's principle of goodness cannot remain unspoiled in the modern world. Whereas in *Moby Dick*, the image of purity evoked by Dante's *Divine Comedy* only fails to touch the mad Captain of the "Pequod," in *Ape*, the principle of goodness is shown to contain in itself the essence of evil. Indeed, it is Mildred's *presence* which hurls Yank to his doom. In *Moby Dick*, on the contrary, the infant whales Melville describes remain totally uncorrupted. Despite these differences in tragic vision, both O'Neill and Melville do make inverted use of the literary quotation drawn from Dante's *Divine Comedy*.[18]

Through the various formal elements I have examined in the sections on symbolism, myth-making, and literary quotation, O'Neill and Melville clearly evolve a kind of poetic realism bearing kinship to Richard Chase's American "romance." Moreover, these techniques, particularly those of literary quotation, reflect a modern vision of reality. In an article quoted before, Jean Weisgerber provides a theoretical survey of such a phenomenon.[19] In the light of that article, it is possible to interpret O'Neill's and Melville's quotations as a means of communicating with the reader. They represent invitations to interpret the work of art along subjective lines. Such literary stance prompts the reader to participate in the artists' search for a poetic realism mirroring their tragic concerns.[20]

CHAPTER VIII. SONGS OF AMERICAN EXPERIENCE

Seeking to define the American character was a task that fascinated O'Neill and Melville. It can be argued that their various works provide an answer to the classic question: what does it mean to be an American? Their realistic novels and plays can be compared in their kindred interpretation of the issues involved. They develop as it were themes which have not ceased to haunt the imagination of American writers for centuries.

They tend to adopt an autobiographical style of writing, a tendency regarded by critics as typically American. In their treatment of the sea motif, the two writers voice essentially American ideas. In their sea novels and plays, they transpose the American spatial disconnectedness and love of freedom. Both artists criticize American institutions derived from New England Puritanism and accordingly reject the so-called American materialism. Similarly, they debunk the harsh deity worshipped by Protestantism: the absence of faith in any organized religious system has often been considered as an essential factor of American experience. In their ever-evolving concept of tragedy, O'Neill and Melville also exhibit profound affinities as they endow the American common man with tragic qualities. They suggest, however, that true tragedy cannot take place on the American continent. Further, in adhering to the symbolistic and mythic methods of the romance genre, they betray their affiliation to an accepted American literary tradition. In summation, O'Neill's and Melville's works present the reader with an ironic reversal of Whitman's optimistic celebration of the possibilities of life in the New World set forth in *Leaves of Grass*.

This strain of pessimism has been regarded by Roy Harvey Pearce and R.W.B. Lewis as an essential component of American literature at large, including the novel and poetry. In other words, Melville and O'Neill express the recurrent preoccupation of American writers about the conflict between society and personal aspirations. Their works reflect what R.W.B. Lewis terms the American rediscovery of man's fall, showing as they do the failure of the pursuit of individual happiness on the American continent.[1]

The confluence of O'Neill's themes and techniques with those of Melville can be detected at all stages of evolution in the dramatist's canon. It would appear, however, that the affinities are most clearly manifested in O'Neill's early one-act plays of the sea, in the period spanning the years 1913 to 1921. In plays such as *Thirst, Cardiff*, and *Ape*, O'Neill's vision of the land/sea dichotomy possesses marked Melvillean overtones. In his middle period, O'Neill started experimenting with form and the land/sea opposition thus remained in the background of his work. In his later years, he reverted to his early realistic style and the land/sea polarity was reintroduced as a major element of meaning into his plays. In *Journey* and *Capricorn*, he explored metaphysical issues in resorting to the land/sea contrast. His plays are in this respect reminiscent of Melville's later works, such as *Billy Budd*. It is during the twenties that O'Neill's style moved closer to European expressionism than to Melville.

Although both O'Neill and Melville adopted a pessimistic viewpoint towards the nature of American experience, the dramatist voiced in a few instances a darker statement than the novelist about the future of American democracy. In *Iceman*, man is abandoned in an absurd universe ruled by death. If *Billy Budd* presents us with an equally godless world, Nature nonetheless offers some relief to the victims of fate. In O'Neill's play, on the contrary, the protagonists are faced with the wilderness of the city and cannot recapture the sense of identification with Nature pervading Melville's novella. But the difference separating O'Neill and Melville does not consist solely in the intense pessimism of the playwright, but also in O'Neill's modification of the models inherited from Melville. O'Neill integrated his sources into a highly personal context. He quoted either from Melville's *Typee* or from *Moby Dick* in order to underline the dissimilarity between the novelist's romantic world and a degraded modern universe. The methods by which O'Neill modified his borrowings are interesting to note. They comprise an examination of the model from various angles of vision—as in *Electra*; the use of ironic contrasts—as in *Ile*, and reduction to imagery—as in *Journey*.

In view of these resemblances and differences, should one use the word "confluence" or "influence" in order to designate the nature of the O'Neill-Melville connection? In most of the cases examined, one is clearly confronted with examples of confluence, i.e., parallels in vision. Instances of influence can however be found in *Ile, Diff'rent*, and *Electra* in which obvious references to Melville's novels can be recognized. However, in the three plays I have mentioned, O'Neill distanced himself from his model to such an extent that the concept of confluence implies a greater similarity with Melvillle's works than the notion of influence. In short, O'Neill's attitude towards his literary model proceeds from a divided vision, one alternating between admiration and rejection. The pattern of O'Neill's kinship with Melville thus duplicates the author's ambivalence towards Orientalism.[2]

The reason for such resemblances between the two writers can be attributed essentially to three factors, i.e., parallels in biography, similar readings, and identical historical background. Not only did O'Neill and Melville share a passion for sea adventures and the classic tragedies of Sophocles and Shakespeare, they also were heavily influenced in their pessimistic philosophy by the nature of the American society in which they lived. As I have mentioned in detail in my introduction, the documents preserved at the Beinecke indicate that O'Neill was an avid reader of books dealing with both the culture, the history, and the economy of the United States. In addition, it appears that Melville also read works relating to the social history of the United States. Merton Sealts reports that the author of *Moby Dick* possessed books about the American revolution and the civil war.[3] During the years in which O'Neill and Melville created their masterpieces, America underwent crises of a comparable intensity. Both writers lived in a time when American confidence was shaken by societal factors. When Melville launched on his artistic career, several financial panics occurred in the New World, in 1837 and 1857. During the Mexican War, around 1848, state deficits reached increasingly high levels. The political situation appeared equally critical as the United States was confronted with the Texas question, the Mexican War, and the acceleration leading to the Civil War. In response to these external elements, Melville voiced a critique of American idealism. Likewise, O'Neill lived in a period during which America experienced difficulty in achieving economic and political stability. The dramatist worked during the delicate period separating the two world wars. As in Melville's time, financial problems arose, first through war debts after 1918 and later through the crash of Wall Street in 1929. Subsequently, the Great Depression led New World citizens to doubt the validity of American democracy.[4] In his cycle of plays, "A Tale of Possessors Self-Dispossessed," O'Neill transcribed his pessimistic vision of American life and dramatized the progressive corruption of its democratic ideals. It can be argued, then, that O'Neill's and Melville's negative attitude towards the possibilities of life in America was motivated by historical factors of a similar nature.

The various motifs I have synthesized above represent only facets of the two authors' overall concept of American experience, one which eventually encompasses, in its varied implications, the human world. This philosophy takes its roots in Alexis de Tocqueville's prophetic study *Democracy in America*, which described the basic component of American culture as a tendency to "see the action of human events as being under the aegis of several antithetical deities: Chance, Mutability, Determinism, and Pantheism."[5] This view is echoed in O'Neill and Melville. In *Moby Dick*, in the chapter entitled "The Mat Maker," Ishmaël interprets modern machinery as a symbol of the Loom of Time, and concludes that "chance, free will, and necessity—(are) no wise incompatible." (p. 316) Elsewhere, in the chapter entitled "The Monkey-Rope," Ishmaël, depending for his survival on the success of Queequeg's dangerous mission, reflects on free will and Providence: "[...] my free will had received a mortal wound [...]. Therefore, I saw that there was a sort of interregnum in Providence [...]." (p. 426) In "The Mast-Head," in a passage quoted in Chapter III, a sailor engages in lengthy lyrical reveries and finally experiences a mystical union with nature, corresponding to Tocqueville's vision of Pantheism. In O'Neill, these motifs culminate, as Raleigh indicates, in *Journey*. Indeed, each of the four Tyrones believes in one of the four deities delineated by Tocqueville, in luck or Chance (James); in Mutability (Jamie); in Pantheism (Edmund); and in Determinism (Mary). Indeed, James Tyrone has more than once relied on Chance in the theatrical career that prompted him to devote all his energies to *The Count of Monte Cristo*; Jamie, a nihilist, affirms the ephemeral quality of all things; Edmund has experienced pantheistic unity in his walk through the fog; finally, Mary is persuaded that no one can avoid the influence of the past. Thus, both O'Neill and Melville reflect the basic uncertainty about fate and free-will that runs throughout American literature.[6]

It would seem correct at this point to submit that O'Neill was working in the context of two traditions, i.e., the European and the American.[7] My examination does not imply, of course, that analyses of the O'Neill canon in the light of European expressionism are no longer valid. On the contrary, I have tried to show that some of the dramatist's works contained elements derived from European writers and from American authors as well. Indeed, O'Neill appeared able to synthesize various types of influence into an original artistic result. In *Dynamo*, one can detect an expressionistic theme in the symbol of the machine. One can also interpret the theme of Prometheus and the electricity symbol of that play in terms of confluence with the American literary tradition. These symbols have been developed by Herman Melville in *Moby Dick*. Likewise, *Ape* includes characteristics inspired by Kaiser's plays while showing correspondences to Melville's *Moby Dick* in its color white symbolism. In other words, it is in the nature of his realism that O'Neill resembles the writers of the American tradition, particularly Melville.

In an article cited in my introduction, "le Jugement de Valeur en Littérature Comparée: Le Comparatisme au Service de l'Evaluation Artistique," Jean Weisgerber suggests that a comparison between the works of two authors can facilitate the task of evaluation.[8] In this case, O'Neill's capacity to reproduce patterns inherited from Melville and to integrate them harmoniously into the fabric of his plays bespeaks the richness of his craft. Moreover, his ability to combine and assimilate influences of both the European and the American traditions indicates the varied nature of his tastes and the broad scope of his literary interests.

The art of O'Neill, then, taking its roots in a double tradition, is a challenge for theatre practitioners of decades to come. Indeed, they will need to devise appropriate scenic devices to translate on the stage the playwright's tragic songs of American experience.

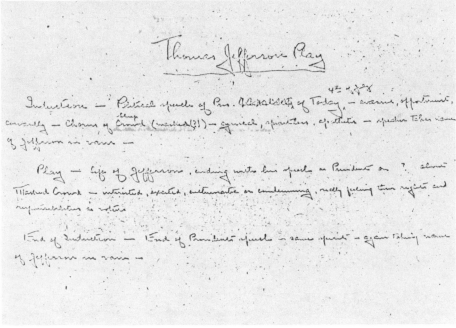

1. Draft for "Thomas Jefferson Play."
This manuscript evidences O'Neill's concern for issues connected with American culture and society.
This and the following three illustrations are reprinted with the kind permission of the Collection of American Literature, Beinecke Rare Book and Manuscript Library, Yale University.

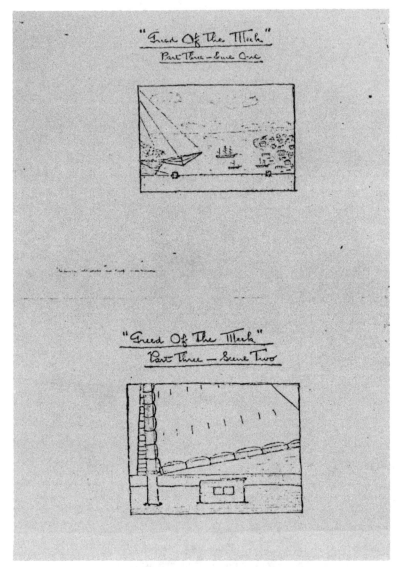

2. Sketches for the "Cycle Plays."
These designs, in the hand of O'Neill, reveal his passion for sailing vessels.

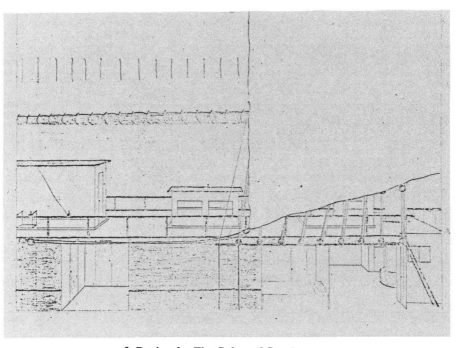

3. Design for *The Calms of Capricorn*.
In this and the following sketch by O'Neill, the playwright's fascination with
clipper ships is manifest.

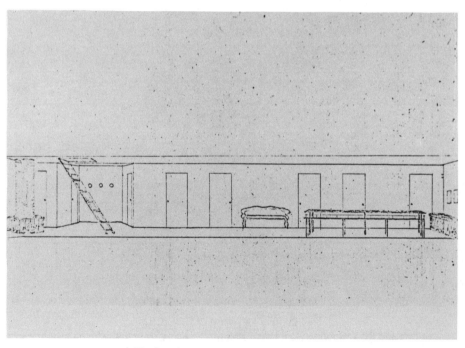

4. Design for *The Calms of Capricorn*.

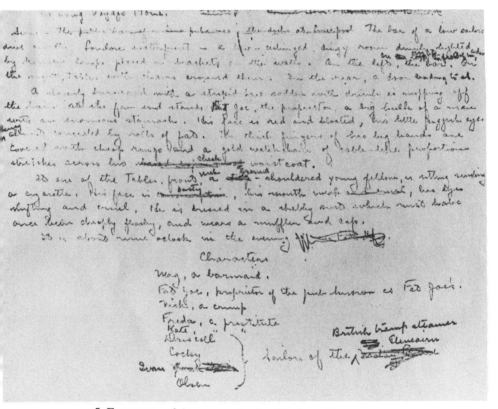

5. Front page of the manuscript for *The Long Voyage Home*.
O'Neill's initial intention for *The Long Voyage Home* was to use a setting
identical to that of Melville's *Redburn*, as his crossing out of the word
"Liverpool" indicates.
This illustration is reprinted with the kind permission of the Theatre Collection
of the Museum of the City of New York.

ENDNOTES

Chapter I. The Vision of O'Neill and Melville

[1]James A. Robinson, *Eugene O'Neill and Oriental Thought. A Divided Vision* (Carbondale and Edwardsville: Southern Illinois University Press, 1984).

Laurin Porter, *The Banished Prince. Time, Memory and Ritual in the Late Plays of Eugene O'Neill* (Ann Arbor and London: U.M.I. Research Press, 1988)

Peter Egri, *Chekhov and O'Neill. The Uses of the Short Story in Chekhov's and O'Neill's Plays* (Budapest: Akademiai Kiado, 1986).

Peter Egri, *The Birth of American Tragedy* (Budapest: Tankönyvkiado, 1988).

[2]Ward B. Lewis, *Eugene O'Neill. The German Reception of America's First Dramatist* (Berne: Peter Lang, 1984).

[3]Virginia Floyd, ed., *Eugene O'Neill at Work. Newly Released Ideas for the Theatre* (New York: Frederick Ungar, 1981).

[4]Judith E. Barlow, *Final Acts. The Creation of Three Late O'Neill Plays* (Athens: University of Georgia Press, 1985).

[5]Travis Bogard and Jackson Bryer, eds., *Selected Letters of Eugene O'Neill* (New Haven and London: Yale University Press, 1988)

Travis Bogard, ed., *The Unknown O'Neill. Unpublished or Unfamiliar Writings of Eugene O'Neill* (New Haven and London: Yale University Press, 1988).

Virginia Floyd, ed., *Eugene O'Neill. The Unfinished Plays. Notes for "The Visit of Malatesta," "The Last Conquest," "Blind Alley Guy."* (New York: Continuun, 1988).

[6]See Susan Harris Smith, "Generic Hegemony: American Drama and the Canon, " *American Quarterly*, 41, no. 1 (March 1989), pp. 112–122.

[7]See in this respect a recent article by C.W.E. Bigsby, "Why American Is Literature." In Debusscher, G. and Schvey, H., eds., *New Essays on American Drama* (Amsterdam and Atlanta: Rodopi, 1989), pp. 3–12. In this article, Bigsby refutes Robert Brustein's well-known assertion according to which American Drama is not literature.

[8]Harold Bloom, ed., *Modern Critical Views. Eugene O'Neill.* (New York: Chelsea House

Publishers, 1987), p. 1.

[9]See Martha Gilman Bower, ed., *Eugene O'Neill. More Stately Mansions. The Unexpurgated Edition* (New York: Oxford University Press, 1988).

[10]*The Calms of Capricorn. A Play. Developed from O'Neill's Scenario by Donald Gallup. With a Transcription of the Scenario* (New Haven and New York: Ticknor and Fields, 1982).

[11]Included in Jackson R. Bryer, ed., *"The Theatre We Worked For." The Letters of Eugene O'Neill to Kenneth Macgowan* (New Haven and London: Yale University Press, 1982), p. 21.

[12]In the Macmillan edition of 1929 published in New York (*Notes*, Beinecke, Za O'Neill 158x, p. 24).

[13]Respectively in the Dutton edition of 1933 (New York) and an edition of 1936 (*Notes*, Beinecke, Za O'Neill 158x, p. 23).

[14]In the New York edition of 1934 (*Notes*, Beinecke, Za O'Neill 158x, p. 22).

[15]In the Century edition published in New York in 1931 (*Notes*, Beinecke, Za O'Neill 158x, p. 36).

[16]The edition in which O'Neill read Clark's study is unkown. He used the Putnam edition of 1931 (New York) for McKay's *Some Famous Sailing Ships* (*Notes*, Beinecke, Za O'Neill 158x, p. 28).

[17]A.M.Saholski's *The Great American Land Bubble* (New York: Harper, 1932); E. Douglas Branch's *The Sentimental Years, 1836–1860* (New York, 1934); Henry Adam's *The Living Jefferson*; Claude G. Bowers's *Jefferson in Power*; Edward Pourne's *Spain in America*; Arthur W. Calhoun's *A Social History of the American Family* (vols. 1–3); George Catlin's *North American Indians* (vol. 2); Samuel Chamberlain's *Behold Williamsburg*; Howard Chapelle's *The History of the American Sailing Ships*; *Confederate States of America*, 2 vols.; Stefan Lorant's *The Emergence of Modern America* and *A History of American Life; Romantic Painting in America*; Thomas Low Nicholos's *40 Years of American Life*; Albert Jay Noch's *Jefferson*; Albert G. Robinson's *Old England Houses*, and Woodrow Wilson's *A History of the American People*. These details are recorded both in O'Neill's *Notes*, Beinecke, Za O'Neill 158x, pp. 25 and 27, and in his private library housed at C.W. Post College (Long Island University).

[18]Shays's rebellion was an uprising, chiefly of farmers, in Massachusetts in 1786–1787. The revolt constituted the culmination of five years of restless dissatisfaction growing out of high taxes, heavy indebtedness, and declining farm prices. The legislature repeal of the legal-tender status of paper money and its refusal to permit the offering of goods to satisfy debts meant that obligations had to be met with hard-to-obtain specie. Insurgents organized regiments, one of them

captained by Daniel Shays, a former Revolutionary War officer who was blamed by some for the entire insurrection. Shays's forces were routed at Petersham on February 4, 1787. The next legislature, sympathetic to the rebels, reduced estate taxes and ended the indefinite jailing of debtors. This above information is derived from Robert J. Taylor, "Shays's Rebellion," *Encyclopedia Americana* (New York: American Corporation, 1977), vol. 24, p. 679.

[19]In his *Notes*, Beinecke, Za O'Neill 158x, pp. 8–10.

[20]In his *Notes*, Beinecke, Za O'Neill 84, pp. 9–11.

[21]See for instance Esther M. Jackson, "The American Drama and the New World Vision," (Madison, Wisconsin: unpublished manuscript, 1981).

[22]Quoted in Jean Chothia, *Forging a Language. A Study of the Play of Eugene O'Neill* (Cambridge: Cambridge University Press, 1979), p. 20.

[23]See Normand Berlin, *Eugene O'Neill* (New York: Grove Press, Inc., 1982), pp. 40 ff.

[24]This survey is inspired by Esther M. Jackson's study quoted in note 21, pp. 1–31.

[25]Ibid., p. 26.

[26]See John Henry Raleigh, "Eugene O'Neill and the Escape from the Château d'If," in John Gassner, ed., *O'Neill. A Collection of Critical Essays* (Englewood Cliffs, N.J.: Prentice-Hall, Inc., 1964), pp. 7–22.

[27]See John Henry Raleigh, *The Plays of Eugene O'Neill* (Carbondale and Edwardsville: Southern Illinois University Press,1965), pp.259–65.

[28]Arthur and Barbara Gelb, *O'Neill* (New York and Evanston: Harper and Row, 1962), p. 155.

[29]In his *Notes*, Beinecke,Za O'Neill 158x, p. 20.

[30]In the manuscript notes for *A Touch of the Poet*, Beinecke, Za O'Neill 111x.

[31]In his *Notes*, Beinecke, Za O'Neill 84, p. 9.

[32]In his *Notes*, Beinecke, Za O'Neill 158x, p. 23.

[33]Robinson, op. cit., pp. 75–79.

[34]Raleigh deals with O'Neill's link with Thoreau in his book on the playwright, op. cit., pp. 64 and 244.

[35]In his notes for *A Touch of the Poet*, pp. 19–21 (Beinecke) and in his private library.

[36]In the Hougthon Mifflin edition published in Boston in 1927.

[37]In the Hougthon Mifflin edition published in Boston in 1939; mentioned in Robinson, op. cit., p. 1.

[38]In the following editions: 1) New York: W.E. Scott, 1936; 2) New York: The Heritage Club, 1939; 3) as edited by G.O. Blake, vol. 3.

[39]Eugene O'Neill, *Long Day's Journey into Night* (London: Jonathan Cape, 1982) p. 117.

I shall use this edition throughout this study.

[40]Jean Chothia, op.cit., p. 199.

[41]See bottom of note 17.

[42]This introduction is preserved in the Berg Collection of English and American Literature at the New York Public Library. It is a four-page typescript with the author's manuscript corrections. Quoted with the kind permission of the Henry W. and Albert A. Berg Collection, The New York Public Library, Astor, Lenox, and Tilden Foundations.

Louis Sheaffer suggests in *O'Neill. Son and Artist* (Boston and Toronto: Little, Brown and C°., 1973) that O'Neill borrowed directly from section 32 of *Song of Myself* in a piece he wrote in 1940 on the death of his dog. The short poem is entitled, "The Last Will and Testament of Silverdene Emblem O'Neill," pp. 518–579.

[43]See bottom of note 17.

[44]Joyce D.Kennedy, "*Pierre*'s Progeny: O'Neill and the Melville Revival," *English Studies in Canada*, 3, i (spring 1977), pp. 103–117.

James Mathews, "The House of Atreus and the House of the Seven Gables," *Emerson Society Quarterly*, 63 (spring 1971), pp. 31–36.

[45]Raleigh,*The Plays of Eugene O'Neill*, op. cit., pp. 246–248.

[46]Gelbs, op. cit., p. 613.

[47]See note 42.

[48]Esther Timar, "Possible Sources for Two O'Neill One-acts," *The Eugene O'Neill Newsletter*, 6, iii (winter 1982), pp. 2O–23.

[49]Joyce D. Kennedy, "O'Neill's Lavinia Mannon and the Dickinson Legend," *American Literature*, 49, i (1977), pp. 108–113.

[50]See my article "Translation as Communication of the Self: Jamesian Inner Monologue in O'Neill's *Strange Interlude* (1927)," In *Communicating and Translating. Essays in Honour of Jean Dierickx*, ed. G. Debusscher and J.-P. van Noppen (Bruxelles: Editions de l'Université de Bruxelles, 1985), pp. 319–328.

[51]Chothia, op. cit., pp. 199ff.

Peter Egri, "The Genetic and Generic Aspects of Stephen Crane's *The Red Badge of Courage*," in *Acta Litteraria Academiae Scientiarum Hungaricae*, 22 (1980), pp. 333–348.

[52]Van Wyck Brooks, *The Confident Years* (New York, 1952), pp. 551–552.

Oscar Cargill et al., *Eugene O'Neill and His Plays* (New York University Press, 1961), pp. 271–282.

Brooks also mentions similarities between O'Neill and authors such as Mencken, Steinbeck, Norris, London, and Hemingway.

O'Neill's reference to O.W. Holmes in *More Stately Mansions* should also be noted. The title of that play is borrowed directly from Holmes's poem "The Chambered Nautilus."

[53]Chothia, op. cit., p. 201.

[54]Letter to Beatrice Ashe, July 25, 1916; preserved in the Berg Collection.

[55]Susan Tuck, "House of Compson, House of Tyrone: Faulkner's Influence on O'Neill," *The Eugene O'Neill Newsletter*, 5, iii (winter 1981), pp. 10–16.

Susan Tuck, "The O'Neill–Faulkner Connection," In James J. Martine, ed., *Critical Essays on Eugene O'Neill* (Boston: G.K. Hall, 1984), pp. 196–206.

Susan Tuck, "O'Neill and Faulkner: Their Kindred Imaginations," *The Eugene O'Neill Newsletter*, 4, iii (winter 1980), pp. 19–20.

[56]See Travis Bogard, *Contour in Time. The Plays of Eugene O'Neill* (New York: Oxford University Press, 1972), pp. 91 and 353. Frank R. Cunningham's dissertation indirectly sheds light on the O'Neill-Melville relationship: "Eugene O'Neill's Romantic Phase, 1921–1925," Lehigh University, 1970; a more recent dissertation examines the link between between O'Neill and Melville exclusively from the perspective of their use of the myth of Dionysus: Marleen Lowel: "Melville and O'Neill in Search of a Nocturnal Paradise: the Myth of Dionysus Rediscovered," The George Washington University, 1988. Lowel's work differs considerably from my own study in that it restricts its focus on very few works by the two authors; further, it considers solely the authors' myth-making; it confers perhaps too much importance upon O'Neill's *The Ancient Mariner*, which was after all not until recently made available to the public and does not constitute an essential work of his canon; finally, it does not deal with the two writers' sea symbolism. The present study is far more encompassing in the motifs it is concerned with; further, Frederic I. Carpenter's *Eugene O'Neill* (New York: Twayne Publishers, 1979 [2]) is also of use to the student of the O'Neill-Melville connection, pp. 30, 72, 81, 130, 168–169.

[57]Raleigh, op. cit., pp. 250–258.

[58]Kennedy, op. cit., p. 114.

[59]Ronald T. Curran, "Insular Typees: Puritanism and Primitivism in *Mourning Becomes Electra*," *Revue des Langues Vivantes*, 41 (1975), pp. 371–377.

[60]Chothia, op. cit., p. 199.

[61]Louis Sheaffer, *O'Neill. Son and Playwright* (Boston and Toronto: Little, Brown, and C°, 1968), pp. 405–406 and 415–416. Personal letter dated 11 June 1984.

[62]*New York Herald Tribune*, 13 February 1921.

[63]Donald C. Gallup, former curator of the O'Neill Collection of the Beinecke Library, argued, in a private conversation, that this introduction had not been written by O'Neill. As no definite evidence has been offered, I have included quotations from this introduction. It is

composed in much the same manner as other O'Neill manuscripts, i.e., as a typed draft with subsequent handwritten corrections. Louis Sheaffer does not hesitate to lend credence to the authenticity of this introduction (*O'Neill. Son and Playwright*, pp. 207–208).

[64]See note 42 for bibliographical information on this Introduction.

[65]See *The Complete Poems of Hart Crane*, ed. Waldo Frank (New York: Doubleday Anchor Books, 1933), pp. 100–101.

[66]A copy of the list of books owned by O'Neill is preserved in the files of the O'Neill Collection at the Beinecke.

[67]in Kennedy,op. cit., p. 113.

In the collection of O'Neill's *Selected Letters* mentioned in note 5, no reference to Melville can be found. It is true, however, that O'Neill's epistles are not essentially literary, except perhaps those to Nathan, Macgowan, and Commins.

[68]Eugene O'Neill, *Mourning Becomes Electra* in *Nine Plays* (New York: The Modern Library, 1941), pp. 683–867. I shall use this edition throughout the present study.

[69]The first draft of *Mourning Becomes Electra* is housed at the Beinecke in file: Za O'Neill + 40x. Quoted with the kind permission of the Collection of American Literature, Beinecke Rare Book and Manuscript Library, Yale University, and of the Yale Committee on Literary Property.

[70]René Wellek, "The Crisis of Comparative Literature," in *Concepts of Criticism*, Stephen G. Nichols, Jr., ed. (New Haven and London: Yale University Press, 1963) pp. 282–295. This quotation is lifted from page 285.

[71]Jean Weisgerber, *Faulkner and Dostoevsky: Influence and Confluence*, translated by Dean McWilliams (Athens: Ohio University Press, 1974).

[72]Jean Weisgerber, "Le Jugement de Valeur en Littérature Comparée: le Comparatisme au Service de l'Evaluation Artistique," *Etudes Littéraires*, 7, ii (1974), pp. 229–243.

[73]Thornton Wilder, *American Characteristics and Other Essays* (New York: Harper and Row publishers, 1979). This quotation is lifted from "The American Loneliness," p. 35.

Chapter II. Autobiographical Journeys

[1]Whitman's quotation is lifted from the following edition: *Leaves of Grass* (New York: The New American Library, 1980).

Several theoretical studies have been useful in the composition of this chapter: Brigitte Scheer-Schäzler, "From Paracriticism to Parabiography? Ihab Hassan's Autobiography *Out of*

Egypt. Scenes and Arguments of an Autobiography," in Gilbert Debusscher, ed., *American Literature in Belgium* (Amsterdam: Rodopi, 1988), pp. 239–250; Albert E. Stone, "Autobiography in American Culture: Looking Back at the Seventies." *American Studies International*, 19, iii & iv (spring–summer 1981), pp. 3–14; Albert E. Stone, ed., *The American Autobiography. A Collection of Critical Essays* (Englewood Cliffs, NJ: Prentice-Hall, Inc., 1981); and James Olney, *Autobiography* (Princeton: Princeton University Press, 1980). Brigitte Scheer Schäzler interprets the autobiographical form as an attempt to analyze and justify the self as well as a desire to mythicize one's life. In an autobiographical work, the writer structures life through imagination and reconciles divergent selves. Albert E. Stone emphasizes the difference between the various components of autobiography: he distinguishes *bios*, or biographical sources; *graphein*, or writing process, and he finally stresses the role of autobiography as a device to exorcise memories of the past. The American autobiography, he argues, conflates personal history and community values so that an individual story often becomes a narrative with sociological implications.

2Bibliographical references for the Sheaffer study will be found in notes 42 and 61 from Chapter I. The biographical information with which I shall be concerned in this part of my study is derived from *O'Neill. Son and Playwright*.

Edwin Haviland Miller, *Melville* (New York: George Braziller, Inc., 1975).

3 See Miller, op. cit, p. 96.

4Miller, op. cit., p. 96 and p.103. I shall use the following edition of that novel: Herman Melville, *White-Jacket. The World in a Man of War* (Boston: the St Botolph Society, 19235).

5See Sheaffer, *O'Neill. Son and Playwright*, op. cit., pp. 54 and 102.

6I shall use the following edition of this play: *A Moon for the Misbegotten* (New York: Vintage Books, 1974).

7Miller, op. cit., pp. 53–72.

8*Redburn* (Harmondsworth: Penguin Books, 1982).

9Miller, op. cit., pp. 165–166.

10Sheaffer, *O'Neill. Son and Playwright*, op. cit., pp. 160–161, 215–216, 387–388.

11Preserved in the Beinecke, file Za O'Neill, Eq. 185x.

12Miller, op. cit. pp. 73–79.

13The following edition of *Moby Dick* will be used: *Moby Dick* (Harmondsworth: Penguin Books, 1984).

14*Pierre or, the Ambiguities* (New York: E.P. Dutton & Co., Inc., 1929).

15Sheaffer describes O'Neill's relationship with his mother in great detail in *O'Neill. Son and Playwright*, op. cit., pp. 156–157 and 467–468.

[16]Information derived from Miller, op. cit., pp. 19–117.

[17]This information is derived from Sheaffer, *O'Neill. Son and Playwright*, op. cit., pp. 90–208.

[18]Throughout this study, the following edition will be consulted: Herman Melville, *Typee* (Harmondsworth: Penguin Books, 1981).

The autobiographical aspect of *Typee, Moby Dick, Clarel* and *Billy Budd* is discussed in Miller, op. cit., pp. 118–219, and pp. 326–368.

[19]A more detailed analysis of the mythical structure of *Moby Dick* will be found in Gerard M. Sweeney, *Melville's Use of Classical Mythology* (Amsterdam: Rodopi, 1975), pp. 35–98.

[20]Albert Camus, *The Myth of Sysyphus*, trans. Justin O'Brien (New York: Alfred A. Knopf, 1955).

[21]See Robert Penn Warren, "Melville the Poet," in Richard Chase, ed., *Melville. A Collection of Critical Essays* (Englewood Cliffs, NJ: Prentice-Hall, 1962), pp. 144–145. See in particular p. 154.

[22]*Billy Budd (An Inside Narrative)* (Chicago and London: the University of Chicago Press, 1962). This edition will serve in all chapters of my study. In another of his later short stories of the sea: "John Marr," the novelist reverts to his early romantic tone when describing the fate of an old sailor having abandoned the sea.

Although the action of *Billy Budd* does not take place on an American vessel, I have chosen to include it in this analysis because critics have detected in this short story patterns reflective of the quality of American life, including the "melting pot" motif and the elevation of the ordinary person. Moreover, *Billy Budd* certainly reflects the American Adam theme running throughout 19th century American literature. See F.O. Matthiessen, *American Renaissance* (New York: Oxford University Press, 1941) pp. 500–514.

[23]A more detailed discussion of this aspect of American culture is provided by Thornton Wilder, op. cit., pp. 1–64.

[24]The autobiographical sources of *Cardiff* are asserted by Sheaffer, *O'Neill. Son and Playwright*, pp. 278–279.

[25]Sheaffer, *O'Neill. Son and Playwright*, p. 196.

[26]Eugene O'Neill, *Bound East for Cardiff* in *Seven Plays of the Sea* (New York: Vintage Books, 1972), pp. 31–51. In all subsequent chapters, quotations will be taken from this edition.

[27]It is interesting to note that in the first version of *Cardiff*, entitled "Children of the Sea," the playwright described the predicament of sailors with a greater degree of compassion than in the published work. See Sheaffer, *O'Neill, Son and Playwright*, pp. 278–279.

Although neither the setting nor the characters of *Cardiff* are typically American, I have chosen to consider this play because it can be viewed as O'Neill's dramatic presentation of the American "melting pot." Yank's fierce individualism also dramatizes an essential theme in the tradition of American literature. See Bogard, op. cit., pp. 3–44 and 63–94.

[28]In the *Electra* trilogy, O'Neill draws from his personal experience to describe both the North and South Seas. While the realistic presentation of the ships anchored in the harbor of East Boston (Act IV of *The Hunted*) indicates O'Neill's familiarity with the Atlantic ocean, it is also conceivable that his travels to the Far East in 1928 should have influenced him in the shaping of the South Sea Islands motif running through the work. While sailing through seas of a quality akin to Orin's enchanted South Seas, O'Neill was composing his play (in the *Notes for Mourning Becomes Electra* preserved at the Beinecke, file Za O'Neill 125).

[29]In *Electra*, it should be remarked, O'Neill deals with the question of God in oblique terms, i.e., through theatrical language. Instead of naming the Puritan divinity pursuing the Mannons directly, the playwright chooses to show the effects of the revenge of that deity in a dramatic fashion. One will find a detailed analysis of that technique in Stephen L. Fluckiger, "The Idea of Puritanism in the Plays of Eugene O'Neill," *Renascence*, 30 (1978), pp. 152–162.

[30]Sheaffer has defined the autobiographical strain of *Iceman* in *O'Neill. Son and Artist*, pp. 489–499. Quotations will be from *The Iceman Cometh* (New York: Vintage Books, 1957)

[31]For the autobiographical sources of *Journey*, see Sheaffer, *O'Neill. Son and Artist*, pp. 510–512.

[32]In *Misbegotten*, a play written in 1943, O'Neill uses a modified form of sea symbolism, that ties in to some extent with his existential vision. Jamie Tyrone defines the nature of his pipe-dreams in terms of sea imagery: "Whether it's the bottom of a bottle, or a South Sea Island, we'd find our own ghosts there waiting to greet us [...]." (p. 87) Memories of the sea thus serve to epitomize man's illusions.

[33]For a definition of the concepts of *bios* and *graphein*, see the bottom of note 1 in this chapter.

[34]Some exceptions to that chronological pattern exist. Melville's *Israël*, written after *Moby Dick*, goes back to the romantic vision of the sea found in the early romances such as *Typee*. O'Neill's *Wilderness*, composed after *Electra*, shows a sentimental treatment of the sea motif.

[35]See Albert E. Stone, op. cit., pp. 1–10.

Chapter III. Mariners and Mystics

[1]Walt Whitman, "In Cabin'd Ships at Sea" in *Leaves of Grass*, op. cit., pp. 31–32.

[2]Two critics have analyzed Conrad's influence on the early plays of Eugene O'Neill: Louis Sheaffer in *O'Neill. Son and Paywright*, pp. 149–150 and Travis Bogard, op. cit., pp. 38–42.

[3]Joseph Conrad, *The Nigger of the Narcissus* (Harmondsworth: Penguin Books, 1977), pp. 15–143.

[4]Bogard, op. cit. p. 4O. The difference between O'Neill's and Conrad's sentimentalism is essentially one of degree. Although *Cardiff* contains sentimental and melodramatic overtones which may be compared with the tone of Conrad's story, the overall effect the playwright achieves departs slightly, through the delineation of a harsh God figure, from the British novelist's brand of realism.

[5]Professor Paul Voelker, from the University of Wisconsin Center-Richland, detailed O'Neill's indebtedness to Conrad in *Bound East for Cardiff* at the 1986 special session of the "Eugene O'Neill Society " at the New York MLA Convention. The topic of the session was "O'Neill: the Composition Process." The title of Professor Voelker's presentation was: "The Evolution of *Bound East for Cardiff*: From Conrad's novel to the Theatre on the Wharf."

[6]See Harold Beaver in his introduction to the edition of *Moby Dick* used throughout the present study, op. cit., p. 2O.

See also Leon Seltzer, *The Vision of Melville and Conrad. A Comparative Study* (Athens: Ohio University Press, 1970), pp. 54ff.

[7]See Merton Sealts, *Melville's Reading. A Cheklist of Books Owned and Borrowed* (Madison, Milwaukee and London: the University of Wisconsin Press, 1966), p. 52.

[8]This play was performed by the Provincetown Players in 1924.

[9]Gaston Bachelard, *L'Eeau et les Rêves. Essai sur l'Imagination de la Matière* (Paris: Corti, 1947).

When referring to O'Neill's and Melville's vision of the sea, I shall use either the terms "sea motif" or "sea symbol," depending on the type of approach I shall be using, i.e., whether literary or linguistic. According to Raymond Trousson in *Un Problème de Littérature Comparée: Les Etudes de Thèmes. Essai de Méthodologie* (Paris: Lettres Modernes, 1965), the term "motif" can be used to designate concerns of a generic nature whereas "theme" has a more specific connotation. I shall favor the term "motif" to emphasize the link between the works I shall analyze and sea literature at large.

My definition of symbolism lies in a theoretical study by Lambros Couloubaritisis, "Symbole et Métaphore," *Cahier du Groupe de Recherches sur la Philosophie et le Langage*, 9 (1988), pp.190–211.

According to Couloubaritsis, the symbol transforms a mere sign by integrating it into a semantic field differing from the one to which it would normally belong. As such, the symbol allows us to see the invisible and unspeakable realms of experience. Thus, Couloubaritsis uses the phrase "sur-déterminé par rapport à un champ sémantique donné " ("over-determined *vis-à-vis* any given semantic field") to describe the nature of symbol (pp. 204–206). Needless to say, Couloubaritsis' definition admirably works for O'Neill's and Melville's romantic symbolism, which explores the depths of the "unspeakable and the invisible" levels of human life.

[10]See Ronald T. Curran, op. cit., p. 169, and Joyce Deveau Kennedy, op. cit., p. 168.

[11]See note 69, Chapter I.

[12]Jean Weisgerber, "The Use of Quotations in Recent Literature," *Comparative Literature*, XXII (winter 1970), pp. 36–45.

[13]The subject-matter of this chapter was first printed in *Eugene O'Neill and the Emergence of American Drama*, ed. Marc Maufort (Amsterdam and Atlanta: Rodopi, 1989), pp. 85–96, under the title "*Typee* Revisited: O'Neill's *Mourning Becomes Electra* and Melville."

[14]See Travis Bogard, op. cit., pp. 91-92; and John H. Raleigh, op. cit., pp. 52–53 and 256–258.

[15]All quotations from *Ile* will be lifted from the same edition: *Seven Plays of the Sea*, op. cit., pp. 109–134.

[16]For a detailed definition of the concept of ironic fate, see Travis Bogard, op. cit., pp. 6–94.

[17]See F.O Matthiessen, *American Renaissance*, op. cit., p. 406 and pp. 455–456.

[18]See note 35, Chapter I.

[19]The following edition will be used throughout this study: *Where the Cross Is Made* in *Seven PLays of the Sea*, op. cit., pp. 135–162.

[20]See note 61, Chapter I.

[21]Subsequent references from *Diff'rent* will be from *Six Short Plays of Eugene O'Neill* (New York: Vintage Books, 1951), pp. 195–253.

[22]In her dissertation quoted above, Lowel deals with the theme of mysticism in Melville and O'Neill from a perspective differing radically from the one I have chosen to adopt. She relates this mysticism to the myth of Dyonysus, without considering it as a part of the writers' sea imagery.

[23]Subsequent quotations will refer to the same edition: *Omoo, A Romance of the South Seas* (Boston: the St Botolph Society, 1922[5]).

[24]See F.O. Matthiessen, op. cit., note 17, Chapter III.

[25]I shall use the following edition of *Beyond the Horizon*: (New York: Dramatists Play Service, Inc., 1947).

[26]All further quotations will be from: *Chris Christopherson* (New York: Random House, 1982).

[27]All quotations from *Anna Christie* will be from this edition:*The Hairy Ape and other Plays* (London: Jonathan Cape, 1936).

[28]I shall quote from this edition of *Ape: Nine Plays* (New York: The Modern Library, 1941), pp. 37–88.

[29]See Raleigh, op. cit., pp. 278–280.

[30]See Raleigh, op. cit., 259–265, and Frederick Wilkins's review of Roger Asselineau's *The Transcendentalist Constant in American Literature* in *The Eugene O'Neill Newsletter*, VI, 2 (S/F 1982), pp. 43–45 (especially p. 45).

[31]See Perry Miller, *Errand into the Wilderness*, (Cambridge, MA: the Belknap Press of Harvard University Press, 1956), pp. 217ff; and T. Wilder, op. cit., pp. 13–14. Wilder emphasizes the disconnectedness of the American citizen, his impossibility of belonging in any definite setting.

The subject-matter of the "sea mystique" section of this chapter first appeared in a modified version in *The Theatre Annual*, XLII (1988), pp. 31–52, under the title: "Mariners and Mystics: Echoes of *Moby Dick* in O'Neill."

Chapter IV. Tragic Tensions of Land and Sea

[1]John Henry Raleigh has suggested the existence of such basic polarity in his book cited earlier. He does not specifically analyze O'Neill's land/sea dichotomy in close connection with Melville's.

[2]John Henry Raleigh mentions a parallel between *Journey* and *Redburn* very briefly, without analyzing O'Neill's possible borrowing in depth, op. cit., p. 252.

[3]Lesser known works by O'Neill prolong the sea imagery of his published works. Shortly after completing *Cardiff*, O'Neill started working on another sea play, which he never finished, "The Personal Equation, or the Second Engineer." Törnqvist signals in *A Drama of Souls* (New Haven: Yale University Press, 1969) that this work dates back to 1915 (p. 259). This manuscript is preserved in the Houghton Library of Harvard University (file n°. Ms Thr. 18.10). The plot of this projected play can be summarized as follows: the International Workers of the World want to

provoke a universal revolution in order to prevent war. Tom and Olga, the heroes of "The personal Equation," are involved in the conflict and Tom accepts to act a revolutionary role on the "S.S. San Francisco," on which his father serves as a second engineer. The father, Perkins, loves the engines of his ship and when Tom attempts to destroy them, almost kills his son. After the accident, Tom is condemned to live in a perpetual state of mental retardation. Perkins and Olga decide to devote their life to curing him. "The Personal Equation" gives another instance of O'Neill's fascination for life at sea through his depiction of Perkins' admiration for this ship. "The Personal Equation" has recently been published in Travis Bogard, ed., *The Unknown O'Neill*, op. cit., pp. 3–75. During the same period, O'Neill was working on the scenarios of other sea plays, as his notes housed in the Beinecke indicate. In his *Notebook, 1918–1920* (file Za O'Neill + 80x), O'Neill made notes for three plays, of which the setting would have resembled that of Melville's novels: their action would have taken place in the South Seas. Therefore, they deserve to be briefly considered here. The first of these scenarios can be likened to *Typee*: the dramatist intended to write about an abandoned sailor of a whaling vessel in the Marquesas, a Polynesian environment reminiscent of that of Melville's novels. The sailor would have been taken care of by the natives but would eventually have escaped (p. 17). In a second scenario, the playwright would have dealt with the theme of reincarnation in China and would have alluded to a South Sea Island, of which many can be found in Melville's works (p. 18). A third scenario focuses on the story of a Spanish sailor on board a ship called "The Antilles" (p. 19). O'Neill's manuscripts prolong the motifs detected in his published works.

[4]Throughout this study, I shall use the following edition of *The Long Voyage Home*:*Seven Plays of the Sea* , op. cit., pp. 53–77.

[5]On page 1 of O'Neill's manuscript for *Long Voyage,* preserved at the Museum of the City of New York.

[6]Quotations from *Thirst* will be taken from *Ten Lost Plays* (New York: Random House, 1964), pp. 1–32.

[7]Quotations from *Capricorn* will be taken from the edition mentioned in note 10 of Chapter I.

[8]*Fog*, in *Ten Lost Plays*, op. cit., pp. 83–107. All citations will refer to this edition.

[9]Chothia, op. cit., p. 199.

[10]*Mardi* (Boston: the St Botolph Society, 1923[5]). Subsequent quotations will be from the same edition.

[11]Quotations from *Marco* will be from this edition: *Nine Plays*, op. cit., pp. 207–303.

[12]Quotations from *Zone* will be from this edition:*Seven Plays of the Sea*, op. cit., pp. 79–107.

13Travis Bogard relates O'Neill's "Blessed Islands" to the philosophy of Nietzsche, op. cit., p. 351.

14"The Encantadas", in *Billy Budd, Sailor and other stories* (Harmondsworth: Penguin Books, 1982), pp. 129–194.

15"Benito Cereno" in *Billy Budd, Sailor and other stories*, op. cit., pp. 215–307.

Chapter V. Tales of Yankees and Puritans

1Several studies have been useful in the composition of this chapter: Perry Miller, *The American Puritans: Their Prose and Poetry* (Garden City, New York: Doubleday Anchor Books, 1956) and *Errand into the Wilderness*, op. cit.; Ursula Brumm, *Die Religiöse Typologie im Amerikanischen Denken* (Leiden: E.J. Brill, 1963); Sacvan Bercovitch, *The Puritan Origins of the American Self* (New Haven and London: Yale University Press, 1975); Jean Béranger and Robert Rouge, *Histoire des Idées aux U.S.A. Du XVIIème siècle à nos jours* (Paris: Presses Universitaires de France, 1981); and Emory Elliott, ed., *Puritan Influences in American Literature* (Urbana, Chicago, London: University of Illinois Press, 1979). Throughout this chapter, the term "Puritanism" will be meant in a generic sense, as synonymous with Protestantism at large, rather than as designating a specific historical movement. My notion of the term "Yankee" as signifying secular, rational, is derived from Gilbert Debusscher's "Profils de la Littérature des Etats-Unis." In Dorsingfang-Smets, A., ed., *L'Amérique du Nord. Histoire et Culture* (Bruxelles: Meddens, 1975), pp. 158–214.

2See Edwin H. Miller, op. cit., pp.172–191 and Sheaffer, *Son and Playwright*, pp.50–54.

3Sacvan Bercovitch considers at length the failure of America to become a New Jerusalem in the study cited above, chapter 5 "The Myth of America," pp. 136–186. See also Frederick Wilkins,"The Pressure of Puritanism in Eugene O'Neill's New England Plays" in Virginia Floyd, ed., *Eugene O'Neill. A World View* (New York: Frederick Ungar, 1979), pp. 237–244.

4In interpreting Melville's critique of American materialism, I have been aided by two articles: Robert Zoellner, "Queequeg: The Well-Governed Shark" in Michael T. Gilmore, ed. *Twentieh Century Interpretations of Moby Dick* (Englewood Cliffs, NJ: Prentice-Hall, Inc., 1977), pp. 87–93; and Richard Harter Fogle, "Benito Cereno" in *Melville. A Collection of Critical Essays*, edited by Richard Chase, pp. 116–124.

Throughout this chapter, I shall use the terms "satire" and "irony" as defined by Jean Weisgerber in "Irony and Satire as Means of Communication," *Comparative Literature Studies*,

10, ii (June 1973), pp. 157–172. Weisgerber argues that satire conveys something positive as a norm is opposed to a real but allegedly unsatisfactory state of affairs. Second, satire communicates indirectly by taking the shape of an attack shedding light on the very reverse of what is actually being recommended. It is important to note that satire is often directed towards a particular person.This will be the case of O'Neill's satire of Reverend Dickey.

Irony, Weisgerber argues, prompts the reader to search for truth, a wisdom that is different from a real but allegedly unsatisfactory state of affairs. The communication imparted through irony is indirect because it takes the shape of a veiled attack. Unlike satire, irony can concentrate on elusive persons. This ironic mode, abstract by definition, is one O'Neill and Melville most often employ.

5In two early works, O'Neill had already criticized American optimism. In *Thirst* (1913), the playwright focuses on three individuals lost on a raft in the middle of the ocean after the sinking of their ship. Among them, a gentleman refuses to admit the terrible predicament with which he is confronted. If in this first one-act play of the sea, O'Neill's critique of American optimism is not specifically related to American materialism, in *Fog* (1914), the dramatist satirizes the exaggerated optimism of an American businessman lost on a raft in the fog of the North Atlantic ocean, near Newfoundland. O'Neill's protagonists risk to collide with an iceberg. In this threatening environment, the businessman adopts an optimistic attitude. Because O'Neill's criticism of American materialism is not yet fully developed in those works, I have preferred to leave them out of consideration.

6One will find a historical study of Puritan racial intolerance in Viola Sachs, ed., *Le Blanc et le Noir chez Melville et Faulkner* (Paris, The Hague: Mouton, 1974), pp. 11–12.

7My interpretation of the role of Pip in *Moby Dick* was influenced by Charles Olson's article: "Ahab and his Fool" in Michael T. Gilmore, ed., op. cit., pp. 55–58.

8In his study *Eugene O'Neill in Ireland. The Critical Reception* (Westport, CT: Greenwood Press, 1988), Edward L. Shaughnessy explains that Catholicism in America had marked Jansenist characteristics, comparable to those of Protestantism. In this respect, the 1885 Baltimore Cathechism may have been responsible for the emergence of an authoritarian form of Catholicism in America, p. 16.

9Eugene O'Neill, *All God's Chillun Got Wings* in *Nine Plays*, pp. 89–133. The same edition will serve throughout this study.

10Raleigh has insisted on the importance of the past in O'Neill, op. cit., pp. 37–95.

11*Israël Potter. His Fifty Years of Exile* (Boston: the St Botolph Society, 1925).

12*A Touch of the Poet* (New York: Vintage Books, 1983).

13Three critics have noted the parallels existing between Puritanism, Transcendentalism, and the American Renaissance: Ursula Brumm, op. cit., pp. 86-90; P. Miller, *Errand into the Wilderness*, pp. 185–192; and Sacvan Bercovitch, op. cit., p. 163.

[14]Quoted by F.O. Matthiessen, op. cit., p. 472.

[15]Ibid, p. 472.

[16]All quotations will be lifted from the following edition: *The Confidence-Man* (London: John Lehmann, 1948).

[17]F.O. Matthiessen, op. cit., p. 472, and Daniel G. Hoffman; "The Confidence-Man: His Masquerade" in Richard Chase, op. cit., pp. 125–143.

[18]See note 30, chapter I.

[19]All quotations will be from *More Stately Mansions* (New Haven and London: Yale University Press, 1979 [7]).

[20]Quoted in Floyd, *A World View*, p. 5.

[21]This information is derived from T. Walter Herbert, Jr., *Moby Dick and Calvinism. A World Dismantled* (New Brunswick, NJ: Rutgers University Press, 1977), pp. 21–56.

[22]Quoted by Joseph Wood Krutch in his introduction to O'Neill's *Nine Plays*, p. XVII.

[23]T. Walter Herbert argues that Melville translated in *Moby Dick* the nineteenth century controversy between Calvinism (the harsh God of Ahab) and Unitarianism (the gentle God Ishmaël is questing). Melville was apparently exposed to the two conflicting influences through his parents (pp. 21–56).

[24]See Virginia Floyd, *A World View*, p. 191.

[25]See note 20, Chapter II.

[26]See Margot Seidel, *Bibel und Christentum in Dramatischen Werk Eugene O'Neills* (Frankfurt, Berne und New York: Peter Lang, 1984), pp. 86–90.

[27]*Clarel. A Poem and Pilgrimage in the Holy Land* (New York: Hendricks House, 1960)

[28]For a fuller treatment of Melville's vision of faith in *Clarel*, see Stan Goldman, "The Small Voice of Silence: Melville's Narrative Voices in *Clarel*" *Melville Society Extracts*,76 (February 1989), p. 9.

[29]For a fuller treatment of this double language in O'Neill, see Shaughnessy, op.cit., p. 18.

[30]In other words, O'Neill's dramatization of these religious issues is sometimes "oblique." One will find a detailed study of O'Neill's indirect delineation of the Puritan God in Stephen L. Fluckiger, op. cit., note 29, Chapter II.

[31]All quotations will from now on be lifted from the following edition: *Desire Under the Elms* in *Nine Plays*, op. cit., pp. 135–206.

[32]Eugene O'Neill, *The Great God Brown* in *Nine Plays*, pp. 305–377. I shall quote from this edition in subsequent chapters as well.

[33]*Strange Interlude*, in *Nine Plays*, op.cit., pp. 483–682.

[34]*Dynamo*, in *Lazarus Laughed and other Plays* (London: Jonathan Cape, 1929).

[35]More information on O'Neill's treatment of the biblical "Joseph" motif can be found in Kurt Eisen, "Eugene O'Neill's Joseph: A Touch of the Dreamer," *Comparative Drama*, vol. 23 , no. 4 (winter 1989–90), pp. 344–358.

[36]An analysis of American religious thoughts is provided by William T. Going, "Eugene O'Neill, American," *Papers on Language and Literature*, 12 (1976), pp. 384–401.

Chapter VI. An American Tragedy

[1]The title of this chapter is directly inspired by Theodore Dreiser's novel, *An American Tragedy*, which belongs to the tradition in which O'Neill and Melville are working.

[2]For more information on the antecedents of the domestic tragedy, see Oscar G. Brockett, *History of the Theatre* (Boston: Allyn and Bacon, 1982 [4]), pp. 367–368, 396–398, and 546–548.

[3]Matthiessen, op. cit., pp. 406 ff.

[4]This information is derived from F.O. Matthiessen, op. cit., pp. 186–197, and pp. 412–413. Melville read Shakespeare in 1849, Hawthorne in 1850.

[5]Quoted in Clifford Leech, *O'Neill* (New York: Barnes and Noble, Inc., 1965), pp. 75–76.

[6]Quoted in Doris V. Falk, *Eugene O'Neill and the Tragic Tension. An Interpretive Study of the Plays* (New Brunswick, NJ: Rutgers University Press, 1958), p. 26.

[7]Quotations from Emerson's essays are lifted from the following edition: "Tragedy " in *The Early Lectures of Ralph Waldo Emerson*, ed. Robert E. Spiller and Wallace E. Williams, 3 vols. (Cambridge, MA: Harvard University Press, 1959–1972).

[8]This quotation is derived from Robert Martin, ed., *The Theatre Essays of Arthur Miller* (New York: The Viking Press, 1978). I have focused on two essays: "Tragedy and the Common Man ", pp. 3–7 and "The Nature of Tragedy", pp. 8–11.

[9]This theme is developed by R.W.B. Lewis in his study: *The American Adam* (Chicago: Chicago University Press, 1955).

[10]I have included a discussion of *Long Voyage* in this study despite its Scandinavian protagonist because it reflects the motif of the fall from innocence, a theme which, according to R.W.B. Lewis, recurs in all major American literature.

[11]See Travis Bogard, op. cit., pp. 199–225.

[12]One will find a more detailed analysis of the relationship between Ishmaël and Ahab in an

article by Marius Bewley, "Melville and the Democratic Experience," in Richard Chase, op. cit., pp. 91–115. Bewley remarks that although Ahab is a common man, the novelist ironically compares him to the Ancient King Ahab, who was punished for his pride, pp. 96–98.

[13]C.W.E. Bigsby mentions a parallel between O'Neill's work and *Moby Dick*, although he does not explore it in depth: in *A Critical Introduction to Twentieth-Century American Drama*, vol. I, 1900–1940 (Cambridge: Cambridge University Press, 1982), p. 91 and p. 94.

[14]Ibid., pp. 87–91.

[15]This section was first published in *The Recorder,* vol. 3, no. 1 (summer 1989), pp. 27–36, under the title "Tragedy and Solipsism: The Kinship of *Moby Dick* and *The Iceman Cometh*."

[16]In the article mentioned in note 44, Chapter I.

[17]This section was first published in *The Eugene O'Neill Newsletter,* vol. XI, no. 2 (1987), pp. 23–28, under the title: "The Legacy of Melville's *Pierre*: Family Relationships in *Mourning Becomes Electra*."

[18]In his article "Billy Budd, Foretopman," in Richard Chase, ed., op. cit., pp. 157–158, Matthiessen argues that the events taking place on board the ship depicted in *Billy Budd* duplicate historical events which took place aboard the U.S. Somers. Moreover, the fate of Billy Budd reflects the fall of the American Adam, a view corroborated by the fact that Melville made references to Jonathan Edwards, a representative of Puritanism, in the drafts of his novella. These elements prompt me to include *Billy Budd* in a discussion of Melville's "American" vision.

[19]In his introduction to the edition of *Moby Dick* already cited (pp. 20–42), Harold Beaver asserts that Camus was influenced by *Moby Dick* in composing *The Myth of Sysyphus* (p. 38).

[20]In *Journey,* Catholicism has almost completely disappeared. Indeed, Tyrone reproaches his sons for having abandoned their faith in the following terms: "[…] you've flouted the faith you were born and brought up in—the one true faith of the Catholic church—and your denial has brought nothing but self-destruction." (p. 66)

[21]The phrase "exile without remedy" is borrowed from an essay by Denis J. Rich: "Exile Without Remedy: The Late Plays of Eugene O'Neill," in Floyd, *A World View,* pp. 257–276.

[22]Quoted in Sculley Bradley, ed., *The American Tradition in Literature* (New York: W.W. Norton , 1967), vol. I, p. 315.

[23]Matthiessen, op.cit., p. 459.

[24]This phrase is directly borrowed from the title of Doris V. Falk's study mentioned in note 6, Chapter VI.

[25]The phrase "ungodly god-like" is lifted from Captain Peleg's description of Ahab in the chapter entitled "The Ship" from *Moby Dick,* p. 176.

[26]See Michael Manheim, "The Transcendence of Melodrama in *Long Day's Journey into Night.*" In Shyamal Bagchee, ed., *Perspectives on O'Neill: New Essays, English Literary Studies*, 43 (1988), pp.33–42.

Chapter VII. In Search of Poetic Realism

[1]This connection between Kazan and poetic realism is a notion derived from Brenda Murphy's paper entitled: "Miller, Kazan, and Mielziner: American Drama as a Collaborative Art." This presentation was part of the MLA special session on American Drama, which took place at the 1986 MLA convention in New York on Monday, 29 December.

[2]This quotation is lifted from Richard Chase, *The American Novel and Its Tradition* (Garden City, New York: Doubleday Anchor, 1957) pp. ix, 13. One will find an analysis of O'Neill's indebtedness to the American romance genre in more general terms in Michael Hinden's article "*Desire Under the Elms*: O'Neill and the American Romance," *Forum Houston*, 15, i (1977), pp. 44–51. Likewise, Richard Chase has provided an insightful examination of the elements derived from the romance genre in Melville's *Moby Dick* in an article entitled "Melville and *Moby Dick*," in *Melville. A Collection of Critical Essays*, Richard Chase, ed., pp. 49–61.

[3]For a definition of my use of the concept of "symbolism " in the romantic sense, see note 9, Chapter III.

[4]In *Electra*, O'Neill also endows the color white with negative overtones in associating it with Puritanism. Christine feels repulsed by that unsavory feature of the Mannon house: "Each time I come back after being away it appears more like a sepulchre! The 'Whited' one of the Bible—pagan temple front stuck like a mask on Puritan gray ugliness!" (p. 699)

[5]As suggested by John Henry Raleigh, op. cit., p. 248.

[6]See W. H. Auden, *The Enchafed Flood. Or the Romantic Iconography of the Sea* (New York: Vintage Books, 1967).

[7]See note 1, Chapter II for full bibliographical references.

[8]*The Rope* in *Seven Plays of the Sea* (New York: Vintage Books, 1972), pp. 163–199.

[9]See Bogard, op. cit., pp. 105–107. The ending of *Rope* offers yet a second ironic twist to the biblical story of Abraham. While at first, the father seems willing to kill his son when presenting him the rope, O'Neill makes it eventually clear that the elder protagonist's intentions were not essentially murderous. Indeed, towards the end of the play, it is revealed that above the rope was hidden the father's inheritance. Had he followed his father's seemingly cruel orders,

Luke would have been enriched.

[10]Mircea Eliade, *Aspects du Mythe* (Paris: Gallimard, 1963) and *Mythes, Rêves et Mystères* (Paris: Gallimard, 1972).

[11]Roger Caillois, *Le Mythe et l'Homme* (Paris: Gallimard, 1972).

[12]Joseph Fontenrose, *The Ritual Theory of Myth* (Berkeley–Los Angeles: University of California Press, 1966).

[13]See Gerard M. Sweeney, op. cit., p. 105 for a treatment of the myth of Orestes in Melville's works; for O'Neill's vision of the same pattern, see Joyce D. Kennedy, op. cit., p. 221.

[14]See Gerard M. Sweeney, op. cit., p. 38.

[15]Raleigh, p. 248.

[16]Marius Bewley, "Melville and the Democratic Experience" in *Melville. A Collection of Critical Essays,* Richard Chase, ed., pp. 91–115. Bewley's reference to Dante can be found on p. 103.

[17]Robert J. Andreach, "O'Neill's Use of Dante in *The Fountain* and *The Hairy Ape,*" *Modern Drama,* 10 (1967), pp. 48–56.

[18]Further, the two writers sometimes allude to Shakespeare's *Hamlet.* For Melville's treatment of these *Hamlet* quotations, see Gerard M. Sweeney, op. cit., pp. 102–103.

For O'Neill's indebtedness to the Hamlet story, see Horst Frenz and Martin Mueller, "More Shakespeare and Less Aeschylus in Eugene O'Neill's *Mourning Becomes Electra,*" *American Literature,* 38 (Mr. 1966), pp. 85–100.

[19]Jean Weisgerber, "The Use of Quotations in Recent Literature," op. cit., see note 8, Chapter II.

[20]Several critics have regarded O'Neill as being at the crossroads of modernism and postmodernism. See for instance John V. Antush, "Eugene O'Neill: Modern and Postmodern", *The Eugene O'Neill Review,* vol. 13, no. 1 (spring 1989), pp. 14–26. The playwright's ironic stance in his use of citations defines him as a postmodern rather than as a modernist. Indeed, modernism tended to resort to literary quotation as a means of reasserting the supremacy of tradition.

Chapter VIII. Songs of American Experience

[1]See Roy Harvey Pearce, *The Continuity of American Poetry* (Princeton: University Press, 1961); and R.W.B. Lewis, *The American Adam* (Chicago University Press, 1955).

[2]As has been documented abundantly by James A. Robinson, op. cit. (note 1, Chapter I). The very subtitle of Robinson's study indicates O'Neill's ambivalence towards his model: *A Divided Vision*.

[3]See Merton Sealts, op. cit., pp. 57, 60, 67, 77, 82, 85, 86, 89, 97, 98, 102, 104.

[4]This information is derived from Richard Morris, ed., *Encyclopedia of American History* (New York: Harper & Row, 1976[5]), pp. 144–292, 374–429, and 686–777.

[5]Raleigh, op. cit., pp. 275–276.

[6]Raleigh, op. cit., pp. 278 and 280.

[7]In *Eugene O'Neill. A Study* (Bombay: Popular Prakasham, 1965), D.V.K. Raghavacharyulu reaches almost similar conclusions about O'Neill's double literary indebtedness, after having reviewed some of the thematic bonds between the dramatist and American novelists. This critic concentrates, however, on O'Neill's American concept of the self and does not focus on the playwright's specific relationships with American nineteenth century artists. He concludes that O'Neill formed the link between the American novel and drama and the European form. Although this idea seems tantalizing, I would hesitate to generalize to such an extent the O'Neill legacy to American literature. A more careful approach is offered here, which consists in showing how an analysis of O'Neill's plays within a simultaneously American and European context can enrich the significance of his work.

[8]See note 72, Chapter I.

SELECTED BIBLIOGRAPHY

This bibliography does not aim at comprehensiveness: I have only included books and articles which have been useful in the composition of this study. In the case of O'Neill, emphasis has been laid on recent criticism, such as appeared primarily in the excellent *The Eugene O'Neill Newsletter* and its successor *The Eugene O'Neill Review*. This bibliography includes as many as possible of those articles that appeared up to 1989 and in the early months of 1990. It reflects the wealth of material that was published around the time of the celebration of O'Neill's centenary in 1988. In addition, the reader is advised to turn to the excellent periodical *Melville Society Extracts* for recent criticism on Herman Melville. In the references of articles published in volumes of essays, the title of the collection is abbreviated through the name of the editor. Full bibliographical indications can then be found in the section dealing with the book length studies of the appropriate author.

I. Herman Melville

A. Works by Melville

Billy Budd, Sailor (An Inside Narrative). Chicago and London: The University of Chicago Press, 1962.

"Benito Cereno." In *Billy Budd, Sailor and other stories*. Harmondsworth: Penguin Books, 1982, pp. 215–307.

Clarel. A Poem and Pilgrimage in the Holy Land. New York: Hendricks House, 1960.

The Confidence-Man. London: John Lehmann, 1948.

"The Encantadas." In *Billy Budd, Sailor and other stories*, pp. 129–194.

Israël Potter. His Fifty Years of Exile. Boston: the St Botolph Society, 1925.

Journal Up the Straits. October 11, 1856–May 5, 1857. New-York: Copper Square Publishers,

Inc., 1971.

Journal of a Visit to London and the Continent, 1849–1850. Cambridge: Harvard University Press, 1948.

The Letters of Herman Melville. New Haven: Yale University Press, 1960.

Mardi. Boston: the St Botolph Society, 1923[5].

Moby Dick. Harmondsworth: Penguin Books, 1984.

Omoo. A Romance of the South Seas. Boston: the St. Botolph Society, 1922[5].

Some Personal Letters of Herman Melville and a Bibliography. Freeport: Books for Libraries Press, 1969[2].

Pierre, or the Ambiguities. New York: E.P. Dutton & Co, Inc., 1929.

The Collected Poems of Melville in Complete Works of Herman Melville, vol. XIV. Chicago: Packard & Co., 1947.

Redburn. Harmondsworth: Penguin Books, 1982.

Short Stories in *Selected Writings of Herman Melville.* New York: The Modern Library, 1952.

Typee. Harmondsworth: Penguin Books, 1981.

White-Jacket. The World in a Man-of-War. Boston: the St. Botolph Society, 1923[5].

B. Critical Studies

Allen, Gay Wilson. *Melville and his World.* New York: the Viking Press, 1971.

Arvin, Newton. *Herman Melville.* London: Methuen & Co., Ltd., 1950.

Baird, James. *Ishmaël.* Baltimore: Johns Hopkins University Press, 1956.

Bercaw, Mary K. *Melville's Sources.* Evanston: Northwestern University Press, 1987.

Bickley, R. Bruce, Jr. *The Method of Melville's Short Fiction.* Durham, NC: Duke University Press, 1975.

Brodhead, Richard H. *Hawthorne, Melville, and the Novel.* Chicago and London: the University of Chicago Press, 1976.

Brodtkorb, Paul, Jr. *Ishmaël's White World. A Phenomenological Reading of Moby Dick.* New Haven and London: Yale University Press, 1965.

Bryant, John, ed. *A Companion to Melville Studies.* Westport, CT: Greenwood Press, 1986.

Chase, Richard. *Herman Melville. A Critical Study.* New York: Hafner Publishing Co., 1977.

Chase, Richard, ed. *Melville. A Collection of Critical Essays.* Englewood Cliffs, NJ.: Prentice-Hall, Inc., 1962.

Dillingham, William B. *Melville's Short Fiction: 1893–1856*. Athens: The University of Georgia Press, 1977.

Fisher, Marvin. *Going Under. Melville's Short Fiction and the American 1850s*. Baton Rouge and London: Louisiana State University Press, 1977.

Frank, Stuart M. *Herman Melville's Picture Gallery. Sources and Types of the "Pictorial" Chapters of "Moby Dick."* Fairhaven, Mass.: Edward J. Lefkowicz, Inc., 1986.

Gale, Robert L.*Plots and Characters in the Fiction and Narrative Poetry of Herman Melville.* Hamden, CT: Archon Books, 1969.

Gilmore, Michael T., ed. *Twentieh-Century Interpretations of Moby Dick*. Englewood Cliffs, NJ: Prentice-Hall, Inc., 1977.

Goldman, Stan. "The Small Voice of Silence: Melville's Narrative Voices in *Clarel*." *Melville Society Extracts*,76 (February 1989), p. 9.

Herbert, T. Walter, Jr. *Moby Dick and Calvinism. A World Dismantled*. New Brunswick, NJ: Rutgers University Press, 1977.

Higgins, Brian. *Herman Melville: A Reference Guide, 1931–1960*. Boston: G.K. Hall, 1988.

Howard Leon. *Herman Melville. A Biography*. Berkeley and Los Angeles: University of California Press, 1951.

Leyda, Jay. *The Melville Log. A Documentary Life of Herman Melville: 1819–1891*. 2 vols. New York: Gordian Press, 1969.

Miller, Edwin Havilland. *Melville*. New York: George Braziller, Inc., 1975.

Mumford, Lewis. *Herman Melville. A Study of his life and Vision*. London: Secker and Warburg, 1962[3].

Olson, Charles. *Appelez-moi Ismaël*. Paris: Gallimard, 1962.

Parker, Hershel, ed. *The Recognition of Herman Melville. Selected Criticism since 1846*. Ann Arbor: University of Michigan Press, 1967.

Rosenberry, Edward H. *Melville and the Comic Spirit*. New York: Octagon Books, 1969.

Sachs, Viola. *Le Blanc et le Noir chez Melville et Faulkner*. Paris–La Haye: Mouton, 1974.

Sealts, Merton M., Jr. *The Early Lives of Melville*. Madison: the University of Wisconsin Press, 1974.

Sealts, Merton M. *Melville's Reading. A Checklist of Books Owned and Borrowed*. Madison, Milwaukee, and London: the University of Wisconsin Press, 1966.

Seelye, John. *Melville. The Ironic Diagram*. Evanston: Northwestern University Press, 1970.

Seltzer Leon. *The Vision of Melville and Conrad. A Comparative Study*. Athens: Ohio University Press, 1970.

Sweeney, Gerard M. *Melville's Use of Classical Mythology*. Amsterdam: Rodopi, 1975.

200

Tolchin, Neal L. *Mourning, Gender, and Creativity in the Art of Herman Melville.* New Haven: Yale University Press, 1988.

Trimpi, Helen. *Melville's Confidence Men and American Politics in the 1850's.* Hamden, CT: Archon Books, 1987.

Weaver, Raymond M. *Herman Melville. Mariner and Mystic.* New York: Pageant Books, Inc., 1961.

Winters, Yvor. *In Defense of Reason.* Denver: the University of Denver Press, 1937.

II. Eugene O'Neill

A. Works by O'Neill

Ah, Wilderness! A Comedy of Recollection in three Acts. New York: Samuel French, Inc., 1933.

The Ancient Mariner. Donald Gallup, ed. Yale University Library Gazette, 35 (1960), pp. 61–86.

Anna Christie. In *The Hairy Ape and other plays.* London: Jonathan Cape, 1936.

Beyond the Horizon. New York: Dramatists Play Service, Inc., 1947.

The Calms of Capricorn. A Play. Developed from O'Neill's Scenario by Donald Gallup. With a Transcription of the Scenario. New Haven and New York: Ticknor and Fields, 1982.

Children of the Sea and three other unpublished plays. J.M. Atkinson, ed. Washington: NCR Microcard Editions, 1972.

Chris Christophersen. New York: Random House, 1982.

The Complete Plays (3 vols). Travis Bogard, ed. New York: The Library of America, 1988.

Days Without End. In *The Plays of Eugene O'Neill.* Vol. I. New York: Random House, 1946, pp. 493–573.

Dynamo in *Lazarus Laughed and other plays.* London: Jonathan Cape, 1929.

The Fountain in *The Great God Brown, The Fountain, The Moon of the Caribbees.* New York: Boni and Liveright, 1926, pp. 103–197.

Hughie. New York: Dramatists Plays Service, 1959.

The Iceman Cometh. New York: Vintage Books, 1957.

Long Day's Journey into Night. London: Jonathan Cape, 1982.

A Moon for the Misbegotten. New York: Vintage Book, 1974.

More Stately Mansions. New Haven: Yale University Press, 1979[7].

More Stately Mansions (the unexpurgated edition). Martha Bower, ed. New York: Oxford University Press, 1988.

Nine Plays. New York: the Modern Library, 1941.

Poems, 1912–1944. Donald Gallup, ed. New Haven: Ticknor and Field, 1980.

Seven Plays of the Sea. New York: Vintage Books, 1972.

Six Short Plays of Eugene O'Neill. New York: Random House, 1951.

Ten Lost Plays. New York: Random House, 1964.

Tomorrow. Seven Arts Magazine, (June 1917), pp. 147–170. Reprinted in The Eugene O'Neill Newsletter, VII, iii (1983), pp. 3–13.

A Touch of the Poet. New York: Vintage Books, 1983.

Work Diary, 1924–1943. Transcribed by Donald Gallup. 2 vols. New Haven: Yale University Library, 1981.

B. Critical Studies

1. Books

Alexander, Doris. *The Tempering of Eugene O'Neill.* New York: Harcourt, Brace and World, Inc., 1962.

Barlow, Judith E. *Final Acts. The Creation of Three Late O'Neill Plays.* Athens: University of Georgia Press, 1984.

Berlin, Normand. *Eugene O'Neill.* New York: Grove Press, Inc., 1982.

Berlin, Normand. *Eugene O'Neill: Three Plays. A Selection of Critical Essays.* London: Macmillan, 1989.

Bogard, Travis. *Contour in Time. The Plays of Eugene O'Neill.* New York: Oxford University Press, 1972.

Bogard, Travis. *Eugene O'Neill Songbook.* Ann Arbor: UMI Research Press, 1990.

Bogard, Travis. *The Unknown O'Neill: Unpublished or Unfamiliar Writings of Eugene O'Neill.* New Haven and London: Yale University Press, 1988.

Boulton, Agnes. *Part of a Long Story. Eugene O'Neill as a Young Man in Love.* London : Peter Davies, 1958.

Bowen, Croswell, with the assistance of Shane O'Neill. *The Curse of the Misbegotten. A Tale of*

202

the House of O'Neill. London: Rupert Hart-Davis, 1960.

Bryer, Jackson R., ed. *"The Theatre We Worked For." The Letters of Eugene O'Neill to Kenneth Macgowan.* New Haven and London: Yale University Press, 1982.

Cargill, Oscar et al., eds. *Eugene O'Neill and his Plays.* New York: New York University Press, 1961.

Carpenter, Frederic I. *Eugene O'Neill.* New York: Twayne Publishers, Inc., 1964, rev. 1979.

Chabrowe, Leonard. *Ritual and Pathos. The Theatre of O'Neill.* Lewisburg: Bucknell University Press, 1976.

Chothia, Jean. *Forging a Language. A Study of the Plays of Eugene O'Neill.* Cambridge: Cambridge University Press, 1979.

Commins, Dorothy, ed. *"Love, Admiration and Respect." The O'Neill–Commins Correspondence.* Durham: Duke University Press, 1986.

Eaton, Richard, and Smith, Madeline, eds., *Eugene O'Neill: An Annotated Bibliography.* New York: Garland, 1988.

Egri, Peter. *The Birth of American Tragedy.* Budapest: Tankönyvkiado, 1988.

Egri, Peter. *Chekhov and O'Neill. The Uses of the Short Story in Chekhov's and O'Neill's Plays.* Budapest: Akademiai Kiado, 1986.

Engel, Edwin A. *The Haunted Heroes of Eugene O'Neill.* Cambridge, MA: Harvard University Press, 1953.

Falk, Doris V. *Eugene O'Neill and the Tragic Tension. An Interpretive Study of the Plays.* New Brunswick, NJ: Rutgers University Press, 1958.

Floyd, Virginia. *The Plays of Eugene O'Neill. A New Assessment.* New York: Frederick Ungar, 1985.

Floyd, Virginia, ed. *Eugene O'Neill: The Unfinished Plays—Notes for "The Visit of Malatesta," "The Last Conquest" and "Blind Alley Guy."* New York: Continuum, 1988.

Floyd, Virginia, ed. *Eugene O'Neill. A World View.* New York: Frederick Ungar, 1979.

Floyd, Virginia, ed. *Eugene O'Neill at Work. Newly Released Ideas for Plays.* New York: Frederick Ungar, 1981.

Frazer, Winifred. *E.G. and E.G.O.: Emma Goldman and the Iceman Cometh.* Gainesville: University of Florida Press, 1974.

Frazer, Winifred. *Love as Death in The Iceman Cometh.* Gainesville: University of Florida Press, 1967.

Frenz, Horst. *Eugene O'Neill.* New York: Frederick Ungar, 1971.

Frenz, Horst and Tuck, Susan, eds. *Eugene O'Neill's Critics. Voices from Abroad.* Carbondale and Edwardsville: Southern Illinois University Press, 1984.

Gassner, John, ed. *O'Neill. A Collection of Critical Essays*. Englewood Cliffs, NJ: Prentice-Hall, Inc., 1964.

Gelb, Arthur and Barbara. *O'Neill*. New York and Evanston: Harper and Row, 1962.

Halfmann, Ulrich. *"Unreal Realism." O'Neills Dramatisches Werk im Spiegel seiner Szenischen Kunst*. Bern und München: Francke Verlag, 1969.

Halfmann, Ulrich, ed. *Eugene O'Neill: Comments on the Drama and the Theater. A Source Book*. Tübingen: Gunter Narr Verlag, 1987.

Kobernick, Mark. *Semiotics of the Drama and the Style of Eugene O'Neill*. Amsterdam: John Benjamins, 1989.

Leech, Clifford. *O'Neill*. New York: Barnes & Noble, Inc., 1965.

Lewis, Ward B. *Eugene O'Neill. The German Reception of America's First Dramatist*. Berne: Peter Lang, 1984.

Manheim Michael. *Eugene O'Neill's New Language of Kinship*. Syracuse: Syracuse University Press, 1982.

Martine, James J., ed. *Critical Essays on Eugene O'Neill*. Boston: G.K. Hall, 1984.

Maufort, Marc, ed. *Eugene O'Neill and the Emergence of American Drama*. Amsterdam and Atlanta: Rodopi: 1989.

McDonough, Edward J. *Quintero Directs O'Neill*. Ann Arbor: UMI Research Press, 1990.

Orlandello, John. *O'Neill on Film*. Rutherford, Madison, Teaneck: Fairleigh Dickinson University Press, 1982.

Porter, Laurin. *The Banished Prince: Time, Memory, and Ritual in the Late Plays of Eugene O'Neill*. Ann Arbor: UMI Research Press, 1988.

Raleigh, John Henry. *The Plays of Eugene O'Neill*. Carbondale and Edwardsville: Southern Illinois University Press, 1965.

Raleigh, John Henry, ed. *Twentieth-Century Interpretations of The Iceman Cometh. A Collection of Critical Essays*. Englewood Cliffs, NJ: Prentice-Hall, Inc., 1968.

Ranald, Margaret Loftus. *The Eugene O'Neill Companion*. Westport, CT: Greenwood Press, 1984.

Robinson, James A. *Eugene O'Neill and Oriental Thought. A Divided Vision*. Carbondale and Edwardsville: Southern Illinois University Press, 1982.

Roberts, Nancy L. and Arthur W., eds. *" As Ever, Gene." The Letters of Eugene O'Neill to George Jean Nathan*. Rutherford, Madison, Teanecke: Fairleigh Dickinson University Press, 1987.

Shaughnessy, Edward L. *Eugene O'Neill in Ireland. The Critical Reception*. Westport, CT: Greenwood Press, 1988.

Sheaffer, Louis. *O'Neill. Son and Artist*. Boston and Toronto: Little, Brown, & Co., 1973.

Sheaffer, Louis. *O'Neill. Son and Playwright*. Boston and Toronto: Little, Brown, & Co., 1968.

Skinner, Richard Dana. *Eugene O'Neill. A Poet's Quest*. New York and Toronto: Longmans, Green, & Co., 1935.

Stroupe, John, ed. *Critical Approaches to O'Neill*. New York: AMS Press, 1988.

Tiusanen, Timo, *O'Neill's Scenic Images*. Princeton, NJ: Princeton University Press, 1968.

Törnqvist, Egil. *A Drama of Souls. Studies in O'Neill's Super-Naturalistic Techniques*. New Haven and London: Yale University Press, 1969.

Vena, Gary. *O'Neill's The Iceman Cometh. Reconstructing the Premiere*. Ann Arbor: U.M.I. Research Press, 1988.

Wainscott, Ronald H. *Staging O'Neill: The Experimental Years*, 1920–1934. New Haven: Yale University Press, 1988.

Winther, Sophus K. *Eugene O'Neill: A Critical Study*. New York: Russell and Russell, 1961.

2. Articles in Books and Periodicals

Adler, Thomas P. "'Through a Glass Darkly:' O'Neill's Esthetic Theory as Seen through His Writer Characters." *Arizona Quarterly*, 32 (1976), pp. 171–183.

Alexander, Doris. "Hugo of *The Iceman Cometh*: Realism and O'Neill." In *Raleigh*, pp. 63–71.

Alexander, Doris. "*Lazarus Laughed* and Buddha." *Modern Language Quarterly*, 17 (D.1956), pp. 357–365.

Alexander, Doris. "Psychological Fate in *Mourning Becomes Electra*." *PMLA*. 68, v (Dec. 1953) pp. 923–934.

Alexander, Doris. "*Strange Interlude* and Schopenhauer." *American Literature*, 25, ii (May 1953), pp. 213–228.

Andreach, R.J. "O'Neill's Use of Dante in *The Fountain* and *The Hairy Ape*." *Modern Drama*, 10 (1967), pp. 48–56.

Andreach, R.J. "O'Neill's Women in *The Iceman Cometh*." *Renascence*, 18, ii (winter 1966), pp. 89–98.

Antush, John V. "Eugene O'Neill: Modern and Post-Modern." *The Eugene O'Neill Review*, vol. 13, no. 1 (spring 1989), pp. 14–26.

Astington, John H. "Shakespeherian Rags" *Modern Drama*, Vol. 31 (1988), pp. 73–80.

Barlow, Judith E. "*Long Day's Journey into Night*: From Early Notes to Finished Play."

Modern Drama, 22 (1979), pp. 19–28.

Barlow, Judith E. "'Mother, Wife, Mistress, Friend, and Collaborator:' Carlotta Monterey and *Long Day's Journey into Night.*" In *Maufort*, pp. 123–131.

Barlow, Judith E. "O'Neill's Many Mothers: Mary Tyrone, Josie Hogan, and their Antecedents." *Perspectives on O'Neill: New Essays, English Literary Studies*, 43 (1988), pp. 7–16.

Ben Zvi, Linda. "*Exiles, The Great God Brown*, and the Specter of Nietzche." *Modern Drama*, 24 (1981), pp. 251–269.

Ben-Zvi, Linda. "Freedom and Fixity in the Plays of Eugene O'Neill." *Modern Drama*, 31 (1988), pp. 16–27.

Berlin, Normand. "The Beckettian O'Neill." *Modern Drama*, 31 (1988), pp. 28–34.

Berlin, Normand."O'Neill's Shakespeare." *The Eugene O'Neill Review*, vol. 13, no. 1 (spring 1989), pp. 5–13.

Bigsby, C.W.E. "O'Neill's Endgame." In *Maufort*, pp.159–168.

Black, Stephen A. "Tragic Anagnorisis in *The Iceman Cometh.*" *Perspectives on O'Neill: New Essays, English Literary Studies*, 43 (1988), pp. 17–32.

Bloom, Stephen F. "Drinking and Drunkenness in *The Iceman Cometh*: A Response to Mary McCarthy." *The Eugene O'Neill Newsletter*, 9, i (spring 1985), pp. 3–12.

Bloom, Stephen F. "Empty Bottles, Empty Dreams: O'Neill's Use of Drinking and Alcoholism in *Long Day's Journey into Night.*" In *Martine*, pp. 159–177.

Bloom, Stephen F. "The Role of Drinking and Alcoholism in O'Neill's Late Plays." *The Eugene O'Neill Newsletter*, 8, i (spring 1984) pp. 22–27.

Bogard, Travis. "First Love: Eugene O'Neill and 'Boutade.'" *The Eugene O'Neill Newsletter*, XII, no 1 (1988), pp. 3–9.

Brashear, W.R. "O'Neill and Shaw: the Play as Will and Idea." *Criticism*, 8 (1966), pp. 155–69.

Brashear, W.R. "O'Neill's Schopenhauer Interlude." *Criticism*, 6 (1964), pp. 256–65.

Brashear, W.R. "'Tomorrow' and 'Tomorrow:' Conrad and O'Neill." *Renascence*, 20 (1967), pp. 18–21, 55.

Brashear, W.R. "The Wisdom of Silenus in O'Neill's *Iceman.*" *American Literature*, 36 (1964), pp. 180–188.

Bryer, Jackson R., ed. "Eugene O'Neill's Letters to Donald Pace: A Newly Discovered Correspondence." In *Maufort*, pp. 133–150.

Bryer, Jackson R. "'Peace Is an Exhausted Reaction to Normal:' O'Neill's Letters to Dudley Nichols." In *Martine*, pp. 33–55.

Chothia, Jean. "Theatre Language: Word and Image in *The Hairy Ape.*" In *Maufort*, pp. 31–46.

Colakis, Marianthe. "Eugene O'Neill's *The Emperor Jones* as Senecan Tragedy." *Classical and*

Modern Literature: A Quarterly, vol. 10, no. 2 (winter 1990), pp. 153–159.

Cunningham, Frank R. "The Ancient Mariner and the Genesis of O'Neill's Romanticism." *The Eugene O'Neill Newsletter*, 3, i (1979), pp. 6–9.

Cunningham, Frank R."'Authentic Tidings of Invisible Things:' Beyond James Robinson's *Eugene O'Neill and Oriental Thought*." *The Eugene O'Neill Review*, vol. 13, no. 1 (spring 1989), pp. 29–39.

Cunningham, Frank R. "*The Great God Brown* and O'Neill's Romantic Vision." *Ball State University Forum*, 14, iii (1973), pp. 69–78.

Cunningham, Frank R. "Romantic Elements in Early O'Neill." in *Martine*, pp. 65–72.

Curran, Ronald T. "Insular Typees: Puritanism and Primitivism in *Mourning Becomes Electra*." *Revue des Langues Vivantes*, 41 (1975), pp. 371–377.

Egri, Peter. "'Belonging' Lost: Alienation and Dramatic Form in Eugene O'Neill's *The Hairy Ape*." *Acta Litteraria Academiae Scientiarum Hungaricae*, 24 (1982), pp. 157–190.

Egri, Peter. "European Origins and American Originality: the Adoption, Adaptation and Reinterpretation of Some European Models in Eugene O'Neill's *The Iceman Cometh*." *Annales Universitatis Scientiarum Budapestinensis de Rolando Eötvös Nominatae*, 11 (1980), pp. 83–107.

Egri, Peter. "The Electra Complex of Puritan Morality and the Epic Ambition of O'Neillian Tragedy." *Perspectives on O'Neill: New Essays, English Literary Studies*,43 (1988), pp. 43–60.

Egri, Peter. "The Merger of the Dramatic and the Lyric in Chekhov's *The Sea-Gull* and O'Neill's *Long Day's Journey into Night*." *Annales Universitatis Scientiarum Budapestinensis: Sectio Philologica Moderna*, 12 (1981), pp. 65–86.

Egri, Peter."The Psychology of Alienation, or What Parodies Are Good for: A Note on O'Neill's Modernity." *The Recorder*, vol. 3, no. 1 (summer 1989), pp. 37–44

Egri, Peter. "The Reinterpretation of the Chekhovian Mosaic Design in O'Neill's *Long Day's Journey into Night*." *Acta Litteraria Academiae Scientiarum Hungaricae*, 22, i–ii (1980), pp. 29–71.

Egri, Peter. "The Use of the Short Story in O'Neill's and Chekhov's One-Act Plays." In *Floyd*, pp. 115–144.

Eisen, Kurt. " Eugene O'Neill's Joseph: A Touch of the Dreamer." *Comparative Drama*, vol.23 (winter 1989–90), pp. 344–358.

Floyd, Virginia. "Eugene O'Neill: Gift of a Celtic Legacy." *The Recorder*, vol. 3, no. 1 (summer 1989), pp. 5–14.

Fluckiger, Stephen L. "The Idea of Puritanism in the Plays of Eugene O'Neill." *Renascence*, 30

(1978), pp. 152–162.

Frazer, Winifred. "'Revolution' in *The Iceman Cometh*." *Modern Drama*, 22 (1979), pp. 1–8.

Frazer, Winifred. "Chris and Poseidon: Man Versus God in *Anna Christie*." *Modern Drama*, 12 (1970), pp. 279–285.

Frazer, Winifred. "King Lear and Hickey: Bridegroom and Iceman." *Modern Drama*, 15 (1972), pp; 267–278.

Frenz, Horst. "Eugene O'Neill and Georg Kaiser." In *Floyd*, pp. 172–185.

Frenz, Horst and Martin Mueller. "More Shakespeare and Less Aeschylus in Eugene O'Neill's *Mourning Becomes Electra*." *American Literature*, 38 (1966), pp. 85–100.

Garvey, Sheila Hickey. "The Origins of the O'Neill Renaissance: A History of the 1956 Productions of *The Iceman Cometh* and *Long Day's Journey into Night*." *Theatre Survey*, XXIX, 1 (1988), pp. 51–68.

Gilmore, Thomas B. "*The Iceman Cometh* and the Anatomy of Alcoholism." *Comparative Drama*, 18, iv (1984) pp. 335–347.

Going, William T. "Eugene O'Neill, American." *Papers on Language and Literature*, 12 (1976), pp. 384–401.

Griffin, Ernest G. "O'Neill and the Tragedy of Culture." *Modern Drama*, Vol. 31, n° 1 (1988), pp. 1–15.

Grimm, Reinhold. "A Note on O'Neill, Nietzsche, and Naturalism: *Long Day's Journey into Night* in European Perspective." *Modern Drama*, 26 (1983), pp. 331–334.

Halfmann, Ulrich. "'With Clenched Fist...:' Observations on a Recurrent Motif in the Drama of Eugene O'Neill." In *Maufort*, pp. 107–121.

Hall, Ann C. "High Anxiety: Women in Eugene O'Neill's *The Iceman Cometh*." *The Recorder*, vol. 3, no.1 (summer 1989), pp. 45–51.

Hartman, Murray. "*Desire Under the Elms* in the light of Strindberg's Influence." *American Literature*, 33 (1961), pp. 360–369.

Hartman, Murray. "Strindberg and O'Neill." *Educational Theatre Journal*, 18 (1966), pp. 216–223.

Highsmith, James M. "The Cornell Letters: Eugene O'Neill on His Craftsmanship to George Jean Nathan." *Modern Drama*, 15 (1972), pp. 68–88.

Highsmith, James M. "A Description of the Cornell Collection of Eugene O'Neill's Letters to George Jean Nathan." *Modern Drama*, 14 (1971), pp. 420–425.

Highsmith, James M. "O'Neill's Idea of Theater." *South Atlantic Bulletin*, 23, iv (1968), pp. 18–21.

Highsmith, James M. "'The Personal Equation:' Eugene O'Neill's Abandoned Play." *Southern*

Humanities Review, 8, (1974), pp. 195–212.

Hinden, Michael. "*The Birth of Tragedy* and *The Great God Brown*." *Modern Drama*, 16 (1973), pp. 129–140.

Hinden, Michael. "Desire and Forgiveness: O'Neill's Diptych." *Comparative Drama*, 14 (1980), pp. 240–250.

Hinden, Michael. "*Desire Under the Elms*: O'Neill and the American Romance." *Forum*, 15, i (1977), pp. 44–51.

Hinden, Michael. "Liking O'Neill" *Forum*, ll, iii (1973), pp. 59–66.

Hinden, Michael. "Missing Lines in *Long Day's Journey into Night*." *Modern Drama*, XXXII, No 2 (1989), pp. 177–182.

Hinden, Michael "Paradise Lost: O'Neill and American History." *The Eugene O'Neill Newsletter*, Vol. XII, No 1 (1988), pp. 39–48.

Hornby, Richard. "O'Neill's Death of a Salesman." *Journal of Dramatic Theory and Criticism*, Vol. 2, No 2 (1988), pp. 53–59.

Hornby, Richard. "O'Neill's Metadrama." *The Eugene O'Neill Newsletter*, Vol XII, No 2 (1988), pp. 13–18.

Jackson, Esther M. "Dramatic Form in Eugene O'Neill's *The Calms of Capricorn*." *The Eugene O'Neill Newsletter*, Vol. XII, No 3 (1988), pp. 35–42.

Kennedy, Joyce Deveau. "O'Neill's Lavinia Mannon and the Dickinson Legend." *American Literature*, 49, i (1977), pp. 108–113.

Kennedy, Joyce Deveau. "*Pierre*'s Progeny: O'Neill and the Melville Revival." *English Studies in Canada*, 3, i (1977), pp. 103–117.

King, W.D. "'It Brought the World to this Coast:'The World Premiere of Eugene O'Neill's *Lazarus Laughed* at the Pasadena Community Playhouse." *Theatre Survey*, XXIX, No 1 (1988), pp. 1–36.

Jiji, Vera. "Reviewers' Responses to the Early Plays of Eugene O'Neill: A Study in influence." *Theatre Survey*, XXIX, No 1 (1988), pp. 69–86.

Krafchick, Marcelline. "Film and Fiction in O'Neill's *Hughie*." *Arizona Quarterly*, 39 (1983), pp. 47–61.

McDermott, Dana S. "Robert Edmond Jones and Eugene O'Neill: Two American Visionaries." *The Eugene O'Neill Newsletter*, 8, i (1984), pp. 3–10.

McDonald, David. "The Phenomenology of the Glance in *Long Day's Journey into Night*." *Theatre Journal*, 31 (1979), pp. 343–356.

Mandl, Bette. "Absence as Presence: The Second Sex in *The Iceman Cometh*." *The Eugene O'Neill Newsletter*, 5, ii (S/F 1982), pp. 10–15.

Manheim, Michael. "Dialogue Between Son and Mother in Chekhov's *The Sea Gull* and O'Neill's *Long Day's Journey into Night*." *The Eugene O'Neill Newsletter*, 6, i (spring 1982), pp. 24–29.

Manheim, Michael. "Eugene O'Neill and the Founders of Modern Drama." In *Maufort*, pp. 47–57.

Manheim, Michael. "O'Neill's Transcendence of Melodrama in *A Touch of the Poet* and *A Moon for the Misbegotten*." *Comparative Drama*, 16, iii (1982), pp. 238–250.

Manheim, Michael. "The Transcendence of Melodrama in *Long Day's Journey into Night*." *Perspectives on O'Neill: New Essays, English Literary Studies*, 43 (1988), pp. 33–42.

Manheim, Michael. "The Transcendence of Melodrama in O'Neill's *The Iceman Cometh*." In *Martine*, pp. 145–158.

Mann, Bruce J. "O'Neill's 'Presence' in *Long Day's Journey into Night*." *The Theatre Annual*, XLIII (1988), pp. 15–30.

Marcus, Mordecai. "O'Neill's Debt to Thoreau in *A Touch of the Poet*." *Journal of English and Germanic Philology*, 62 (April 1963), pp. 270–279.

Mason, Jeffrey D. "The Metatheatre of O'Neill: Actor as Metaphor in *A Touch of the Poet*." *The Theatre Annual*, XLIII (1988), pp. 53–66.

Maufort, Marc. "American Flowers of Evil: *Long Day's Journey into Night* and Baudelaire." In *New Essays on American Drama*, eds. Gilbert Debusscher and Henry Schvey. Amsterdam and Atlanta: Rodopi, 1989, pp. 13–28.

Maufort, Marc. "Communication as Translation of the Self: Jamesian Inner Monologue in O'Neill's *Strange Interlude* (1927)." In Debusscher, Gilbert and Van Noppen, Jean-Pierre, eds. *Communicating and Translating. Essays in Honour of Jean Dierickx*. Bruxelles: Editions de l'Université de Bruxelles, 1985, pp. 319–328.

Maufort, Marc. "Eugene O'Neill's innovative Craftsmanship in the 'Glencairn' Cycle (1914–1917)." *The Eugene O'Neill Newsletter*, Vol. XII, No 1 (1988), pp. 27–33.

Maufort, Marc. "Eugene O'Neill's and the Shadow of Edmond Dantès: the Pursuit of Dramatic Unity in *Where the Cross is Made* (1918) and *Gold* (1920)." *American Literature in Belgium*. Ed. Gilbert Debusscher. Amsterdam: Rodopi, 1988, pp. 89–97.

Maufort, Marc. "The Legacy of Melville's *Pierre*: Family Relationships in *Mourning Becomes Electra*." *The Eugene O'Neill Newsletter*, Vol. XI, No 2 (1987), pp. 23–28.

Maufort, Marc. "Mariners and Mystics: Echoes of *Moby Dick* in O'Neill." *The Theatre Annual*, XLII, (1988), pp. 31–52.

Maufort, Marc. "O'Neill's Variations on an Obituary Motif in *Bound East for Cardiff* and *Hughie*." *Revue Belge de Philologie et d'Histoire*, Vol. LXVI, No 3 (1988), pp. 602–612.

Maufort, Marc. "Tragedy and Solipsism: The Kinship of *Moby Dick* and *The Iceman Cometh*." *The Recorder*, vol. 3, no.1 (summer 1989), pp. 27–36.

Maufort, Marc. "*Typee* Revisited: O'Neill's *Mourning Becomes Electra* and Melville." In *Maufort*, pp. 85–96.

Metzger D.P. "Variations on a Theme: A Study of *Exiles* by James Joyce and *The Great God Brown* by Eugene O'Neill." *Modern Drama*, 8 (1965), pp. 174–184.

Onunwa, Father Paschal."Eugene O'Neill: A Voice for Racial Justice." *The Recorder*, vol. 3, no.1 (summer 1989), pp. 15–24.

Porter, Laurin R. "*The Iceman Cometh* as Crossroad in O'Neill's long Journey." *Modern Drama*, Vol. 31, No 1 (1988), pp. 52–62.

Raleigh, John Henry. "Communal, Familial, and Personal Memories in O'Neill's *Long Day's Journey into Night*." *Modern Drama*, Vol. 31, No 1 (1988), pp. 63–72.

Raleigh, John Henry. "Eugene O'Neill and the Escape from the Château d'If."*In Gassner*, pp. 7–22.

Raleigh, John Henry. "The Historical Background of *The Iceman Cometh*." In *Raleigh*, pp. 54–62.

Raleigh, John Henry. "The Irish Atavism of *A Moon for the Misbegotten*." In *Floyd*, pp. 229–236.

Raleigh, John Henry. "The Last Confession. O'Neill and the Catholic Confessional." In *Floyd*, pp. 212–228.

Raleigh, John Henry. "Strindberg in Andrew Jackson's America: O'Neill's *More Stately Mansions*." *Clio*, 13 (1983), pp. 1–15.

Raleigh, John Henry. "Strindberg and O'Neill as Historical Dramatists." In *Maufort*, pp. 59–75.

Pasquier, Marie-Claire. "You Are One of Us, You Are a russian." In *Maufort*, pp. 77–83.

Rich, J. Dennis. "Exile Without Remedy: the Late Plays of Eugene O'Neill." In *Floyd*, pp. 257–278.

Robinson, James A. "Buried Children: Fathers and Sons in O'Neill and Shepard." In *Maufort*, pp. 151–157.

Robinson, James A. "The Metatheatrics of *A Moon for the Misbegotten*." *Perspectives on O'Neill: New Essays, English Literary Studies*, 43 (1988), pp. 61–75.

Robinson, James A. "O'Neill's Grotesque Dancers." *Modern Drama*, 19 (1976), pp. 341–349.

Robinson, James A. " O'Neill's Indian *Elm*." *The Eugene O'Neill Review*, vol. 13, no. 1 (spring 1989), pp. 40–46.

Robinson, James A. "O'Neill's Symbolic Sounds." *Modern Language Studies*, 9, ii (1979), pp. 36–45.

Robinson, James A. "Taoism and O'Neill's *Marco Millions.*" *Comparative Drama*, 14 (1980), pp. 251–262.

Rust, R.D. "The Unity of O'Neill's *S.S. Glencairn.*" *American Literature*, 37 (1965), pp. 280–290.

Sarlos, Robert K. "'Write a Dance:' Lazarus Laughed as O'Neill's Dithyramb of the Western Hemisphere." *Theatre Survey*, XXIX, No 1 (1988), pp. 37–50.

Schvey, Henry I. "'·The Past Is the Present, Isn't?:' Eugene O'Neill's *Long Day's Journey into Night.*" *Dutch Quarterly Review of Anglo-American Letters*, 10 (1980), pp. 84–99.

Selmon, Michael. "Past, Present and Future Converged: The Place of *More Stately Mansions* in the Eugene O'Neill Canon." *Modern Drama*, 28, iv (December 1985), pp. 553–562.

Smith, Madeline. "Anna Christie's Baptism." *The Recorder*, vol.3, no.1 (summer 1989), pp. 57–63.

Smith, Madeline C, and Eaton, Richard. "Four Letters by Eugene O'Neill." *The Eugene O'Neill Newsletter*, Vol. XI, No 3 (1987), pp. 12–18.

Smith, Susan Harris. " Actors Constructing an Audience: *Hughie*'s Post-Modern Aura." In *Maufort*, pp. 169–180

Stroupe, John H. "O'Neill's *Marco Millions*: A Road to Xanadu." *Modern Drama*, 12 (1970), pp. 377–382.

Törnqvist, Egil. "Ibsen and O'Neill." *Scandinavian Studies*, 37 (1965), pp. 211–235.

Törnqvist, Egil. "Jesus and Judas: On Biblical Allusions in O'Neill's Plays." *Etudes Anglaises*, 24 (1971), pp. 41–49.

Törnqvist, Egil. "*Miss Julie* and O'Neill." *Modern Drama*, 19 (1976), pp. 351–364.

Törnqvist, Egil. "Nietzsche and O'Neill: A Study in Affinity." *Orbis Litterarum*, 23 (1968), pp. 97–126.

Törnqvist, Egil. "O'Neill's Lazarus: Dionysus and Christ." *American Literature*, 41 (1970), pp. 543–554.

Törnqvist, Egil. "O'Neill's Work Method." *Studia Neophilologica*, 49 (1977), pp. 43–58.

Törnqvist, Egil. "Personal Addresses in the Plays of O'Neill." *Quarterly Journal of Speech*, 55 (1969), pp. 126–130.

Törnqvist, Egil. "Personal Nomenclature in the Plays of O'Neill." *Modern Drama*, 8 (Feb. 1966), pp. 362–373.

Törnqvist, Egil. "Platonic Love in O'Neill's *Welded.*" In *Floyd*, pp. 73–83.

Törnqvist, Egil. "From *A Wife for a Life* to *A Moon for the Misbegotten*. On O'Neill's Play Titles." In *Maufort*, pp. 97–105.

Tuck, Susan. "'Electricity Is God Now:' D.H. Lawrence and O'Neill." *The Eugene O'Neill*

Newsletter, 5, ii (1981), pp. 10–15.

Tuck, Susan. "House of Compson, House of Tyrone: Faulkner's Influence on O'Neill. "*The Eugene O'Neill Newsletter*, 5, iii (1981), pp. 10–16.

Tuck, Susan. "The O'Neill-Faulkner Connection." In *Martine*, pp. 196–206.

Tuck, Susan. "O'Neill and Faulkner: Their Kindred Imaginations." The *Eugene O'Neill Newsletter*, 4, iii (1980), pp. 19–20.

Tuck, Susan. "O'Neill and Frank Wedekind." *The Eugene O'Neill Newsletter*, 6, i (1982), pp. 29-35 and 6, ii (1982), pp. 17–21.

Voelker, Paul D. "Eugene O'Neill's Aesthetic of the Drama." *Modern Drama*, 21, i (1978), pp. 87–99.

Voelker, Paul D. "Eugene O'Neill and George Pierce Baker: A Reconsideration." *American Literature*, 49, ii (1977) pp. 206–220.

Voelker, Paul D. "Success and Frustration at Harvard: O'Neill's Relationship with George Pierce Baker (1914-1915)." In *Maufort*, pp. 15–29.

Voelker, Paul D. "The Uncertain Origins of Eugene O'Neill's 'Bound East for Cardiff.'" *Studies in Bibliography*, 32 (1979), pp. 273–281.

Werner, Bette Charlene. "Eugene O'Neill's Paradise Lost: The Theme of the Islands in *Mourning Becomes Electra*." *Ball State University Forum*, 27, 1 (winter 1986), pp.46–52.

Wilkins, Frederick C. "The Pressure of Puritanism in Eugene O'Neill's New England Plays." In *Floyd*, pp. 237–244.

Wilkins, Frederick C. "'Arriving with a Bang:' O'Neill's Literary Debut." In *Maufort*, pp. 5–13.

Williams, Gary Jay. "The Dreamy Kid: O'Neill's Darker Brother." *The Theatre Annual*, XLII (1988), pp. 3–13.

Williams, Gary Jay. "Turned Down in Provincetown: O'Neill's Debut Reexamined." *Theatre Journal*, 37, ii (May 1985), pp. 155–166.

Yu, Zhao. "O'Neill's Tragedies: A Chinese View." *The Recorder*, vol. 3, no.1 (summer 1989), pp. 52–56.

Zapf, Hubert. "O'Neill's Hairy Ape and the Reversal of Hegelian Dialectics." *Modern Drama*, Vol. 31, No 1 (1988), pp. 35–40.

III. General Criticism

A. American Drama

Bigsby, C.W.E. *A Critical Introduction to Twentieth-Century American Drama*, 3 vols. (Cambridge: Cambridge University Press, 1982, 1984, 1985).

Bigsby, C.W.E." Why American Drama Is Literature." In G. Debusscher and H. Schvey, eds.*New Essays on American Drama*. Amsterdam and Atlanta: Rodopi, 1989, pp. 3–12.

Grimsted, David. *Melodrama Unveiled: American Theater and Culture*, 1800–1850. Chicago and London: University of Chicago Press, 1968.

Jackson, Esther M. "The American Drama and the New World Vision." Unpublished manuscript, Madison, WI, 1981.

Jackson, Esther M. *The Broken World of Tennessee Williams*. Madison, Milwaukee and London: University of Wisconsin Press, 1966[2].

Sievers, David. *Freud on Broadway*. New York, 1955.

Smith, Susan Harris. "Generic Hegemony: American Drama and the Canon." *American Quarterly*, 41, no. 1 (March 1989), pp. 112–122.

B. American Literature

Atkinson, Brooks, ed. *The Selected Writings of Ralph Waldo Emerson*. New York: The Modern Library, 1968[3].

Bercovitch, Sacvan. *The Puritan Origins of the American Self*. New Haven and London: Yale University Press, 1975.

Bradley, Sculley, ed. *The American Tradition in Literature*. 2 Vols. New York: W.W. Norton, 1967.

Brumm, Ursula. *Die Religiöse Typologie im Amerikanischen Denken*. Leiden: E.J. Brill, 1963.

Chase, Richard. *The American Novel and its Tradition*. Garden City, NY: Doubleday, 1957.

Debusscher, Gilbert."Profils de la Littérature des Etats-Unis." In Dorsinfang-Smets, A., ed., *L'Amérique du Nord. Histoire et Culture*. Bruxelles: Meddens, 1975, pp. 158–214.

Elliott, Emory, ed. *Puritan Influences in American Literature*. Urbana, Chicago, London:

University of Illinois Press, 1979.

Feidelson, Charles. *Symbolism and American Literature*. Chicago: Chicago University Press, 1953.

Lewis, R.W.B. *The American Adam*. Chicago: Chicago University Press, 1955.

Matthiessen, F.O. *American Renaissance. Art and Expression in the Age of Emerson and Whitman*. London, Oxford, New York: Oxford University Press, 1941.

Miller, Perry. *The American Puritans. Their Prose and Poetry*. Garden City, NY: Doubleday, 1956.

Miller, Perry. *Errand into the Wilderness*. Cambridge, MA: the Belknap Press of Harvard University Press, 1956.

Pearce, Roy Harvey. *The Continuity of American Poetry*. Princeton: Princeton University Press, 1961.

Philbrick, Thomas. *James Fennimore Cooper and the Development of American Sea Fiction*. Cambridge, MA: Harvard University Press, 1961.

Whitman, Walt. *Leaves of Grass*. London: Secker and Warburg, 1960.

Wilder, Thornton. *American Characteristics and other Essays*. D. Gallup, ed. New York: Harper and Row, 1979.

C. Theory of Literature

Aristotle: *Art of Poetry*. Hamilton Fyfe, ed. Oxford: Claredon Press, 1940.

Auden, W.H. *The Enchafed Flood or the Romantic Iconography of the Sea*. New York: Vintage Books, 1967.

Bachelard, Gaston. *L'Eau et les Rêves. Essai sur l'Imagination de la Matière*. Paris: Corti, 1947.

Berry Ralph. "The Frontier of Metaphor and Symbol." *The British Journal of Aesthetics*, 7, i (Ja. 1967), pp. 76–83.

Caillois, Roger. *Le Mythe et l'Homme*. Paris: Gallimard, 1972.

Campbell, Joseph. *The Hero with a Thousand Faces*. New York: Meridian Books, 1956.

Camus, Albert. *The Myth of Sisyphus and Other Essays*. Trans. Justin O'Brien. New York: Alfred A. Knopf, 1955.

Conrad, Joseph. *The Nigger of the Narcissus, Typhoon and other Stories*. Harmondsworth: Penguin Books, 1963.

Eliade, Mircea. *Aspects du Mythe*. Paris: Gallimard, 1963.

Mircea, Eliade. *Mythes, Rêves et Mystères*. Paris: Gallimard, 1972.

Fontenrose, Joseph. *The Ritual Theory of Myth*. Berkeley–Los Angeles: University of California Press, 1966.

Langer, Susanne K. *Philosophy in a New Key. A Study in the Symbolism of Reason, Rite, and Art*. New York: The New American Library of World Literature, Inc., 1955[7].

Langer, Suzanne K. *Feeling and Form. A Theory of Art Developed from Philosophy in a New Key*. New York: Charles Scribner's sons, 1953.

Matoré, Georges. *L'Espace Humain. L'Expression de l'Espace dans la Vie, la Pensée et l'Art Contemporain*. Paris: Nizet, s.d.

Monnerot, Jules. *Les Lois du Tragique*. Paris: Presses Universitaires de France, 1969.

Olney, James, ed. *Autobiography*. Princeton: Princeton University Press, 1980.

Osborn, Michael. "The Evolution of the Archetypal Sea in Rhetoric and Fiction." *Quarterly Journal of Speech*, 63, iv (1977), pp. 347–363.

Steiner, George. *The Death of Tragedy*. London: Faber and Faber, 1961.

Trousson, Raymond. *Un problème de Littérature Comparée: Les Etudes de Thèmes. Essai de Méthodologie*. Paris: Lettres Modernes, 1965.

Weisgerber, Jean. *L'Espace Romanesque*. Lausanne: L'Age d'Homme, 1978.

Weisgerber, Jean. *Faulkner and Dostoevsky: Influence and Confluence*. Athens: Ohio University Press, 1974.

Weisgerber, Jean. "Irony and Satire as Means of Communication." *Comparative Literature Studies*, 10, ii (1973), pp. 157–172.

Weisgerber, Jean. "Le Jugement de Valeur en Littérature Comparée: le Comparatisme au Service de l'Evaluation Artistique." *Etudes Littéraires*, 7, ii (1974), pp. 229–243.

Weisgerber, Jean. "The Use of Quotation in Recent Literature." *Comparative Literature*, 22 (winter 1970), pp. 36–45.

Williams, Raymond. *Modern Tragedy*. London: Chatto and Windus, 1966.

D. Theory of the Theatre

Brustein, Robert. *The Theatre of Revolt*. Boston, 1964.

Burke, Kenneth. *A Grammar of Motives*. New York: George Braziller, 1955.

Esslin, Martin. *An Anatomy of Drama*. London: Temple Smith, 1976.

Fergusson, Francis. *The Idea of a Theatre*. Princeton: Princeton University Press, 1972[5].

Gorelik, Mordecai. *New Theatres for Old*. New York: Octagon Books, 1975[2].

Heilman, Robert B. *The Iceman, the Arsonist, and the Troubled Agent. Tragedy and Melodrama on the Modern Stage*. London: George Allen and Unwin, Ltd., 1973.

Macgowan, Kenneth. *The Theatre of Tomorrow*. New York: Boni and Liveright, 1921.

Miller, Arthur. *The Theatre Essays of Arthur Miller*. Robert A. Martin, ed. New York: the Viking Press, 1978.

E. American Culture

Beard, Charles A. and Mary R. *The Rise of American Civilization*. London: Jonathan Cape, 1930.

Channing, Edward. *A History of the United States*. 7 Vols. New York: Octagon Books, 1977.

Commager, Henry Steele. *Documents of American History*. 2 Vols. Englewood Cliffs, NJ : Prentice-Hall, Inc., 1973.

Morris, Richard B., ed. *Encyclopedia of American History*. New York: Harper and Row, 1976[5].

Tocqueville, Alexis de. *De la Démocratie en Amérique*. Paris: Librairie de Médicis, 1951[2].

INDEX

This index includes proper names (those of writers—with the exception of Eugene O'Neill and Herman Melville, for whom the reader must turn to their respective novels and plays; of critics; and, of historical figures) and works of primary literature cited in the text.

Abortion, 7

Adams, Henry, 10

Albee, Edward, 6

Anderson, Sherwood, 11

André, 5–6

Andreach, Robert J., 161

Anna, 11, 34, 58–59,076, 83, 93

Anthony and Cleopatra, 126

Antoine, André, 5

Ape, 34, 59–60, 76, 84–85, 149–150, 151, 160, 161, 164, 167

Ashe, Beatrice, 11

Auden, W.H., 153

Bachelard, Gaston, 42, 55, 62, 65

Barlow, Judith, 2

"Bartleby, the Scrivener," 154

Beaver, Harold, 41

"Benito Cereno," 94–95, 100–101, 103

Bewley, Marius, 160–161

Billy Budd, 20, 32–33, 36, 81–84, 133, 138, 140–142, 164

Biographia Literaria, 41

Bird, Robert Montgomery, 6

Bogard, Travis, 2, 11, 48

Boucicault, Dion, 6

Boulton, Agnes, 13, 28, 53

Brahm, Otto, 5

Brown, 7, 145

Brumm, Ursula, 153–154

Bryer, Jackson R., 2

Caillois, Roger, 157

Camus, Albert, 31–32, 113, 115, 122, 141

Capricorn, 3, 52, 67, 71, 74–75, 82, 94–95, 117, 120–123, 164

Cardiff, 4, 10, 13, 20, 33–34, 36, 40–41, 66–69, 76–80, 84–85, 89, 93, 130, 164

Caribbees, 13, 34

Chase, Richard, 147, 162

Chillun, 105

"Choice," 8

"Choices," 11

Chothia, Jean, 9, 11, 13

Chris, 58–59

Clarel, 20, 31–33, 36, 116–117, 123

Clemens, Samuel Langhorne (MarkTwain), 1O

Coleridge, Samuel Taylor, 41

"Compensation," 8

Confidence, 110–111, 145

Conrad, Joseph, 39–41

The Contrast, 5

Cook, George Cram, 5

The Count of Monte Cristo, 7, 53, 146, 166

Crane, Hart, 9–11, 14–15

Crane, Stephen, 11

Cross, 13, 24–25, 34, 48, 53, 55, 82, 91, 118

Cunningham, Frank R., 11

Curran, Ronald T., 12–13, 43

The Dance of Death, 125

Dante Alighieri, 160–162

Days, 117

Democracy in America, 61, 166

Democratic Vistas, 4

Desire, 7, 25, 119, 129, 132–133, 154

Dickinson, Emily, 10

Diderot, Denis, 125

Diff'rent, 13–14, 48, 53, 55, 91, 164

Divine Comedy, 160–162

A Doll's House, 125

Dostoevsky, Fedor Mikhailovich, 16

Dreiser, Theodore, 11

Dunlap, William, 5

Dynamo, 10, 120, 123, 151–153, 159, 167

The Education of Henry Adams, 10

Edwards, Jonathan, 154

Egri, Peter, 2, 11

Electra, 7, 9–12, 15, 34–36, 39, 42–44, 46–48, 53–55, 90, 108, 114, 120–121, 125, 138–140, 143, 158, 164

Eliade, Mircea, 157

Emerson, Ralph Waldo, 1, 2, 3, 4, 7, 8, 10, 17, 52, 57–58, 61, 90, 110–112, 127–128, 153

Emperor, 7

"The Encantadas," 91–92

The Enchafed Flood, 153

The Faith Healer, 6

Falk, Doris V., 146

"The Fall of the House of Usher," 10

Fashion, 6

The Father of a Family, 125

Faulkner, William, 11, 16

Fish, Carl Russell, 3

Fiske, John, 3

Floyd, Virginia, 2

Fog, 76, 92

Fontenrose, Joseph, 157

Fountain, 3, 161

Franklin, Benjamin, 99–100, 106–108

Freud, Sigmund, 21–22, 26

Gallup, Donald C., 3

Gelb, Arthur and Barbara, 8, 10

Ghosts, 125

Gierow, Karl Ragnar, 3

The Gladiator, 6

Glaspell, Susan, 5

Godfrey, Thomas, 5

The Great Divide, 6

Hawthorne, Nathaniel, 1, 8–9, 17, 27, 126

Herne, James A., 4, 6

Horizon, 58, 72, 74–75, 89

The House of the Seven Gables, 9

Huckleberry Finn, 10

Hughie, 7

Ibsen, 1, 125

Iceman, 7, 11, 20, 35–36, 47, 50, 82, 89, 103, 114, 117, 122–123, 125, 129, 136–138, 143–144, 154, 164

Ile, 13, 39, 48–53, 55, 164

The Illegitimate Son, 125

Interlude, 11, 119–120, 151–153

Introduction to Hart Crane's *White Buildings*, 9, 10, 14

Israël, 15, 106–109

Jackson, Esther Merle, 7

James, Henry, 11

Jefferson, Thomas, 4, 143

"Thomas Jefferson Play," 4

Josephson, Mathew, 3

Journey, 7, 9, 20, 22, 24–25, 35–36, 39, 48, 54–56, 58–62, 77, 81–82, 93, 96, 117, 122, 125, 129, 138, 140–144, 164, 166

Kaiser, Georg, 1, 167
Kazan, Elia, 147
Kennedy, Joyce D., 9, 10, 12, 15, 43, 138
King Lear, 126
Krutch, Joseph Wood, 113

Leaves of Grass, 9,19,39
Lessing, Gotthold Ephraim, 125
Lewis, R.W.B., 128, 163
Lewis, Sinclair, 11
Lewis, Ward B., 2
Little, Frances, 3
Long Voyage, 13, 15, 34, 67–70, 85, 89, 131

Macgowan, Kenneth, 3
Manheim, Michael, 146
Mansions, 3, 10, 52, 61, 109, 112, 114
Marco, 3, 82, 101–102
Mardi, 30, 34, 81–83, 90–91, 94–95
Margaret Fleming, 6
Mariner, 41
Mathews, James, 9
Matthiessen, F.O., 110, 125, 126, 143, 153
Melville, Allan, 22, 25
Melville, Gansevoort, 21
Melville, Maria, 25
Metamora, 5
Miller, Arthur, 127–128
Miller, Edwin H., 2O–21, 23
Miller, Perry, 110
Misbegotten, 7, 22, 92, 122
Miss Sara Sampson, 117
Moby Dick, 1, 13–15, 20, 23, 25, 30–31, 33–34, 39–42, 48–57, 59–60, 70–75, 77, 80, 85–86, 88–89, 94–96, 104–105, 113–123, 125–126, 129, 133, 135–138, 140, 142–144, 148, 150–154, 159–162, 164–167

"A Model of Christian Charity," 99

Monterey, Carlotta, 28

Moody, William V., 4, 6

Mosses from an Old Manse, 9, 126

The Myth of Sisyphus, 31–32

"The Nature of Tragedy," 128

Nietzsche, Friedrich, 1, 32, 90, 127

The Nigger of the Narcissus, 40–41

Notes and Lectures upon Shakespeare, 41

"The Oblong Box," 10

The Octoroon, 6

Omoo, 30, 34, 55, 77–80, 90–91

O'Neill, Ella Quinlan, 25

O'Neill, James, Sr., 7, 24

O'Neill, James, Jr., 21–22

Pearce, Roy Harvey, 163

Pierre, 12, 15, 47, 133, 138–140, 143, 146, 151–153, 158

Poe, Edgar Allan, 3, 10

"Poem 47," 96

Porter, Laurin R., 1

The Portrait of a Lady, 11

The Prince of Parthia, 5

Raleigh, John Henry, 7, 10, 12–13, 48, 61, 159, 166

The Red Badge of Courage, 11

Redburn, 23, 30, 56, 59–60, 65–70, 72–73, 75–76, 81–83, 86, 92–93, 129–132

The Rime of the Ancient Mariner, 41

Ritchie, Anna Cora Mowatt, 6

Robinson, James A., 1, 8

Rope, 7, 154–157

Sandburg, Carl, 11, 14

Miss Sara Sampson, 125

The Scarlet Letter, 9

Schopenhauer, Arthur, 127

Sealts, Merton, 41, 165

Seltzer, Leon, 41

Shakespeare, William, 125–127, 129, 165

Shays, Daniel, 4

Sheaffer, Louis, 13, 14, 20, 21, 33, 53

Shepard, Sam, 6

Shore Acres, 6

Sister Carrie, 11

Sniper, 7

Sophocles, 125, 128, 129, 146, 165

Stone, John Augustus, 6

Stowe, Hariet Beecher, 6

Strindberg, August, 1, 125

Synge, John M., 1

"A Tale of Possessors Self-Dispossessed," 3, 165

Tate, Allen, 14

Thirst, 71–72, 80, 88–89, 117–118, 121, 130, 164

Thoreau, Henry D., 1, 2, 8, 9, 17, 52, 111

Timar, Esther, 10

Tocqueville, Alexis de, 61, 166

Toller, Ernst, 1

Touch, 3, 8, 52, 61, 108, 111

"Tragedy," 127

"Tragedy and the Common Man," 128

Tuck, Susan, 11

Tyler, Royall, 5

Typee, 12–13, 15, 20–21, 29, 33–34, 42–47, 90, 129,–130, 164

Uncle Tom's Cabin, 6

Van Vechten, Carl, 15

Voelker, Paul Duane, 41

Walden, 8–9

Web, 11

Weisgerber, Jean, 16, 47, 162, 167

Wellek, René, 16–17

White Buildings, 10, 14

White-Jacket, 21, 23, 30, 56, 60, 77–82, 84, 86–89

Whitman, Walt, 1, 2, 4, 8, 9, 14, 17, 19, 37, 39, 146, 163

Wilder, Thornton, 17, 19

Wilderness, 24, 25

Williams, Tennessee, 6

Wilson, Lanford, 7

Winthrop, John, 99

Zola, Emile, 147

Zone, 10, 13, 34, 76, 85–87